HISTORICAL
ATLAS
— OF —
EXPEDITIONS

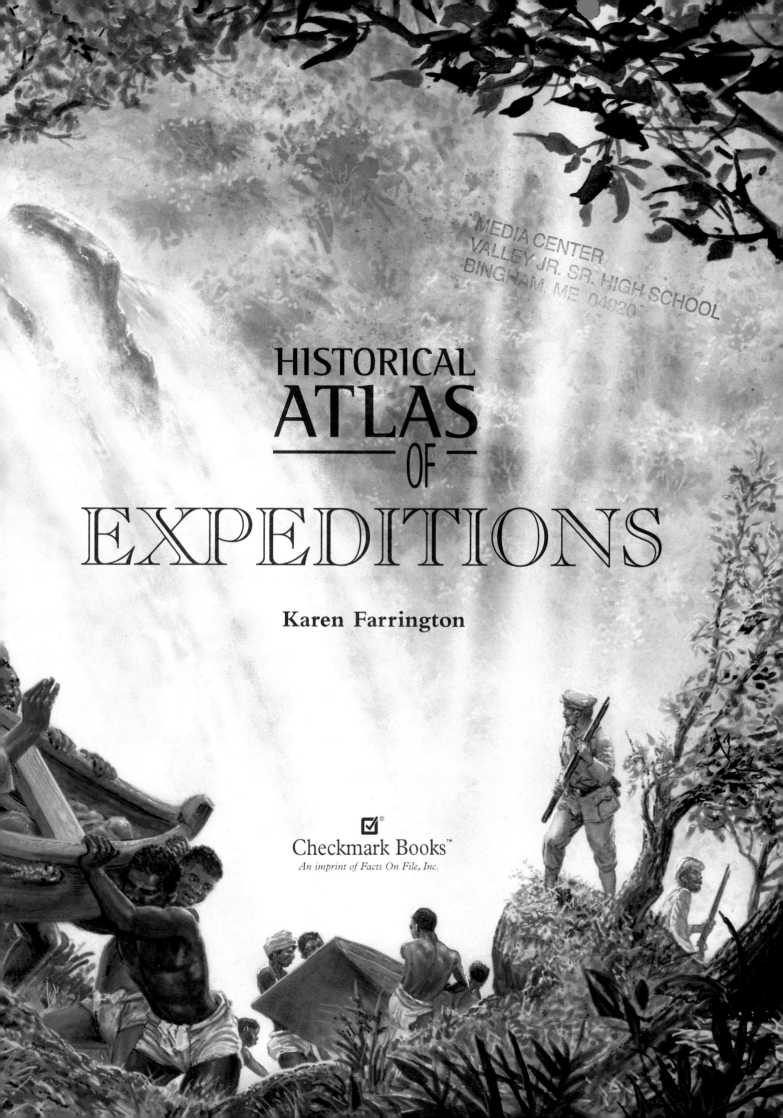

HISTORICAL ATLAS OF EXPEDITIONS

Karen Farrington

Checkmark Books®

An imprint of Facts On File, Inc.

Historical Atlas of Expeditions

Text and Design © 2000 Thalamus Publishing

Library of Congress Cataloging-in-Publication Data available on request from Facts On File.

Checkmark Books are available at special discounts when purchased in bulk quantities for businesses, associations, institutions or sales promotions. Please call our Special Sales Department in New York at: (212) 967-8800 or (800) 322-8755.

You can find Facts On File on the World Wide Web at:
http://www.factsonfile.com

For Thalamus Publishing
Commissioning editor: Lucian Randall
Project editor: Neil Williams
Maps: Keith Williams and Roger Kean
Illustrations: Oliver Frey
Four-color separation: Thalamus Studios

Printed and bound in India by Thomson Press

ISBN: 0-8160-4432-5

PICTURE ACKNOWLEDGMENTS
Picture research by Nathan Grainger/Images Select International limited
AKG London: 12–13, 24, 30–31, 36 (left), 37, 38, 39, 41 (top), 43 (bottom), 46, 47, 50, 62, 86, 90, 100, 113, 158, 169 (bottom), 170 (left); Ancient Art & Architecture Collection: 59, 143; Ancient Art & Architecture Collection/ Murat Ozby: 16; Ancient Art & Architecture Collection/ Ronald Sheridan: 10, 23; Ann Ronan Picture Library: 1, 12, 20, 30, 33, 35 (both), 40, 43 (top), 45 (top), 51, 68, 72, 74 (top), 75, 79 (both), 80 (both), 81, 82 (top), 83, 87 (bottom), 89, 92, 93, 96 (both), 101, 112, 119, 120 (both), 121, 122 (both), 123, 125, 126, 131, 135, 137, 140 (both), 141, 142 (bottom), 144, 145, 147, 148 (bottom), 149, 150, 151, 152, 153 (both), 154, 155, 172 (both), 173, 174 (right), 182, 186, 188; Bettemann Archive/ BBC Hulton: 76; BPCC/ Aldus Archive: 44; Chris Fairclough Colour Library: 21, 183; Culver Pictures: 106, 107, 110, 115, 128, 130, 133, 134; Detroit News: 160, 161 (both); E.T Archive: 52 (right), 53, 84, 169 (top), 170 (bottom), 171, 187; Fox Photos: 163 (bottom); Gamma: 77; Hulton Deutsch: 78, 156, 159, 178 (top); Hulton Getty: 67 (top), 95 (Laing engraving), 103 (bottom), 114, 116, 127, 132, 136, 163 (top), 176, 181, 184 (top); Kit Houghton: 58 (bottom); NASA/ Image Select: 189; Oldrich Karasek/ Still Pictures: 65; Pictor Uniphoto: 69, 95 (background), 109; Pictures Colour Library: 29, 41 (bottom), 55, 56–7, 74 (bottom), 85, 117, 131 (top), 175, 177; Rex Features/ Adrian Sherratt: 164, 165; Spectrum Colour Library: 6–7, 14, 18 (bottom), 32, 45 (bottom), 66–7, 73, 111, 128–9, 157, 184–5; Spectrum Colour Library/ D. & J. Heaton: 118, 178–9; Spectrum Colour Library/ E.J. Chalker: 22; Still Pictures/ Bill O'Connor: 61; Thalamus Publishing: 11 (bottom), 77 (top), 82 (bottom), 87 (top), 88 (both), 95 (inset), 98 (bottom), 99 (both), 102 (both), 103 (top), 129 (top); Thalamus Studios: 2–3, 28, 34, 42, 52 (left), 54, 58 (top), 60 (top), 64, 94, 98 (top), 108, 124, 142 (top), 146, 174 (left), 180, 186 (top); Werner Forman Archive: 19, 25, 91; Werner Forman Archive/ Egyptian Museum, Cairo: 11 (top); Werner Forman Archive/ Gulistan Imperial Library, Teheran: 36 (right); Werner Forman Archive/ Spink & Son, London: 60 (bottom); Werner Forman Archive/ Tanzania National Museum, Dar Es Salaam: 18

Half title: *Ptolemy's Map of the World was originally drawn c.AD 150. This version is taken from the first printed edition of 1472. It would be more than 11 centuries before cartographers would become as accurate again as Ptolemy.*

Previous pages: *Henry Morton Stanley is mostly remembered for his famous meeting with Dr. Livingstone in the African jungles, but Stanley undertook several expeditions across Africa and contributed greatly to the growing core of knowledge about the "Dark Continent."*

Contents

INTRODUCTION

There was a time, not too long ago, when words like "remote" and "unexplored" applied to most of the planet. Humankind's reasons for conquering the surrounding wilderness were numerous. In earliest times the aims of explorers were simple and straightforward—find new sources of water, food, and other essential commodities. Gradually, other motivating factors arose—the quest for fabulous riches, the necessity for trade, the desire for greater power and the subjugation of others, piousness of religious conversion, escape, excitement, or just plain curiosity.

It is this last human trait, however, that has probably contributed most to our drive to explore; whether mounting expeditions to cross hostile terrain, navigate unfriendly oceans, or tame impassable mountain barriers, wanting to know what lies on the other side has been irresistible. Without the desire for knowledge and the need to prove a point mankind may well have stayed put in small clusters and remained tribal in nature.

Throughout history, those who have gone awandering have been out of contact with their own kind, sometimes for years on end. Only recently have explorers benefitted from technological devices: radio, satellite links, geo-positional navigation, email. When Marco Polo journeyed to China no one at home in Venice knew whether he was dead or alive, until he returned. We take communications for granted today, so it is difficult to understand how early explorers ever managed. When Americans landed on the Moon, the whole planet watched and heard the astronauts speak on television. The achievement of this expedition was certainly no lesser than that of the Polos, but how much more comforting it must have been for the NASA astronauts to be in contact with Houston.

One of the problems with looking at any historic period is that it is impossible to see events as they would have appeared to those experiencing them. To most modern readers, the values and motives of these explorers from the past are almost meaningless, since they frequently bear little relation to those of modern

society. We have become used to the idea that modern expeditions are largely scientific in their purpose and may feel inclined to see greed—as well as curiosity—as the prime motivation behind the treks that many detailed in this book undertook. Yet we should not forget that after the conquest of the Moon came the desire to mine its ores for financial gain—once the scientists are done, commerce moves in. In fact this is really very similar to the way expeditions prior to the 20th century worked out.

In the course of discovery there have been tales of heroism and also of heroic failure. Along with every triumph came a catastrophe of epic proportions. Thousands of souls have been sacrificed on the pyre of such enterprise, the optimism and sense of adventure of each one cruelly dashed. As this book shows, some great discoveries have resulted from shrewd cunning, others have been happy accidents. Human endeavor has rarely been as animated and arousing as in the course of conquering the unknown world. To learn how mankind has brought about a world without physical frontier is to understand human nature itself and what makes it tick.

Right: Strangers to Australian history might find the sight of camels in the continent unusual. Camels were introduced by European settlers to aid expeditions into the Australian outback, and are an example of how exploration is a process of cross-fertilization of cultures, flora, and fauna. This picture shows the Australian Exploring Expedition of 1876 traveling through the scrub.

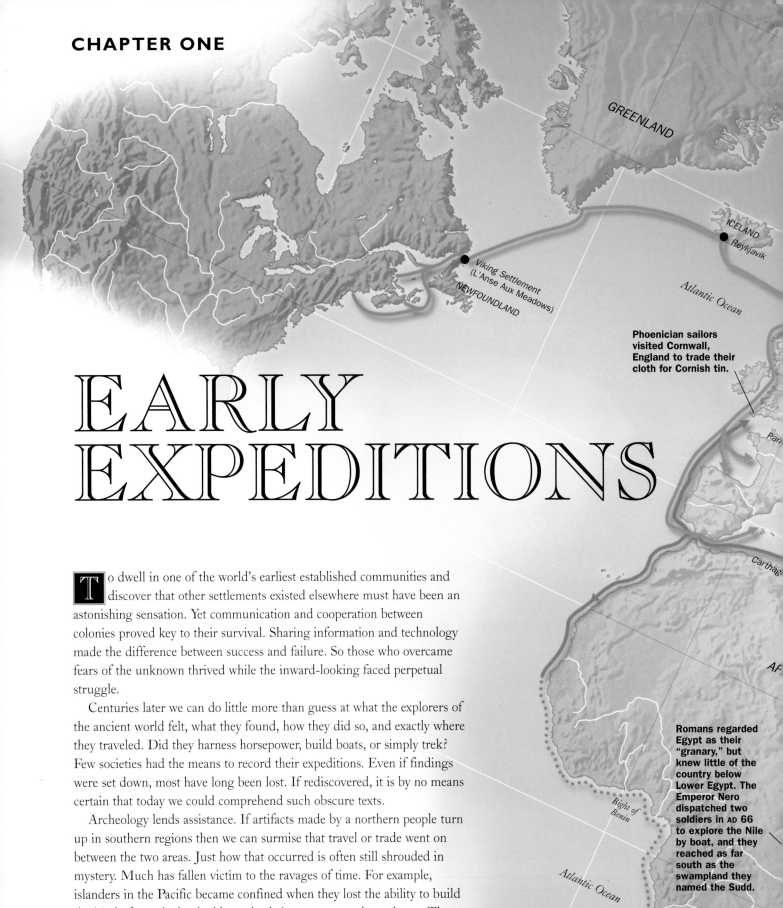

CHAPTER ONE

GREENLAND

ICELAND
Reykjavik

Atlantic Ocean

Viking Settlement
(L'Anse Aux Meadows)
NEWFOUNDLAND

**Phoenician sailors
visited Cornwall,
England to trade their
cloth for Cornish tin.**

Par

Carthag

AF

EARLY EXPEDITIONS

Carthag

T o dwell in one of the world's earliest established communities and discover that other settlements existed elsewhere must have been an astonishing sensation. Yet communication and cooperation between colonies proved key to their survival. Sharing information and technology made the difference between success and failure. So those who overcame fears of the unknown thrived while the inward-looking faced perpetual struggle.

Centuries later we can do little more than guess at what the explorers of the ancient world felt, what they found, how they did so, and exactly where they traveled. Did they harness horsepower, build boats, or simply trek? Few societies had the means to record their expeditions. Even if findings were set down, most have long been lost. If rediscovered, it is by no means certain that today we could comprehend such obscure texts.

Archeology lends assistance. If artifacts made by a northern people turn up in southern regions then we can surmise that travel or trade went on between the two areas. Just how that occurred is often still shrouded in mystery. Much has fallen victim to the ravages of time. For example, islanders in the Pacific became confined when they lost the ability to build the kind of vessels that had brought their ancestors to those shores. These pioneers explode our preconceived notions about the limitations of expeditions in ancient times and leave us gasping in wonder, for they traveled thousands of miles in their primitive craft across the Pacific Ocean to launch the island communities we that recognize today. To some civilizations the mountain ranges, raging rivers, and broad oceans formed natural barriers to expansion. To others they did not. Exploration and development are then intertwined.

**Romans regarded
Egypt as their
"granary," but
knew little of the
country below
Lower Egypt. The
Emperor Nero
dispatched two
soldiers in AD 66
to explore the Nile
by boat, and they
reached as far
south as the
swampland they
named the Sudd.**

Bight of
Benin

Atlantic Ocean

**Hanno, a navigator
from the Phoenician
city of Carthage is
believed to have
circumnavigated Africa
at some time between
500–450 BC. There is
evidence that
Carthaginians did
reach down the West
African coast at about
this time.**

A World Unfolds

Ancient Egypt	3200–1450 BC	
Phoenicians	c.600–c.100 BC	
Phoenicians		
Hanno of Carthage	c.500–450 BC	
Alexander the Great	336–323 BC	
The Silk Road	after 120 BC	
Romans under Nero	AD 66	
Roman traders	AD 100	
The Vikings	793–960	

As early as 3500 BC Sumerian traders traveled down the Persian Gulf on expeditions to India.

Norwegian Sea

SCANDINAVIA

Stockholm

Baltic Sea

Riga

ROPE

Venice

Pellas

Black Sea

Byzantium

Astrakhan

Caspian Sea

Aral Sea

terranean

Antioch

Aleppo

Tyre

Alexandria Eschate

Babylon (Baghdad)

Bukhara

Samarkand

Memphis

Red Sea

PERSIA

Persepolis

Gabae

Kabul

Takla Makan Desert

Thebes

ARABIA

Kandahar

Hindu Kush

Bucephala

Persian Gulf

Gobi Desert

(Khartoum)

Arabian Sea

Great India Desert

Himalayas

(Djibouti)

INDIA

CHINA

Luoyang

Sea of Japan

JAPAN

Indian Ocean

Goa

Dhaka

Yellow Sea

Bay of Bengal

Hanoi

Nellore

Quanzhou (Canton)

Equator

CEYLON (SRI LANKA)

Andaman Sea

South China Sea

Philippine Sea

Gulf of Thailand

SCAR

EGYPTIAN EXPLORERS

from 3200 BC

Early Egyptians were nomads whose very existence depended on finding tracks and waterholes for themselves and their livestock. A ring of stones and standing megaliths near Nabta in the Nubian Desert dating back some 7,000 years indicates that they plotted courses with the help of the sun and the stars.

To later generations the Egyptians bequeathed illuminating texts to broaden our understanding of their lives. Thanks to hieroglyphics, which have since been translated, the earliest expeditions of note are generally attributed to the Egyptians. The first recorded voyage by sea was made under the direction of the Pharaoh Snefru in about 3200 BC. Some 400 years later comes the first identifiable explorer, Hannu, who led an expedition from Egypt and chartered the limits of the known world. In effect, it was a trip down the Red Sea but was nonetheless courageous for its time.

One of the most eminent expedition leaders from Egypt was Harkhuf, an Egyptian nobleman who lived in about 2300 BC. His grave at Elephantine (now Aswan) bears his final testimony, telling how he was dispatched by the king to investigate the road to Yam. Two expeditions later he returned with "300 asses, laden with incense, ebony, heknu, grain, panthers, ivory, throw-sticks, and every good product." Of himself he says: "I was more excellent and vigilant than any count, companion, or caravan conductor who had been sent to Yam before."

Nearby is the grave of Pyopi-nakht, another expedition leader of note. It is known that he journeyed down the Red Sea to claim "the body of [his] royal companion, the captain of ships, the caravan-leader Anankht," killed in local skirmishes.

Right: *Tomb model of an Egyptian ship from Thebes, c.2000 BC.*

Conquest and trade

While sailing down the Nile or the Red Sea was an obvious means of exploration for the Egyptians, wood for ship construction was scarce—they favored cedar from the Lebanon. So they were also just as likely to choose the "Oasis Road" which veered away from the Nile in Middle Egypt and followed a succession of water holes.

Like all ancient peoples, the Egyptians were keen to get their hands on the riches of neighboring lands. To the south was Nubia, otherwise known as Kush, which was rich in mineral reserves. The farmers who lived there could not hope to defend themselves against the enormous forces rallied by the Egyptians. Four thousand years ago one Egyptian government official, Antefoker, wrote: "I slaughtered the Nubians on several occasions…setting the fear of Horus among the southern foreign lands to pacify [them]." Included in the booty Egyptian expeditions brought back were animal skins, myrrh, ebony, ivory, incense—and slaves, required for the ambitious building projects undertaken in Egypt. Not until the eighth century BC did the Nubians shake off Egyptian domination.

One particular lure for the Egyptians was the land of Punt, meaning "the Sacred." Although its exact whereabouts remains a mystery, it is generally thought to have been along the southern shore of the Gulf of Aden or on the adjoining Somali coast.

The inscriptions on the temple of Queen Hatshepsut (1479–57 BC) at Deir el-Bahri, near Luxor, explain the nature of an Egyptian expedition during the reign of ancient Egypt's only female pharaoh. After her death her half-brother and successor, Thutmose III, defaced much of her temple, but fortunately enough was left to give us an outline of what occurred. Probably leaving from Thebes (Luxor), the caravan either crossed some 150 miles of desert from the Nile to the Red Sea or used a long-lost canal connecting the two waterways. Then came a journey on the Red Sea that amounted to perhaps 1,500 miles. Onboard ship they carried goods for trading and gifts for Prince Parihu of Punt. The temple inscriptions reveal that relations between Egypt and Punt were cordial, at least at this point in history. On the return voyage the ships were loaded with goods as diverse as scents, gold rings, panther skins, elephant tusks, apes, a giraffe, and myrrh trees in pots.

Left: Queen Hatshepsut depicted as a sphinx at Deir el-Bahri. The only female pharaoh of ancient Egypt (Cleopatra, much later, was of Greek descent), she was still shown with the false beard that male pharaohs wore on formal occasions.

Below: The Punt ship, as described in temple wall paintings, had a sophisticated rigging system for its masts and sails. This scene shows it being loaded for the return journey. Unfortunately, the inscriptions do not reveal Punt's location.

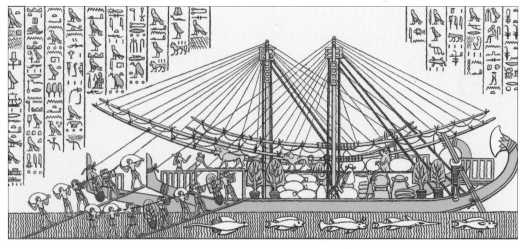

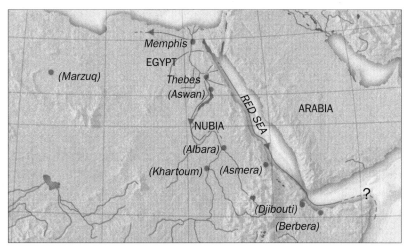

ALEXANDER *the* GREAT

356 BC *to* 323 BC

Right: Conqueror of the known world, Alexander lent his name to cities from the Mediterranean to northern India. This bust is a Roman copy of an original Greek sculpture.

The most enigmatic expedition leader of the ancient world was also the most successful. Alexander the Great led his army on an astonishing 25,000-mile march that took them from Macedonia to Egypt, then on across Asia as far as the Himalayas and back to Persia. He established an impossibly large empire in doing so. But his real achievements lay not in conquest, but rather in going where no European had set foot before.

Alexander was the son of the Macedonian king, Philip II and his wife Olympias. From his father he inherited a masterly grasp of politics and military matters. His mother endowed him with a fascination for mysticism. She was a devotee of the god Dionysus, linked to ecstasy and possession. His parents became estranged—after Philip discovered Olympias in bed with a snake, according to mythology. This tale gave rise to the rumor that Alexander was the product of a liaison between his mother and a god manifesting himself as a reptile. Alexander was certainly happy enough for intimations of his immortality to spread.

There was a third vital influence on the young Alexander and that was his tutor, Aristotle (384–322 BC). From the age of 13 Alexander was taught rhetoric, philosophy, physics, ethics, and poetry by the sage and the short spell under his guidance left a lasting impression. Before becoming king, Alexander astounded Persian ambassadors to the Macedonian court after he intelligently questioned them about the geography of their country.

His intellectual pursuits came to an end with the sudden death of his father, who was assassinated in the theater at Aegea in June 336 BC. Immediately, the 20-year-old Alexander was forced to deal with unrest in the empire his father had created. He stormed Thebes in Greece and burned the long-established city to the ground, sparing only the temples and the home of the Greek poet Pindar. The swift and ruthless vengeance wreaked by Alexander to consolidate his leadership earned him the title "tyrant of Greece." Other states, fearful of the consequences of rebellion against such a man,

began to toe the line. Although short in stature, his violence and personal charisma would carry him far.

An ancient adversary

Initially Alexander planned his expedition to avenge the Greeks for a military humiliation by Persia that had occurred some 150 years before his birth. In addition to fighting men, he took with him geographers, astronomers, scientists, mathematicians, and engineers. There were even men whose sole task it was to assist the cartographers by pacing out each day's march.

His first conflict occurred near the ancient city of Troy, where he triumphed over a Persian army that vastly outnumbered his own. Anecdotes suggest that he lost only 110 men. Darius, the king of Persia, regrouped his forces for a battle at Issus, in what is now Syria. Once again, the honors went to Alexander, and Darius fled, leaving his mother, wife, and children to their fate. As a mark of respect, Alexander treated them nobly.

He then marched his army to Egypt, razing the city of Tyre on the way. In Egypt he founded the famous city of Alexandria in 332 BC, which would become a renowned seat of learning, home to Cleopatra, and the site of the Pharos lighthouse, one of the Seven Wonders of the World. Alexander was crowned Pharaoh of Egypt and consulted with a famous Oracle before leaving his new kingdom. He was told what he wanted to hear—that he was the son of God. He departed from Egypt intending to confront Darius again, and his wish was granted at Gaugamela on October 1, 331 BC, while his army marched toward Babylon. For the third time Alexander was the victor and the Persian king was forced to flee the battlefield, to be murdered by two of his entourage.

The enormous riches of the Persian's capital of Persepolis lay before him. Alexander looted then razed the city. His conquest of the Persian Empire was complete. Dreams of unifying east and west under Macedonian control were coming to fruition for Alexander, but his expedition still had far to go to fulfil his ambitions.

Below: Alexander brought the Persians to battle for a second time at Issus, where he forced Darius, the Persian king, to flee for his life. This Roman mosaic at Pompeii is copied from a Greek painting by Philoxenos.

Above: *The extent of the ruins of Persepolis can only hint at the glory that was the Persian capital. After finally defeating King Darius, Alexander looted the city and then had it razed to the ground in 331 BC.*

A bitter trek

Alexander had his sights set on further gains at the outposts of the Persian Empire in the east. He led his army across what is now Iran and Afghanistan, through the Khyber Pass, and into India, where he carried out an aggressive campaign of conquest. The young king from Macedonia was now operating at the very borders of the ancient known world.

Motivated as much by curiosity as greed, it was only the uncharacteristic opposition of his weary troops that compelled him to stop rather than forge on into the heart of India to the south. With his men yearning for home, Alexander decided on a speedy return by ship and had a fleet built. After embarking half the force, it sailed down the Hydaspes to the Indus river. The remainder, led by Alexander, marched along the river banks, fending off hostile tribes, in a trek to the Indus delta that took nine months to complete.

On the shores of the Arabian Sea Alexander split the army into three groups. The sick and wounded were to march directly overland to Persia, while Alexander led a second force to explore along the unknown shoreline of the Arabian Sea. The third group was to remain on the ships and sail along the coast, survey the shoreline, and provide supplies for Alexander's foot soldiers. It became a bitter test of endurance. Those marching overland to Persia encountered hideously brutal conditions, including Pakistan's Makran Desert, which claimed the lives of many. Alexander, who was forced to march inland to avoid the desert terrain, only managed one of the many planned meetings with his naval fleet.

By the time the army reached Persia they had suffered hardships that can only be guessed at. Food shortages, inadequate clothing, lack of medicines and shelter took a severe toll on the men, but the results of the expedition were unprecedented. The entire known world was in Alexander's control. He had established an

2000 BC	c.1900 BC	1792 BC	1600 BC	1501–1479 BC	c.1500 BC	c.1200 BC	c1000 BC
Early Greeks settle the Peloponnese	Egyptians establish line of forts along Nile as far as Nubia	King Hammurabi of Babylonia extends control over Mesopotamia	Aryan tribes reach the Indus valley	Expeditions to east Africa initiated by Queen Hatshepsut	People from the Philippines settle the Mariana Pacific islands	Barbarian "sea peoples" explore and raid Mediterranean civilizations	Polynesians from Fiji colonize Samoa and Tonga

estimated 17 new cities bearing the name Alexandria, some of which were later renamed and others that did not endure. With Alexander and his army went the Greek language and culture, an influence that would later assist Roman conquests of the region.

Hero or villain?

For Alexander the question of how to maintain his empire was now uppermost. How could he stop it from unraveling? One plan was to establish a shipping route from Babylon to Egypt, around the Arabian peninsula, so linking the two foundation stones of his empire with the mutual benefits of trade. However, his monumental efforts were cut short by his untimely death in 323 BC, at the age of only 33. Some believed he was poisoned, others that he became infected with malaria. Recent theories suggest the cause of death was typhoid fever. In any event, the wars of succession following his death lasted for 40 years and all semblance of unity in the empire quickly disappeared.

Alexander had always been a difficult, ambitious character, notoriously impossible to analyse even for his contemporaries. He had two wives and fathered at least three children, but since most of his adult life was spent with his army, his closest relationships were with his officers and men. Alexander's leadership, though harsh, was innovative and inspired a faithful following, and despite his position, he maintained close friendships. His most intimate friendship was with Hephaistion, whom he had known since childhood; yet being close to Alexander was a risky position. He murdered another friend, Clitus—a man who had once saved his life—following a drinking bout. Afterward he was so grief-stricken that he went into seclusion for three days.

Drink lay at the root of many of his violent outbursts. Macedonian boys were introduced to a culture of heavy drinking at an early age, and the long-term effects of this alcohol dependency may have contributed to the black rages and megalomaniac tendencies that prevailed in Alexander's final years; just before his death he ordered his subjects to worship him as a god.

By modern standards, Alexander was a military dictator of the worst kind. But in an ancient world of tribalism, savagery, cruelty, and political disunion his lasting legacy is to have pushed forward the boundaries of knowledge as far as was practically possible.

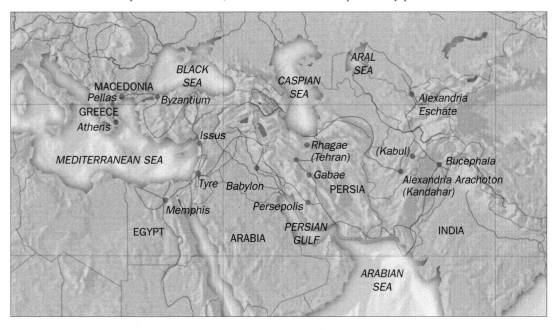

735 BC	620 BC	c.600 BC	600 BC	6th century BC	512 BC	460 BC	c.450 BC
The Greeks create colonies in eastern Sicily	Greek traders establish colonies in the Nile delta	A Phoenician fleet is believed to have circumnavigated Africa, taking three years	Greeks explore and colonise south-west France	Scylax of Caryanda travels into India and Arabia	Persians conquer Greece	Athenians send military expedition to attack Persia	Carthaginian traders make direct voyages to Britain

The SILK ROAD
from 105 BC

The terrain across central Asia from China to the West is some of the most inhospitable in the world. High mountains, baking deserts, empty steppes, and sparse settlements make travel through the vast region arduous. Ruthless bandits were a menace in antiquity, as were bears and wolves. Yet the huge profits that could be made by exchanging luxury goods over long distances made the risks seem worthwhile, and intrepid bands of travelers rose to the challenge.

Early expeditions scythed a path through unyielding Asia in order to barter and exchange. The trump card held by China was silk, a world apart from the hempen fibers, rough woolens, and cottons known in other civilizations. Westerners were beguiled by its softness and strong colors and simply could not fathom how it was made. As late as AD 70 the Roman Pliny believed that strands of silk were gathered on leaves of an indigenous Chinese plant. It wasn't until the fourth century that a Chinese princess smuggled some silk worms out of her native country and enabled the launch of silk farms in other parts of Asia. The secret was out. Silk was no longer the glorious, mysterious fabric it had been for centuries.

Silk was first produced in China about 3000 BC. It provided a healthy internal trade until about 138 BC when Emperor Wu-di of the Han dynasty became dominant in central Asia. At this time China was ignorant about the wider world. Emperor Wu-di wanted to know more. At his instruction, Zhang Qian (Chang Ch'ien) led one of the earliest expeditions and became the first known Chinese traveler to make contact with the Central Asian tribes.

Zhang Qian was a diplomat in the court of emperor Wu-di when he was ordered to make an alliance with an Iranian tribe, who the Chinese called the Yue-Chi, to combat their common enemy, the Huns. His first task was to find the Yue-Chi. In attempting to make contact he was captured by Huns and imprisoned for a decade until he could make an escape. He discovered the Yue-Chi were no longer inclined to make war on the Hun and, while returning to China, he was briefly arrested once more.

In 126 BC he arrived back in China

Below: At either end of the Silk Road, merchants and travelers could ride on horseback, but in the great wastes of Central Asia, camels were the only means of transport, exchanged for mules to climb the intervening mountain ranges.

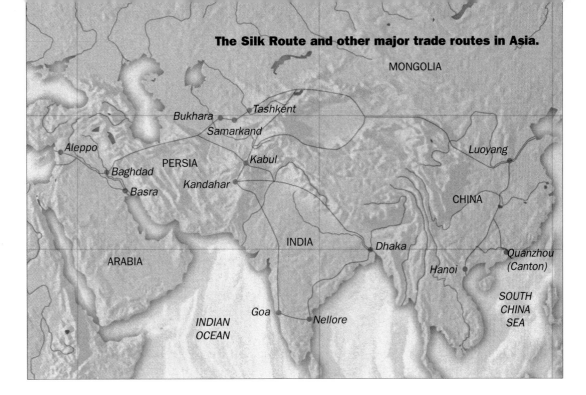

The Silk Route and other major trade routes in Asia.

accompanied by just two of the 100 troops that had originally left with him. His descriptions of the countries he visited outside China's border were intriguing. The possibilities of trade began to dawn on the Chinese court. Zhang Qian was dispatched again, this time with merchandise, to determine new links and with instructions to avoid the marauding Huns at all costs. It is thought that as a direct result of his efforts, what we now know as the Silk Road came into existence in 105 BC. In antiquity the route was not called the Silk Road. The name was coined in modern times by German geographer Ferdinand Freiherr von Richthofen (1833–1905), an early expert in Oriental map-making.

The Silk Road was about 4,000 miles long, a colossal path linking the Yellow River in the east with the Mediterranean in the west. It remained a significant trading route while empires rose and fell around it. Among those who relied on the Silk Road were the Greeks, Romans, Persians, Parthians, Mongolians, and various Chinese dynasties.

The original middlemen

The inhabitants of northwest India seized the opportunity to become middlemen in this lucrative trade and expanded its allure by introducing precious stones and metals including jade, gold, and silver into the exchange. Since the Greeks and Romans rarely, if ever, dealt directly with the Chinese because of the distances involved, they were only dimly aware of their existence. While the exchange of goods occurred on an ongoing basis there was no corresponding exchange in culture.

In the west lay the burgeoning Roman Empire, where republicanism had given way to imperialism. The society was outward looking and hungry for new commodities. Silk became extremely popular in this self-indulgent society. A dozen caravan trains leaving China each year during the Han dynasty provided up to 30 per cent of the Chinese dynasty's revenues. With the door to east-west trade open and its potential clearly evident, the Greeks were also keen to become beneficiaries.

Yet fine silks were not the only goods that China traded. There were also many spices, notably cinnamon—and, a rarity in the west, paper. From the west came wool, gold, silver, and precious stones. And, eventually, along with the hard goods there was a trade in ideas.

One of the most famous finds along the route of the Silk Road was made in 1938 by Belgian archeologists at Begram in Afghanistan. Inside two hidden rooms the Europeans discovered ivory plaques and statues from India, bronze idols and glassware from Egypt, lacquered goods from China, and artifacts from other cultures. The items had been stowed away some 2,000 years previously for reasons we cannot know. Further evidence of the extent of the Silk Road was found at Shosoin Temple in Japan. The temple was built in AD 752 by Emperor Shomu and devoted to his mother. Inside were items from China, India, Persia, and the Mediterranean, all hauled along the Silk Road into China and from there exported to the otherwise isolated society of Japan.

In the east the Silk Road began at Xi'an (Chang'an). It was the capital of the Han dynasty and, in common with other major cities on the route, it fostered great wealth. When

Relics of the route

There have been exciting archeological finds along the Silk Road that indicate a more ancient origin to at least parts of the trade route. The sands of the Takla Makan Desert in Chinese Turkestan have yielded the mummified bodies of people who lived 500 years before the Egyptian pharaoh Tutankhamun. Perplexingly, these were not indigenous people as one might expect but Caucasians—tall blonds and redheads with high-bridged noses. These people migrated east hundreds of years before silk became a trade commodity. Locally they were known as Tokharians. By the tenth century AD they had been absorbed into indigenous local populations. The discovery of these bodies has proved that the Silk Road was established on existing, ancient migratory routes.

Several mummies dating back to the Han dynasty, between 202 BC and AD 220 have been recovered. These bodies, although wrapped in silks, were not embalmed but were preserved by the dry desert air. Among the artifacts found with the bodies were a bow, arrows, arrow shafts, and a scabbard. Associated with the women were a bronze mirror, a double-edged comb, and cosmetics.

camel trains departed from Xi'an they were loaded with cascades of silk.

In addition to hard goods the Silk Road became a way of exchanging ideas. Its existence assisted incalculably with the spread of Buddhism, which was founded in India by Siddhartha Gautama (born about 563 BC). Other important religions also spread along the trading route, including Zoroastrianism from Persia (its adherents became known as Parsis in India), Manicheanism, Mithraism, and Nestorian Christianity.

The never-ending road

Using the network of Buddhist monasteries an early traveler from China, the monk Fu-Hsien, journeyed around India at the end of the fourth century AD. His work, written when he was safely back in Nanking, was called *Memoirs of the Buddha Dominions*, an important source for first-hand facts about life outside China for its literate minority of readers. Another monk, Hsuan-Tsang, provided more enlightenment 130 years later. In travels lasting 15 years, he collected botanical specimens, manuscripts, religious icons, and relics. He also wrote of his experiences in the hefty tome *Memoirs on Western Countries*.

When the trek taken by ancient traders was followed by four English women during eight months of 1999 the primary difficulties were disease—namely dysentery—and boredom. Said Sophia Cunningham, one of the four: "We would have day after day for three and a half months of relentless sand. We all felt as if it would never end." The four, which included Alexandra Tolstoy, daughter of the historian Count Nikolai Tolstoy, traveled on horseback and by camel. Today the route stretches through the modern nations of China, Uzbekistan, Afghanistan, Iran, Iraq, and Syria.

Above: *The ruins of the ancient T'ang city of Gaochang, an outlying command and staging post on the Silk Road.*

STRABO *and the* ROMANS

c63 BC to cAD 24

For 1,000 years Rome held sway in the Mediterranean, notching up an array of conquests. Roman expeditions tended to be military rather than exploratory or scientific. Nevertheless, because Romans governed through knowledge of their territories, there were often geographers attached to the legions, and they made important observations that were preserved for posterity. Strabo enjoyed just such a role. He was a Greek geographer, historian, and philosopher who traveled widely in the Roman Empire and recorded his findings in no fewer than 60 books. Most of the contents of his 43 history books have been lost but his *Geography*, spanning 17 volumes, has survived almost in its entirety. The first two volumes are an introduction, the next ten deal with Europe, four are about Asia, and the final volume focuses on Africa; at least, the part that the Romans knew along the Mediterranean coast and the lower reaches of the Nile in Egypt.

Although born in Greek territory, Strabo spent many years in Rome, witnessing the advent of Augustan rule and with it the birth of Imperial Rome. He first developed a taste for travel when he joined a Nile expedition led by Aelius Gallus, the Roman prefect of Egypt. By his own account he ultimately traveled from Armenia in the east to Britain in the west and from the Black Sea in the north to the borders of Ethiopia in the south.

One of Strabo's heroes was Homer, who he believed to be the founder of the science of geography. In his day the reality of Homer, author of *The Iliad* and *The Odyssey*, was beyond question, but these days it is believed the works of many hands were attributed to Homer. In Strabo's discussion of Homer's geography we can see how the world appeared to the ancients: "In the first place Homer declares that the inhabited world is washed on all sides by Oceanus, and this is true; and then he mentions

Above: The historian and geographer Strabo, from a 15th-century woodcut.

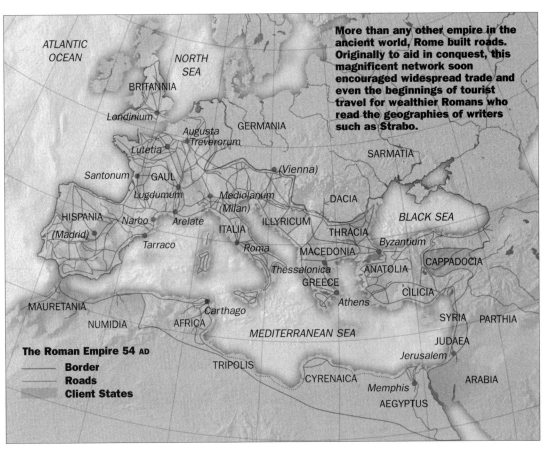

More than any other empire in the ancient world, Rome built roads. Originally to aid in conquest, this magnificent network soon encouraged widespread trade and even the beginnings of tourist travel for wealthier Romans who read the geographies of writers such as Strabo.

ATLANTIC OCEAN

NORTH SEA

BRITANNIA

Londinium

GERMANIA

Augusta Treverorum

Lutetia

SARMATIA

Santonum GAUL

(Vienna)

Lugdumum Mediolanum (Milan)

DACIA

HISPANIA Narbo Arelate ILLYRICUM

BLACK SEA

(Madrid) ITALIA THRACIA

Byzantium

Tarraco Roma MACEDONIA

CAPPADOCIA

Thessalonica ANATOLIA

GREECE CILICIA

MAURETANIA Athens

Carthago SYRIA PARTHIA

NUMIDIA AFRICA

MEDITERRANEAN SEA JUDAEA

The Roman Empire 54 AD Jerusalem

——— **Border** TRIPOLIS

——— **Roads** CYRENAICA ARABIA

Client States Memphis

AEGYPTUS

some of the countries by name, while he leaves us to infer the other countries from hints. For instance, he expressly mentions Libya, Ethiopia, Sidonians, and Erembians—and by Erembians he probably means Arabian troglodytes—whereas he only indicates in general terms the people who live in the far east and the far west by saying that their countries are washed by Oceanus."

Polybius

Strabo's work supplemented that done by Polybius (c.200–120 BC), author of the 40-volume *Universal History*, which illustrated how much of Europe, Asia Minor, and North Africa had fallen under Roman dominion. Polybius gathered much of his information when he joined Scipio Africanus the Younger on the campaigns in North Africa that finally demolished the Carthaginian Empire.

Both Polybius and Strabo wrote with a Roman bias, but in a way that also gives us an insight into contrasts between the societies of the time. Said Polybius: "In all things that regard the acquisition of wealth, the manners also, and the customs of the Romans, are greatly preferable to those of the Carthaginians…

Among the Carthaginians money is openly employed to obtain the dignities of the state; but all such proceeding is a capital crime in Rome." He fondly discussed "the superior excellence of the Roman government" and scorned the lack of sophistication of the Carthaginians. "[Superstition] is impressed with all its terror and influences on both the private actions of the citizens and the public administration also of the state in a degree that can scarcely be exceeded."

Rome began its expansion in 753 BC, first gaining control of other areas on the Italian peninsula, then extending its sphere of influence to Carthage (North Africa), Spain, and Greece. At about the time of Christ, Rome was in control of the Biblical lands and had conquered Germany as far as the River Elbe. France and Britain were later conquered under Caesar and Claudius respectively. Strabo visited Britain where he observed: "The whole race… is madly fond of war, high-spirited, and quick to battle, but otherwise straightforward and not of evil character. And so when they are stirred up they assemble in their bands for battle, quite openly and without forethought, so that they are easily handled by those who desire to outwit them."

Above: *Having destroyed the Punic city of Carthage, the Romans rebuilt in their own mold and graced the new city with splendid buildings, such as the Colosseum.*

ISLAMIC EXPLORERS

from AD 630

When Mohammed delivered the word of Allah to his followers in AD 630 he established a new religion whose far-flung conquests would initiate a new era of exploration. The rapid expansion of Islam carved out a vast swathe of territory, united disparate peoples, and allowed a degree of free movement between the conquered lands. The annual pilgrimage to Mecca that every Muslim must make at least once—the Hajj—meant that most Muslim citizens traveled large distances from home, and consequently travel and exploration became ingrained in Islamic society.

As belief in Islam spread through the Middle East, North Africa, and Asia Minor the number of expeditions that set out each year traveling to Mecca, in present day Saudi Arabia, increased exponentially. New routes were discovered by geographically isolated converts, fresh trade links were established, and inward-looking communities acquired a thirst for adventure.

Since by this time the Western Roman Empire had collapsed, the Eastern Roman, or Byzantine, Empire was encircled by enemies, and Europe was factionalized, the collective Muslim emirates became the most potent civilization west of China. As this religious empire expanded and matured, it gained considerable knowledge of geography and cartography as a by-product of increasing trade.

One of the most significant early geographical works was *The Figures of the Earth*, collated by Mohammad ibn Musa al-Khwarazmi. He had access to the findings of Arab and Persian sailors who voyaged through the Indian Ocean. Mathematical and cultural work was produced by Abu Rayhan al-Biruni (973–1048), an open-minded scholar who pondered on the Earth's rotation about its axis and the geographical changes that had affected places like the Indus Valley. Once again we see the prevailing influence of Islam in his work. He calculated the locations of cities by degree so that the Mosque-builders could site their buildings accurately in line with Mecca.

425 BC	415 BC	340 BC	329 BC	326 BC	321-316	280 BC	c.235 BC
Death of Herodotus, Greek historian and geographer	An Athenian expedition to Sicily ends in disaster	Greek navigator Pytheas circum-navigates Britain	Alexander the Great reaches Afghanistan	Alexander the Great leads his army into India	Alexander the Great's empire breaks up	A canal is built linking the Mediterranean with the Red Sea	Eratosthenes uses geometry to estimate the Earth's circumference

A Christian patron

Another eminent Islamic geographer was al-Idrisi (1100–65). Paradoxically, although he could trace his family lineage directly back to Mohammed, he chose to work for a Christian for most of his life. The man who enticed him was King Roger II of Sicily, a Norman by descent. Al-Idrisi was 45 years old and had already traveled extensively in Spain, North Africa, and Asia and probably Portugal, western France, and southern England as well. He went to Palermo in the knowledge that a considerable Muslim enclave existed there already. His task for the king was to compile a map of the world.

With royal patronage, al-Idrisi was able to dispatch representatives to far-flung places with a brief to note the landfall and shorelines. From the south they returned with descriptions of the River Niger; from the east came the latest in Chinese cartography, which he added to his extensive knowledge of the work of Ptolemy and other Greek and Roman scholars. Indeed, the criticism often leveled at al-Idrisi is that he depended too much on the flawed wisdom of the ancients and insufficiently on the more modern methods becoming available to him.

Left: Roger II is crowned king in 1129, from a mosaic in the Palatine Chapel in Palermo, Sicily. Descended from the Norman family of de Hauteville, who conquered Sicily and southern Italy, King Roger was unusual for his time in his admiration of Muslim culture and manners.

His research culminated in two extensive maps and, for his patron, *The Book of Roger*, devoted to geographical knowledge. In addition he wrote about medicine and was a literary writer and poet. Islamic scholars continued to produce detailed and beautifully-designed maps, which were extremely accurate and ultimately aided European explorers of a later era.

Facing: Arab traders were quick to use the stars as navigational aids, and this, combined with an interest in geography, led to sophisticated observatories throughout Muslim lands. This is the Jantar Mantar Observatory, Jaipur, India.

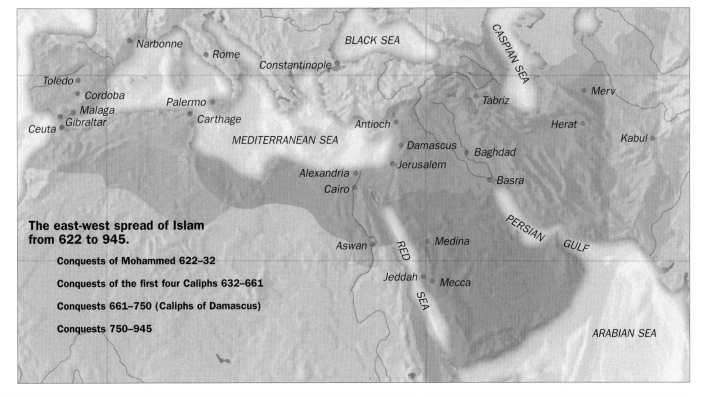

The east-west spread of Islam from 622 to 945.

Conquests of Mohammed 622–32

Conquests of the first four Caliphs 632–661

Conquests 661–750 (Caliphs of Damascus)

Conquests 750–945

c.200 BC	194 BC	126 BC	50 BC	20 BC	1 BC	1 BC	AD 39
Polynesian settlement in the islands of Tahiti	Death of Eratosthenes who attempted to calculate Earth's circumference	Chang Chi'en reaches Samarkand along the Silk Road	Romans begin trade with India	Cornelius Balbus travels 1,000 miles into Africa from Tripoli	The first farming communities arrive in the Caribbean	Madagascar is explored and settled by Indonesians	A wooden ship 233 ft long is constructed on Lake Nemi near Rome

The VIKINGS

790 *to* 1100

Vikings came from Scandinavia and were a force to be reckoned with between 790 and 1100 AD. Northern Europe was warmer then, food production successful, and the well-nourished Norse population of Scandinavia expanded. The need for new lands and the impetus for trade drove the Norse overseas to the west and eastward along rivers into Russia. With a well developed agrarian culture, when the Norse went raiding, or *viking*, overseas, they were a fierce, ruthless, and plundering people. Vikings made their presence felt wherever they turned up. The first major venture out of their own lands was in 793 to Lindisfarne, the monastery on the east coast of England where they slaughtered and stole whatever they could. Assisted by their strongly constructed ships and a working knowledge of astronomy for the purposes of navigation, Viking raids continued along the English, Scottish, Welsh, and Irish coasts and ultimately they went into France. In the tenth century Bjorn Ironside, the son of a Danish king, led 62 ships on a voyage along the Spanish and North African coasts where they clashed with the equally fearsome Moorish warriors.

The aim of the Vikings was to tax or colonize. Their coast-hugging expeditions brought fear to the local populace but dramatically extended the horizons of this northern people. Yet they are best remembered for their exploration of the unknown. Iceland—originally discovered by the Irish—was rediscovered in 860 and became a Viking settlement.

Stepping stones to America

A century later quarrelsome Eric the Red discovered Greenland after being thrown out of Iceland, and started a colony that would last until the 15th century. His son, Leif Eriksson, likewise imbued with an adventuring spirit, sailed further west and made landfall in America. He landed in three places which he named Helluland, Markland, and Vinland. While it has not yet proved possible to locate these landing sites precisely, it is generally accepted that they were on Baffin Island, Labrador, and in Newfoundland at L'Anse aux

Right: The first real evidence of what a Viking longboat looked like was discovered in 1904, when this ninth-century vessel was discovered in Oseberg, Norway.

AD 10	50	83	c.100	c.200	c.300	399-414	c.400
Greek geographer Strabo produces map of Roman world	The first non-stop trading voyages from Egypt to India are undertaken	Romans reach Scotland	New knowledge of monsoon winds allow faster trade between India and Arabia	Bantu peoples reach the east coast of Africa	Polynesians discover Easter Island	Fu-Hsien journeys south of the Takla Makan and returns to China via Sri Lanka	Polynesians discover the Hawaiian islands

Meadows, where excavations have turned up Viking buildings and artifacts. Sustaining an existence in America proved impossible, however, primarily due to the hostility of the local people whom the Vikings called *skraelingar*—meaning "screechers" or "uglies." Nevertheless Vikings continued to visit the North American continent to collect wood for ships.

Modern excavations have enlightened us about the kind of ships used by the Vikings, ships that survived the rigors of the Atlantic. The knorr, or cargo ship, was 54 feet long and 15 feet wide with one mast and a sail. Longships used for raids were larger still. Passengers, crew, livestock, and cargo shared the central space during voyages. There was no way of cooking aboard so food had to be dried and preserved before setting sail.

To the east the Vikings forged routes deep into Europe, to the Black Sea, and finally to Asia and the Middle East. They established trading posts that today are prosperous cities, including Smolensk and Kiev. Most of the trading in the southern and eastern lands was carried out under Arab dominion. The goods the Vikings traded included slaves, furs, animal oils, walrus ivory, ropes, wool, and honey. In exchange they received precious metals, wine, weapons, spices, and silks.

Ships remained essential throughout the Viking era and the rivers Dnieper and Volga were particularly vital arteries of trade. But their expeditions from the north also required overland transport. Vikings generally chose to wait for winter and hauled goods over long distances using sleds.

The exploits of the Vikings are known because they were recorded in the form of sagas. More than simply exciting stories, the sagas contain geographical details that hold up astonishingly well to modern scrutiny.

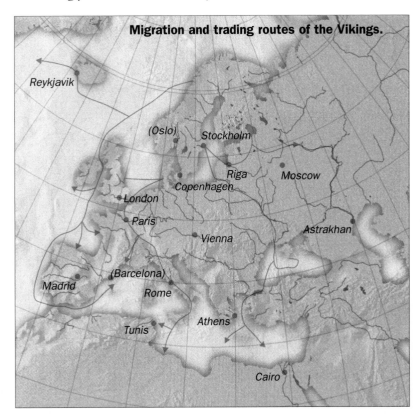

Migration and trading routes of the Vikings.

633	650	670	705	711	c.800	c.860	982
Buddhist monk Xuan Zang travels to India in search of religious texts	Arab traders colonize East African coast	Muslim Arabs reach Tunisia	Arabs reach central Asia	Arabs reach West African coast	Polynesians arrive in New Zealand	Viking Gardar Svarvarsson circumnavigates Iceland	Erik the Red founds colony in Greenland

CHAPTER TWO

TRAVELS
before 1600

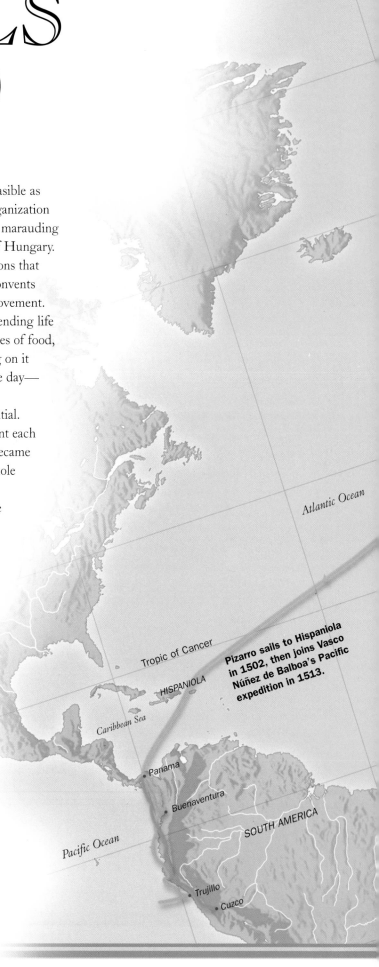

Pizarro sails to Hispaniola in 1502, then joins Vasco Núñez de Balboa's Pacific expedition in 1513.

In the Middle Ages long-distance travel at last became feasible as regional stability in Europe improved. Better military organization allowed the developing nation-states to defend themselves from marauding peoples, such as the Vikings of Scandinavia and the Magyars of Hungary. Towns and cities were at last protected by newly-built fortifications that made journeys much safer, and a network of monasteries and convents provided food and shelter to travelers, thus encouraging free movement. Methods of agriculture improved, giving greater yields and extending life expectancy. With a burgeoning population and frequent surpluses of food, feudal lords who owned both the land and the peasants working on it were in a position to contribute to the military expeditions of the day— the Crusades.

But the perils posed to land-based travelers were still substantial. Enmity increased between Christians and Muslims, which meant each was at risk from the other. To the east were the Mongols who became united under Genghis Khan in 1206 and took control of the whole of Asia. At its height the Mongol Empire was the largest the world had ever seen. But the most effective bar to travel was the scourge of the Black Death, which ripped through Europe in the middle of the 14th century. The outbreak of the plague, carried by the black rat and its fleas, began in Central Asia in 1347, swept through China and India, and accompanied merchants into Europe. It was a virulent epidemic that killed the population and their animals. In some areas the mortality rate exceeded 50% and in all over a third of the population of Europe was wiped out, some 20 million souls. At the time no one knew what caused this dreadful disease, which could bring death within three days. For a while, the risks of journeying to other lands became prohibitive, but in between epidemics of bubonic and pneumonic plague Europeans traveled, explored, and discovered as never before.

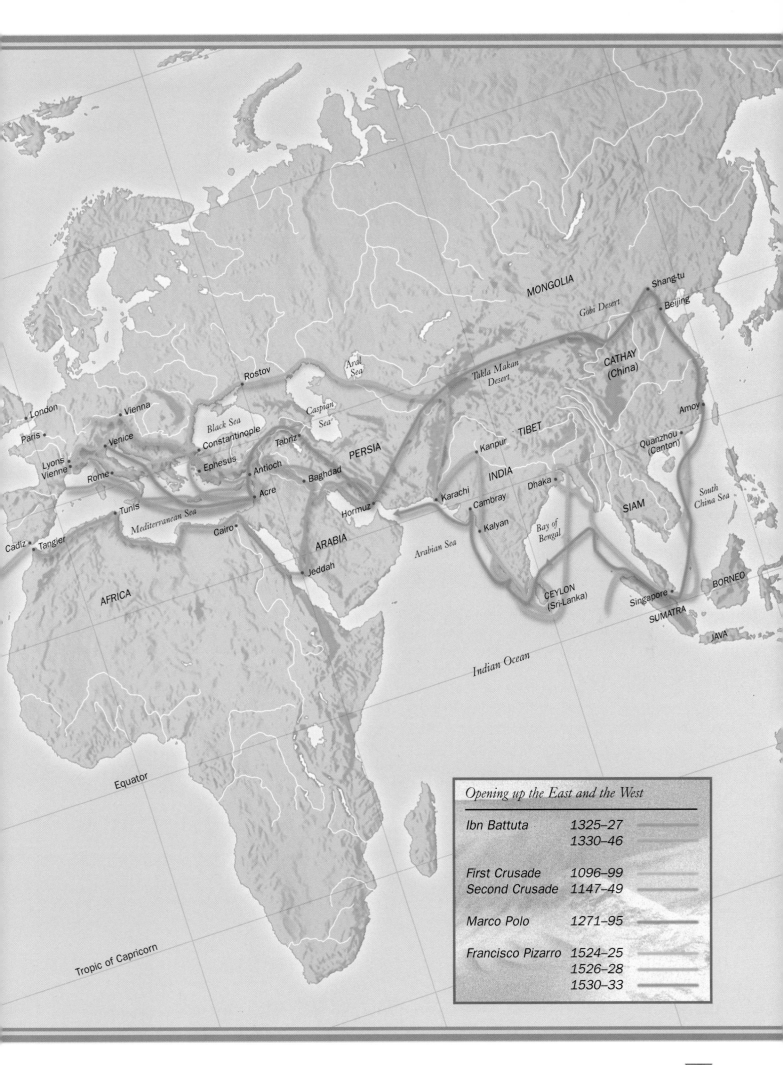

MONGOLIA

Shang-tu

Gobi Desert

Beijing

CATHAY
(China)

Amoy

Aral
Sea

Takla Makan
Desert

Rostov

Caspian
Sea

Quanzhou
(Canton)

London

Vienna

Black Sea

Constantinople

Tabriz

TIBET

Paris

Ephesus

PERSIA

Kanpur

INDIA

Dhaka

South
China Sea

Lyons
Vienne

Antioch

Baghdad

Rome

Acre

Karachi

Cambray

SIAM

Tunis

Hormuz

Kalyan

Mediterranean Sea

Cairo

Bay of
Bengal

BORNEO

Cadiz

Tangier

ARABIA

Arabian Sea

Singapore

Jeddah

CEYLON
(Sri-Lanka)

SUMATRA

AFRICA

JAVA

Indian Ocean

Equator

Tropic of Capricorn

Opening up the East and the West		
Ibn Battuta	1325–27	
	1330–46	
First Crusade	1096–99	
Second Crusade	1147–49	
Marco Polo	1271–95	
Francisco Pizarro	1524–25	
	1526–28	
	1530–33	

IBN BATTUTA
1304 to 1369

Right: One of the most traveled men of his time, Ibn Battuta's recorded observations of his journeys provide an illuminating insight into the medieval Arab world.

I nspired by the vast realm of the Islamic world, Ibn Battuta left his home in Morocco at the age of 21 with the aim of fulfilling the Hajj, or Muslim pilgrimage, to Mecca. "I left Tangier, my city of birth…with the intention of making a pilgrimage to the Holy House and of visiting the Tomb of the Prophet," Ibn Battuta relates in the opening line of his book *Rihlah*, dictated on his return. Outside North Africa he was enthralled by the new lands he found, and began a 26-year expedition that would take him to the remotest corners of the Muslim world, ultimately covering an estimated 75,000 miles.

Ibn Battuta was born into a family of Muslim Berber judges and, we can surmise, was broadly educated at the mosque and widely read. His aim in undertaking the Hajj was not only to fulfil his religious obligations but also to converse with the scholars of the Arab world. As his appetite for adventure grew beyond his original aims of completing the Hajj, he expressed a desire "to travel through the earth" with only one rule rooted in his mind—never to use the same road twice.

At first he traveled along the Mediterranean sea until he reached Alexandria—where he visited the famous library and lighthouse—and Cairo where he boarded a voyage heading up the Nile. His aim was to cross the Red Sea into Arabia but a local conflict prevented him from doing so. He was forced to return to Cairo and go

overland to Mecca, visiting Syria along the way.

Following his pilgrimage, Ibn Battuta visited Basra in present-day Iraq and went up the Euphrates River to Baghdad, then further north into Turkish territory before returning to Mecca. He remained there as a student for a while before the desire to travel overcame him once more. Next he set off by ship across the Red Sea and down the eastern coast of Africa with Arab traders, making stops all the way to Kilwa in present day Tanzania. The journey was not without risk since relations between Muslim

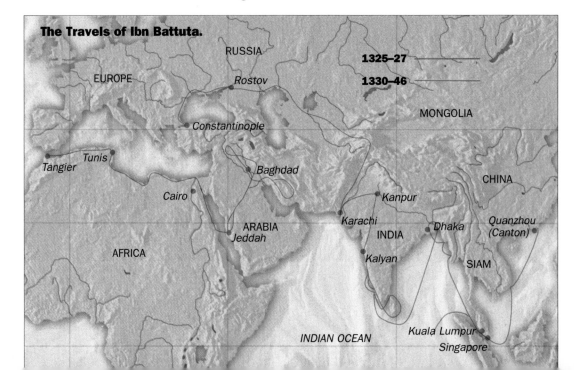

The Travels of Ibn Battuta.

RUSSIA

EUROPE

Rostov

1325–27

1330–46

MONGOLIA

Constantinople

Tunis

Tangier

Baghdad

CHINA

Cairo

Kanpur

ARABIA

Jeddah

Karachi

INDIA

Dhaka

Quanzhou (Canton)

AFRICA

Kalyan

SIAM

Kuala Lumpur

INDIAN OCEAN

Singapore

traders and the Africans they frequently enslaved were precarious.

He returned to Mecca for a third stay (only when approaching and departing the Islamic center did he suspend his rule of not using roads more than once). Soon he set off for India, using a convoluted route to explore other lands on the way. First he headed north overland for the Black Sea port of Sinope, then he went through the Caucasus, up the frozen Volga River, back to the Black Sea and into Constantinople. From there he headed across the steppes of Russia, north of the Caspian Sea, touching the Silk Road before dipping down into Afghanistan and finally India.

In Delhi he was made an honored judge by the ruling Sultan, Mohammed bin Tughlak. At the Sultan's behest Ibn Battuta went to China, but the expedition was to prove far from straightforward. Rebels attacked the diplomatic mission shortly after leaving Delhi, and a second attempt left Ibn Battuta the sole survivor of a storm that sank his expedition's ships in the Indian Ocean off the Malabar Coast—he had been praying in the mosque at Calicut when the tempest struck. Undaunted he sailed to the Maldive Islands, where he worked as a judge, then went on to Sri Lanka to see the island's wealth of gem stones. Finally he headed for

China once more, shadowing first the coast of India and then the Malay peninsula. He landed at Quanzhou and traveled overland to Beijing.

Beyond the Islamic world

Although impressed with Chinese culture, he found the local religions a source of concern. As a Muslim he was offended by the worship of idols, yet this act was central to the religious life of the Chinese. "Whenever I went out I saw many blameworthy things that disturbed me so much that I stayed indoors most of the time and only went out when necessary," he related.

His journey back to Morocco was slow but more direct. En route he witnessed the ravages of the Black Death and made a final pilgrimage to Mecca before arriving back in Morocco in November 1349. His wanderings were not over, however, for the Sultan of Morocco dispatched him first to Spain and then south across the Sahara to Timbuktu.

Ibn Battuta showed a keen interest in the people as well as the places that he visited. When he recounted his adventures to the scribe Ibn Juzavy they were lively and thrilling, and the writer embellished them further, adding his own poetry. Today the book provides us with one of our most comprehensive insights into the medieval Islamic world.

Above: *On his long trip from Constantinople to India, Ibn Battuta traveled around the northern shores of the Caspian Sea, through what today is Kazakhstan.*

The CRUSADES

1095 to 1254

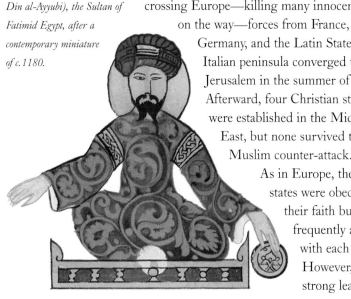

The crusades were military expeditions— holy wars fought in far off places—that entailed moving a large number of people across daunting distances, the logistics of which had never before been attempted. Feeding, transporting, and controlling a mass of people was no easy task, as the crusaders discovered.

With European powers involved in petty squabbles, Pope Urban II attempted to instill unity by creating the common purpose of a universal Christian crusade against Islam. With Jerusalem in Muslim hands, the Christians of the Byzantine Empire appealed for help, and the Pope made his rallying call for action in November 1095 at a council in Auvergne, France, before 14 archbishops, 250 bishops, and 400 abbots as well as assorted noblemen.

The message vibrated throughout Europe and even the Pontiff must have been taken aback by the response. An array of wealthy barons stepped forward, as did numerous penniless knights and, after them, peasants who literally downed tools in the fields to answer the call. While all took a vow to the church and donned the uniform of the cross, the soldiers had little in common. The scale of manpower on the move was probably unprecedented. After crossing Europe—killing many innocent locals on the way—forces from France, Germany, and the Latin States of the Italian peninsula converged to take Jerusalem in the summer of 1099. Afterward, four Christian states were established in the Middle East, but none survived the Muslim counter-attack.

As in Europe, the Islamic states were obedient to their faith but frequently at odds with each other. However, when strong leaders came forward the Muslims carried through a reversal in military fortunes. The first to fall was the Christian state of Edessa, on Christmas Eve, 1144, at the hands of the Muslim leader Zengi.

In France St. Bernard of Clairvaux used all his famous rhetorical skills to summon enthusiasm for a Second Crusade. The initial fervor dwindled as the Second Crusade encountered resistance in Turkey and Syria and ultimately headed for home in an undignified retreat. Zengi was succeeded by Nur ed-Din and then Saladin, the most renowned Muslim commander of the age. His forces stormed through the region, recapturing Jerusalem in 1187 and almost everything else the crusaders had seized except the seaport of Tyre and a nearby stronghold. The Third Crusade was declared that same year by Pope Gregory VIII, winning the allegiance of Richard I Lionheart of England, Philip II Augustus of France, and the Holy Roman Emperor Frederick I Barbarossa. The Christians achieved partial success in winning back some territory in the region but failed to secure Jerusalem.

The ignominious Fourth Crusade occurred between 1202–4. Short of finances, its leaders

Below: Saladin (Salah al-Din al-Ayyubi), the Sultan of Fatimid Egypt, after a contemporary miniature of c.1180.

1003	1088	1096	1154	1215	1231	1245–7	1253
Leif Eriksson charts the coast of Newfoundland	First official university in Europe is established in Bologna, Italy	First Crusade departs for the Holy Land	Abu Abdullah Idrisi completes world survey in *The Book of Roger*	Mongol army reaches the Yellow River in China	Mongols invade Korea	Giovanni del Carpini journeys through Russia to Mongolia	William of Rubruck travels to the Mongol capital of the Karakorams

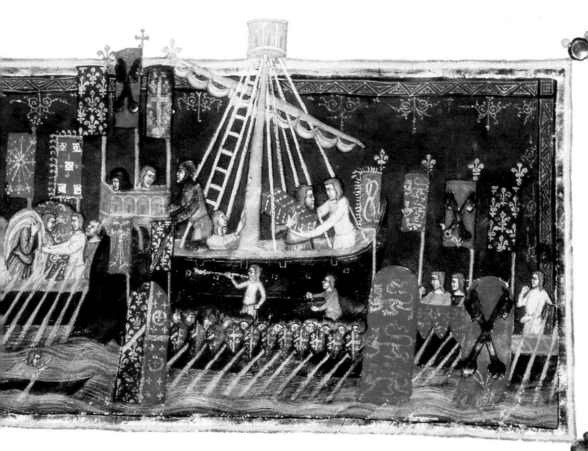

Left: Crusaders embarking for the Holy Land, a manuscript illumination from the 15th-century Statutes de l'Ordre du Grand Esprit au Droit-Desir.

decided to sack Constantinople, which was then a Christian city. The resulting butchery and vandalism outraged Pope Innocent III, who declared: "It was not heavenly riches upon which your minds were set but earthly ones. Nothing has been sacred to you; you have violated married women, widows, even nuns. You have despoiled the very sanctuaries of God's Church." There were a further four crusades during the 13th century and smaller expeditions set out sporadically after that. Not all were in opposition to Muslim states. Pagans and heretics were visited by avenging Church forces too.

Better than glory in this life, those joining a crusade were assured of salvation in the next—a defining motivation at a time when life expectancy was low and people were obsessed with what would become of them after death. The horrors of damnation preached from the pulpit loomed large and by supporting a crusade, they believed their souls would stand a better chance of attaining heaven.

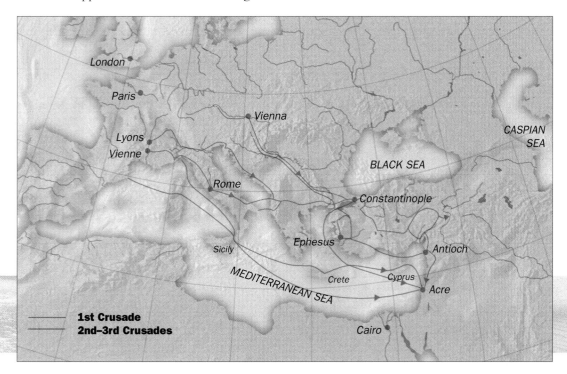

London
Paris
Vienna
Lyons
Vienne
CASPIAN SEA
BLACK SEA
Rome
Constantinople
Ephesus
Sicily
Antioch
MEDITERRANEAN SEA
Crete
Cyprus
Acre
Cairo

—— **1st Crusade**
—— **2nd–3rd Crusades**

1262

Nicolo and Maffeo Polo start travels that lead them to the Great Khan

The crusading impetus

Some knights were zealots who sought to
overthrow the "infidels" as a matter of principle,
while for others belief that Jesus would return to
earth in the Second Coming made liberating the
Holy Land a necessity. The notion that
Jerusalem in Muslim hands somehow put
heaven in peril for all Christians also prevailed.
As the crusades became routine events, many
were lured along in the hope of securing new
wealth or land for themselves.

In reality the lot of a crusader was not a
happy one. Much of the finance for the trips
came from the noblemen, and many were
bankrupted in the process. The lands they
traveled through, even in Europe, were
frequently hostile and there were few ways of
feeding an army along the way. Unaccustomed
to the heat of the Middle East and falling
victim to disease, many men did not survive
long. Crusade leaders had to cope with
ludicrously long supply lines that rendered
feeding and watering their troops a daily crisis.

There was hope among some crusaders that
by liberating Jerusalem they would bring forth
Prester John, a mythical Christian king and
priest, as an ally. Prester John was said to be an
immortal Nestorian Christian with abundant
wealth whose territories nestled in the far reaches
of Asia (a conflicting myth placed his kingdom in
the heart of Africa). A forged letter purporting
to be from Prester John to the Byzantine
emperor, which circulated around Europe,
further excited belief in the enigmatic figure.

The Mongols who ruled central Asia were
another consideration—real rather than fanciful
like Prester John, but equally mysterious. The
unlikely possibility that they would join an
alliance against Muslims prompted Pope
Innocent IV in 1245 to dispatch the Franciscan
friar Giovanni de Plano Carpini (c.1180–1252)
eastward into the unknown. Thirty months and
15,000 miles later he returned to Europe. While
he had succeeded in winning an assembly with
the Mongol leader, all entreaties to form a union
were flatly refused. Carpini nevertheless gave
the West its first insight into Mongol culture
and geography with his *History of the Mongols*.

Into the unknown

Six years after Carpini returned another
Franciscan, William of Rubruck, took up the

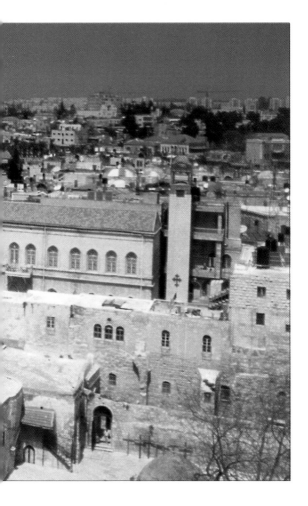

Caspian Sea was land-locked. He also did much to dispel the myth of Prester John (identifying him as King John of the Mongol-Turkish tribe) although the rumors of his existence refused to die. Even in the 19th century the aim of finding Prester John's kingdom was a motivation for European explorers in Africa.

It is easy to dismiss the crusades as an episode of undiluted bigotry, yet both sides gained advantages, mostly through trade. By 1344 an embargo issued by the Pope on trade with Muslims was repealed and Italian cities like Venice and Genoa, on the route to the Holy Land, became significant commercial centers. Like all wars, the crusades increased the pace of warfare technology in the pursuit of building better weapons, armor, and fortifications. Ultimately, Europeans worked alongside Arabs to produce advances like the windmill, the magnetic compass, gunpowder, and timepieces. Valuable experience in conducting large-scale expeditions, often across the sea, pointed the way toward the great Age of Discovery and Europeans learned from the Arabs the new arts of navigation.was also gained, helping to pull Europe into the enlightenment of the Renaissance era, and knowledge about the world outside Europe was gleaned.

challenge, this time at the behest of King Louis IX of France. William and his small party set off from Constantinople on May 7, 1253. The journey that spanned thousands of miles across the Russian steppes was harsh: "There was no end to hunger and thirst, cold, and exhaustion," he wrote afterward. Rubruck was also granted an audience with the Great Khan, and stayed in the Mongol heartland for six months before beginning his arduous return. With him he brought a letter for the King of France which was non-committal and said nothing to suggest the possibility of a future Christian-Mongol alliance against the Muslims.

Rubruck's hardships had not been suffered in vain, however. He brought back more detailed knowledge about the Mongol way of life and established for the first time—for Westerners—that the

Left: *In need of allies, the European crusaders lent strength to the legend of a fabulous Christian king who ruled somewhere in Asia, and who would come to the aid of the Holy Cause. Prester John, however, remained a legend. Title page of* Ho Preste João das Indias, *printed in Lisbon, 1540.*

MARCO POLO
c1254 to 1324

Right: Marco Polo was ridiculed throughout Europe for his tales of the East, and yet later visitors to China would see many of the marvels he described.

H is name is a byword for epic expeditions. For centuries Marco Polo was credited with being the first European to travel extensively through Asia. He inspired countless thousands to follow in his footsteps. Yet modern scholars have cast serious doubt on the authenticity of his tales of life in China under the Mongol emperor Kublai Khan. It is possible that Marco Polo was a fraud with a vivid imagination, who traveled no further east than Persia and was an ordinary merchant rather than an esteemed ambassador.

Polo was born in Venice, a city-state governed as a republic by its Great Council. His father, Nicolo, and uncle, Maffeo, were traders so committed to their business of buying and selling abroad that, having left Venice when Marco was an infant they did not meet again until he was 14. The brothers had been working in the Middle East until they joined a caravan that was headed into China, which was in the dominion of the Mongol Empire under the control of Kublai Khan (1215–94), grandson of the empire's architect Genghis Khan (1167–1227).

A Buddhist by inclination, Kublai Khan was surprisingly open-minded about religion. After entertaining the Polo brothers he asked them to act as envoys to the Pope and to bring back from Europe 100 learned men to his court for debate on the merits of Christianity against other faiths. He also requested some oil from the lamp burning at the Holy Sepulcher in Jerusalem. It was by any standards an exciting enterprise. Back in Venice the Polo brothers invited the teenaged Marco to join their adventure. In 1271 they traveled to Jerusalem to collect the bottle of oil. While they were in the Holy Land a new Pope was inaugurated, Gregory X, who was by chance an old acquaintance. The Pope agreed to make the Polos his ambassadors to Kublai Khan and packed them off with numerous gifts and— instead of the 100 learned men—the services of two friars. The monks, daunted by the perils of the trip, soon turned back, but the Polos persevered.

Heading overland from Palestine they went to Hormuz on the Persian Gulf, through the Iranian deserts and into what is today Afghanistan. There they had a yearlong pause waiting for Marco to recover from illness— possibly malaria. The men then continued through the Pamir Mountains, along a stretch of the Silk Road then across the Gobi Desert, land never before seen by westerners. The slow

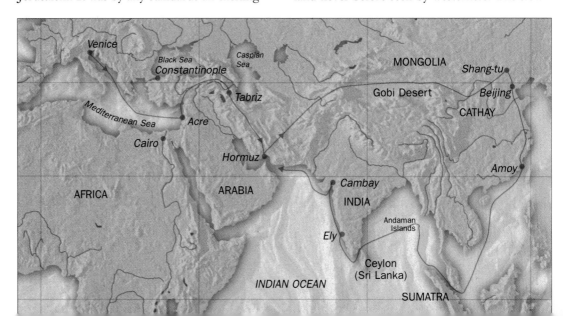

trek east continued until they reached the Yellow River, where they were met by representatives of the Khan and taken to his palace at Shangdu in 1274 or 1275.

Servant of the Kahn

Marco appears to have been a personable man with a flair for languages. He apparently arrived at the court of Kublai Khan when the latter was keen to employ foreigners rather than Chinese in high ranks of government. His exact movements remain unclear. But it is believed he traded salt on behalf of the Khan and visited Burma, Vietnam, and India in an official capacity. His father and uncle appear to have held roles as military advisors.

He was a roving diplomat for about 17 years before the Polos decided to return home due to growing instability in the Mongol Empire of the aging Khan. Although the ruler was unwilling to see them leave the Polos won a westbound passage accompanying a Mongol princess destined to marry the ruler of Persia. This time the journey was made in a fleet of 14 ships, which set sail in about 1292.

The route took the Polos around the Malay peninsula, to Sumatra, Ceylon (Sri Lanka), and around the tip of India into the Gulf of Oman. From there they disembarked and went overland to Persia. When their duties were done they set off for Europe, running the gauntlet of Muslim bandits on the way. In 1295 they reached Venice, almost unrecognizable as the travelers who had set out 24 years before. Although much of their

wealth had been stolen on the return trip, it is said that the Polos astounded bystanders when they produced gems that had been stitched inside the lining of their bedraggled clothing.

Stories related by Marco Polo about his adventures on his return were generally greeted with derision, but the exotic tales reached a wider audience when, while working as a Venetian ship's captain, Polo was captured by the rival Genoan State in 1298 and thrown into jail. While he was incarcerated he met a writer, Rusticello of Pisa, who turned his anecdotes into a book. Still, *Il Milione* (The Million), known in French as *Divisament du Monde* (Description of the World) and in English as the *Travels of Marco Polo*, met a similar, scornful response.

Left: Nicolo, Maffeo and Marco Polo take their leave of Venice. They would not see home again for 24 years.

Below: Kneeling before Kublai, the Khan of all Khans, Nicolo Polo hands over the Pope's letter, while Maffeo and the young Marco look on. The illustration by a westerner has little feel for the Mongolian court.

Right: Marco Polo, who was employed by Kublai Khan as an ambassador, claimed to have witnessed the imperial army in battle on several occasions. This 16th-century Indian illustration depicts Kublai Khan's army laying siege to the Chinese fortress of O-Chou and crossing a pontoon bridge over the river Yang-tse-Kiang.

Above: Kublai Khan, as portrayed by a 20th-century Chinese artist.

A strange eastern world

Much of what Marco Polo described seemed obscure and improbable to contemporary Europeans. For instance, Kublai Khan issued paper money, but to outsiders the notion seemed ridiculous. Also, no one in the west had until then heard about Japan, the islands which the Khan twice tried—and failed—to conquer. There was also skepticism about the "black stones" used for fuel in China, which today we know as coal.

Yet there are as many questions as answers in the book. How did Marco Polo travel in China yet never mention the Great Wall? Why did he not comment on the bizarre trend of foot-binding among women? Did the fascinating Chinese tea-drinking ceremonies really not merit a mention? These startling omissions have led some historians to brand Marco Polo's travels as nothing more than myth.

To cast further doubts, there are also no references in eastern texts to back up claims that Marco Polo was ever in the court of the Khan despite the fact that the presence of foreigners usually warranted comment. His detractors claim that the descriptions that appear in Rusticello's book were concocted by Marco Polo from established Arab and Persian accounts of the time—which would explain why his use of language is mysteriously dominated by Arab and Persian expression. If this is true Marco Polo may have traveled no further than the Black Sea and Constantinople where his family had business concerns.

His writings contain major flaws. There is little statistical or factual information of use to geographers. Dates, distances, climate, and other data have been missed out in favor of lavish descriptive passages. Polo happily repeated rumor without due consideration of the facts. Consequently his assurances that the mythical Prester John existed and was living in Asia inspired many fruitless expeditions. The work has also been branded humorless and unimaginative.

But Rusticello also must bear some responsibility for the weaknesses of the book. As a writer he added embellishments and adopted the same approach one might use for a romantic fable. Written before the advent of printing, different interpretations were added later, probably each time a copy was made. Monks, responsible for copying, felt duty-bound to expunge what they considered to be heresies.

A legacy for later travelers

In his defense, it would have been possible to visit China in those times without learning of the existence of the Great Wall. Also Marco Polo may have been referred to in Kublai Khan's court by a Chinese or Mongolian name hitherto unrecognized in medieval books out of China. Whatever the truth, Polo's writings became the standard for all western travelers in Asia for several centuries afterward. It contained sufficient accurate cultural information to enlighten much of Europe about societies outside of their own.

After he was released from jail Marco Polo married and fathered three daughters. In his home area he was still treated with incredulity for his wild claims. A friar who visited Polo on his deathbed urged him to confess that the stories he told were false. Polo allegedly replied: "I did not write half of what I saw."

Left: Marco Polo was impressed at the lavishness of the Great Khan's court. When he went to war, Kublai commanded operations from his "elephant castle." From a book illustration by Friedrich Justin Bertuch.

FRANCISCO PIZARRO
1474 to 1541

To the Inca of Peru, gold was "the sweat of the sun." To Spanish conquistadors it was justification for the brutal conquest and colonization of Inca territories. The pursuit of gold inspired some of the bloodiest expeditions ever, precipitating the rapid annihilation of the entire Inca civilization.

The man responsible for much of the bloodshed was Spaniard Francisco Pizarro, the illegitimate son of an army officer and a farm girl. Pizarro cut his teeth on expeditions in the company of the charismatic Vasco Núñez de Balboa (1475–1519) who discovered Panama and led his men from the Atlantic to the Pacific Ocean, which he claimed for Spain along with all the surrounding lands. The trek across Panama was a test of endurance. The land was covered with dense jungle, the climate hot and humid. On the return journey the men risked starvation because they chose to carry treasures looted from an Indian village rather than basic supplies. Pizarro settled in Panama, ostensibly to raise cattle. But rumors of abundant gold in the unexplored lands of South America caught his interest. After two abortive attempts to conquer South America a third and better-prepared expedition was initiated at the end of 1530 with the blessing of Charles V, the Holy Roman Emperor.

When strong winds forced their small fleet to anchor, Pizarro and his men were compelled to march along the coast, leaving them subject to disease, the ravages of the climate, and attack by local Indians. When they reached their goal, the Inca city of Tumbes, they found it in ruins due to a raging civil war. The Inca were in turmoil after their king and his heir had died, probably in a smallpox epidemic introduced by colonial Spaniards. In the Inca city of Cajamarca Pizarro tricked Atahualpa, the tribal king into meeting him. Atahualpa believed Pizarro's protestations of peace. But when the unarmed king appeared before the Spanish, Pizarro had him arrested and slaughtered his followers.

Atahualpa is deceived

In an effort to win his freedom, Atahualpa pledged to fill his prison cell once with gold and twice with silver by way of ransom. The duplicitous Pizarro accorded him royal treatment until the treasure was delivered. Then he had Atahualpa garroted in public in the summer of 1533.

Pizarro's next target was Cuzco. In his path lay the high and inhospitable Andes. The key to his success was the existence of a road system built by indigenous Indians—the royal Inca Highway—which ran a total of 3,000 miles. For 750 miles Pizarro, his 100 horsemen, and 30 foot-soldiers forged through the mountain ranges. They encountered hostile Inca on four occasions and each time triumphed thanks to their superior weapons and advanced tactics. After sacking Cuzco Pizarro established a new city on the Rimac river, called the "City of the Kings." Today it is known as Lima.

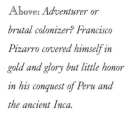

Above: *Adventurer or brutal colonizer? Francisco Pizarro covered himself in gold and glory but little honor in his conquest of Peru and the ancient Inca.*

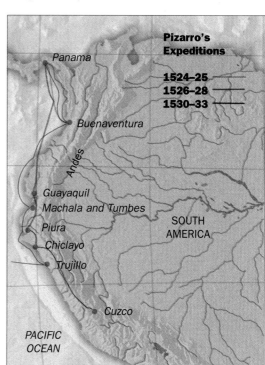

Pizarro's Expeditions

1524–25
1526–28
1530–33

Panama
Buenaventura
Andes
Guayaquil
Machala and Tumbes
Piura
Chiclayo
Trujillo
SOUTH AMERICA
Cuzco
PACIFIC OCEAN

Throughout his adventures in South America Pizarro had been supported by his four half-brothers and Diego Almagro (1474–1538). When conquest of Peru appeared complete, Almagro led a mission down the coast toward Chile looking for new sources of gold. The search was arduous and largely fruitless, remembered mostly for the barbarity shown to the Indians enslaved by the Spanish. When Almagro eventually returned, he found Cuzco under siege by Manco Çapac, the new Inca leader. The Spaniard defeated the Indians and claimed the city as his own, infuriating Pizarro in the process. Now the Spanish faced a civil war and it was Pizarro who was the ultimate victor. At his behest Almagro was executed in July 1538. Pizarro was himself killed in revenge three years later by Almagro's son.

By the time of his death Pizarro had melted down most of the gold artifacts he had seized from the Inca for ease of transport back to Spain. The ancient treasures of the Inca civilization remaining in existence today are mostly those that had been buried in graves as part of funeral rites. With the destruction of the Inca there was no one to work in the established mines or to discover new locations for gold—an illustration of the counter-productive aspects of the colonization, and a factor that would soon lead to the importation of African slaves. Although he was courageous in his travels through uncharted territory, Pizarro is chiefly remembered as a dishonorable and ruthless character motivated entirely by greed.

Below: Pizarro has King Atahualpa seized and his followers slaughtered after deceiving the Inca leader as to his good intentions. An illustration by Theodore de Bry, published in Frankfurt in 1596.

JESUIT MISSIONARIES

from 1540

Facing: A small gouache painting on parchment from the 18th century shows St. Francis Xavier being given minor medical attention.

Above: *Ignatius Loyola founded a Christian movement that would have more impact on South America and the Far East than any other institution. Along the riverbanks of the Amazon basin,* right, *Jesuits saved many Indians from slavery.*

During the 16th century an arm of the Roman Catholic Church reached out to embrace newly discovered lands and peoples. The Society of Jesus, otherwise known as the Jesuits, became responsible for organising foreign missions instigated by the Pope as well as educating the heathens and nursing the sick wherever they encountered them. Quid pro quo for such generous considerations was, of course, conversion to Roman Catholicism.

The Society was founded by Ignatius Loyola (1491–1556), the son of gentry from Spain's Basque region, and who was later canonized. In his youth he was a soldier, but while defending a fortress at Pamplona in 1521 he received leg injuries and, while convalescing, developed a passionate faith. With fellow Christians in Rome he sought to find new ways of serving God. The result was the Society of Jesus, motto *Ad majorem Dei gloriam*—"to the greater glory of God." The order was accepted by Pope Paul III in 1540. The term Jesuit had been a recognized insult until then—Loyola never used it with regard to his new movement. But it was soon adopted by the devout Society members as an easy short-form.

Jesuit teaching hit a chord among Catholics as a means of countering the Protestant Reformation that was sweeping Europe at the time. By the time Loyola died more than 1,000 had joined the fold. A century later the number was 15,000 and still rising.

Uppermost in the minds of Jesuits was the conversion of Muslims. But the threat posed by the Ottoman Turks prevented travel to the Holy Land so they were compelled to look elsewhere. South America was an obvious choice. Jesuits arrived in Brazil as early as 1549. In the face of enormous geographical barriers—raging waterfalls and dense forests—they made their way through the continent to establish links with indigenous peoples, commencing with the Guarani.

To the horror of the Jesuits, slave traders, known as *bandeirantes*, were in avid pursuit of the Indians to provide manpower in the new mines and plantations created by colonists from Spain and Portugal. From 1608 Jesuits organized local populations into self-reliant communities and offered them the protection of the Church. Even the Church's authority was not always sufficient to deter slave traders, but in the protection of the community Indians learned European technology, more advanced methods of agriculture, and defense tactics. The ruins of stone-built churches still mark the sites of settlements across the north and central regions of the continent.

Jesuits undertook some impressive expeditions. In 1629 Father Montoya and Father Macedo led 12,000 persecuted Indians to safety down the remote Parana river, and in 1686 Father Samuel Fritz canoed hundreds of miles up the Amazon to begin new settlements. The general consensus is that Jesuits improved the living conditions of Amazonian tribes, albeit on their own religious terms.

South America was not the only destination for trained Jesuit priests. They went to Africa, China, India, North America, and Japan. Those who traveled to Canada published the newsletter *Jesuit Relations*, which committed to history valuable information about the native tribes there. In Rome all information sent back by the missionaries from every corner of the world was

1271–95	1292	1325–48	1365	1370	1381	1385	1403–33
Marco Polo travels to the Mongol empire and China	Mongols attempt a seaborne invasion of Java	Ibn Battuta travels through Africa, the Middle East, and Asia	Crusade by Cypriots sacks Alexandria in Egypt	Teutonic Knights defeat the Lithuanians	Peasants' Revolt in England	Heidelberg University is established	Zheng Ho voyages from China to the East African coast

noted and filed, providing resource material for future generations.

St. Francis Xavier

Among the most revered of the Jesuits was Francis Xavier (1506–52), one of Loyola's original supporters in the movement. A fellow Basque, Xavier was a pragmatist who installed Christian practices alongside those of the native culture in order that both should survive.

His first stop was Goa in India, where he worked with the pearl fishers, offering them the teachings of the Catholic Church in their own language. From there he went to the Malay Archipelago and the Spice Islands before entering Japan. This was unknown territory to Europe but Xavier was full of enthusiasm. The Japanese were, he said, "the best people yet discovered."

Xavier died in China after contracting a fever before he could carry out his plans for widespread Christian conversion in Japan. He left detailed notes on the places he visited and the people he met, which assisted cartographers and ethnographers of subsequent generations, and he, too, was later canonized.

The Jesuits attracted considerable enmity, not least from within the ranks of the Church itself. Bowing to pressure from European rulers, whose colonial ambitions were being thwarted by devout priests, Pope Clement XIV suppressed the Jesuits in 1773. As a result they were ejected from numerous countries in Europe and the recently discovered lands, and forced to abandon many of the communities they had worked so hard to nurture. Only Frederick II of Prussia and Catherine II of Russia ignored the Pope's order. Jesuits were finally given their full freedoms once more in 1814 on instruction of Pope Pius VII.

WILLEM BARENTS

1550 to 1597

Right: As an explorer, Willem Barents is honored as a commander who put the safety of his men's lives above the results of the expedition.

"*And he had no sooner drunke that he turned his eyes in his head and died presently, and we had no time to call the master out of the other yawl to speak unto him.*" These were the final moments of Willem Barents, the man who discovered Spitsbergen and the first European to survive an Arctic winter.

The story of Barents, who died on the return journey to his native Holland, was faithfully recorded by crew member Gerrit de Veer who in 1598 published the "true and perfect description" of hardy men braced against the elements in an unknown land. It contained geographical and astronomical information as well as elaborations on the icy wastes barely dreamed about in the temperate climes of Europe. It is from de Veer's words that historians gathered so much detail about Barents' expedition. Missions to the region carried out subsequently have backed up his findings.

Willem Barents was a seaman who twice tried—and failed both times—to find a northeast passage that would allow trade between northern Europe and the Orient without running the gauntlet of Spanish and Portuguese shipping in southern seas. He became a trail-blazing expedition leader entirely by accident, when his ship became ice-bound at Novaya Zemlya, in August 1596. He had been attempting to break through the ice into what he believed would be open seas warmed by the midnight sun surrounding the North Pole. There was no choice open to himself, his commander Jacob van Heemskerck, and the crew of 15 other than to hunker down until the worst of the winter was over.

Looming large in their minds was the story of Sir Hugh Willoughby, the English adventurer who had died in 1554 at the very place they were now stranded. Willoughby and his men were found by Russian fishermen frozen to death. Still, the Dutchmen carved out a blueprint for survival. Key to it was the construction of a substantial wooden hut measuring some 33 feet by 20 feet from timber washed up on the shoreline and stripped from their stricken ship. They christened it *Het Behouden Huys*—the Saved House. It offered valuable protection with its constantly glowing fire, although the men often woke in the dark mornings to find their covers and clothes crisp with frost. Using wine barrels from the ship, the men constructed Turkish baths, which they enjoyed regularly. Goods they had taken for trading now became essential to their very existence.

They trapped foxes for food, and sometimes the polar bears that roamed nearby. But the shortage of supplies took its toll on the men's health, and two died that winter, probably from the effects of scurvy caused by the lack of fresh food. It was almost certainly scurvy that claimed the life of Barents the following spring.

By the time the thaw set in their ship was no

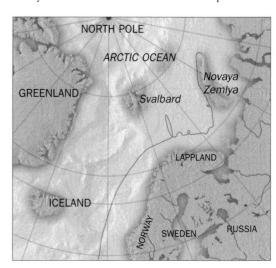

longer seaworthy, which forced them to put to sea in open boats to negotiate a path through treacherous icebergs and row hundreds of miles to safety. Barents died on the seventh day of the voyage moments before the death of another crewmember. The rest battled on for a further 73 days before they reached a mainland settlement.

Find on Novaya Zemlya

The wreck of the Saved House was discovered 273 years later by Norwegian hunter Elling Carlsen. Inside he found evidence of the marooned crew's everyday existence, which he took back to Norway and sold to an English trader. The following year, 1872, the artifacts were displayed in Amsterdam. Much is still unknown about the Barents expedition, however, including the site of his grave. It would be centuries before anyone approached the success of his mission in that wilderness. Indeed, the survival of so many men after such hardships was an amazing triumph in itself.

By the end of the 16th century Spanish dominion of the Atlantic had diminished and southern trading routes became viable to northern European countries, so the need for a northwest or northeast passage evaporated. It was also realized that Arctic routes were beyond

the navigable scope of 16th- and 17th-century vessels.

De Veer's account was greeted with wild enthusiasm, even though he had resisted the temptation to embellish his stories with dragons, gold, or other myths that featured in the travelogs of the time. His maps revealed the climate and features of the lands he visited. Expeditions were coming of age.

Above: Willem Barents' ship in the Arctic ice.

Below: A cutaway drawing of the Saved House, showing the perpetual fire and the turkish bath made from a barrel. Both drawings from Gerrit de Veer's account.

Sir WALTER RALEIGH

1554 to 1618

Right: *The relationship between Raleigh and Queen Elizabeth I deteriorated from court favorite to prisoner. Sir Walter Raleigh and his son, by an unknown artist, 1588.*

As far as explorers go, Sir Walter Raleigh was the stay-at-home kind. He left it to others to steer the ships, plant the flags, and chart the maps, all in his name. Not that he had much choice in the matter. Although Raleigh yearned for adventure, to sail the high seas and journey to new lands, he was a favorite of Queen Elizabeth I of England and was banned from taking risks (he is apochryphally said to have endeared himself to the queen by chivalrously covering a puddle with his cloak in order that her feet should not get wet).

Raleigh was born at Hayes Barton in Devon and grew to be a man of many talents. As a scholar he studied at Oxford University, as a soldier he fought for French protestantism, as a courtier he was a poet, politician, philosopher, and scientist. In 1578 he persuaded the Queen to let him sail to America with his half-brother Sir Humphrey Gilbert, another courtier beloved of Elizabeth. But Gilbert tragically drowned on the return journey across the Atlantic and the queen clipped Raleigh's wings.

Raleigh was forced to content himself with sponsoring the first English colony in America rather than sailing there himself. The forward party left Plymouth in April 1584, claimed a chunk of what is now North Carolina for England, and then returned home. Raleigh was permitted to christen the new colony Virginia, in honor of his virgin Queen.

Subsequently Raleigh indulged in some privateering and sought Elizabeth's patronage to finance an expedition that sailed for America on April 9, 1585 and reached Roanoke Island in three months. Relations between the settlers and the native Americans soon broke down. This proved disastrous since the settlers were ultimately unable to feed themselves and experienced all manner of deprivation. When Sir Francis Drake visited them in the middle of 1586 the would-be colonists needed no persuasion to head home.

A new colony

Undeterred, Raleigh organized another expedition that was destined once again to sail without him. This time 14 families and 78

1410	1416	1419	1469	1482–4	1488	1488	1497
Chinese build largest ever wooden sailing ship, 426 ft with 12 decks	Chinese fleet sails to Yemen	Henry the Navigator establishes Portuguese navigational school at Sagres	Portuguese explorers cross the Equator	Diogo Cão is first European to explore Congo River	Bartholomeu Dias rounds Cape of Good Hope into Indian Ocean	Portuguese establish a settlement on Mauritanian coast	John Cabot reaches Newfoundland

Having only once left English shores, Raleigh had two failed expeditions to his name. These failures were mitigated somewhat by the discovery in America of the potato, samples of which were brought home and planted on Raleigh's estate in Ireland. The introduction of tobacco (also from America and at the time perceived as an aid to health) was another encouraging event.

Raleigh fell from grace when he secretly wooed Bessie Throckmorton, one of the Queen's maids of honor. Elizabeth was so angry that she incarcerated the two lovers in the Tower of London. Raleigh's release, secured by a ransom of treasure, brought about the freedom he had dreamed of. In 1595 he set off to South America in search of the riches of El Dorado. Although the legendary gold eluded him, he journeyed up the Orinoco River and was struck by the beauty of his surroundings.

In 1603 Raleigh's domestic fortunes took a further turn for the worse when Elizabeth died to be succeeded by James I. The new king had Catholic sympathies while Raleigh was an avowed Protestant. Too high-profile to be ignored, Raleigh was once again thrown into the Tower, this time on a charge of treason.

He languished there for 13 years, and busied himself with writing his *History of the World*. On his release, he persuaded James to let him make one make-or-break voyage to Guiana. James agreed on the understanding that relations with Spain were not to be jeopardized. Alas, in a skirmish at a Spanish mine, Raleigh's son Wat was killed; after this disaster Raleigh knew that certain death awaited him in England, but honor made him return and, as anticipated, James invoked the death penalty. Raleigh was beheaded on October 29, 1618.

single men were shipped to Roanoke Island under the governorship of John White. The governor's daughter gave birth to Virginia Dare, the first English child born on American soil. White returned with the ships to England in August 1587 to secure supplies for the new colony. Delayed in part by the war with Spain, White was unable to return to Roanoke Island for three years, and when he did there was no sign of those left behind, only the word "Croatoan" carved in a tree trunk. Croatoan was the name of an island but White was unable to reach it. The fate of the colonists is still unknown, although there is speculation that some married into Indian tribes.

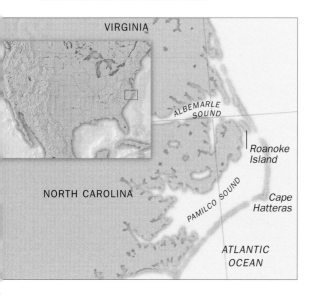

1497–9	1498	1500	1502–07	1507
Vasco da Gama forges sea passage to the East around the Cape of Good Hope	Columbus reaches Orinoco River	Pedro Cabral claims Brazil for Portugal	Lodovico de Varthema travels in Asia and is first Christian known to visit Mecca	Portuguese sack Muscat in Oman

YERMAK TIMOFEYEVICH

1460 to 1524

In the reign of Ivan the Terrible (1530–84) the Russian Empire was hemmed in by the Ural Mountains. Beyond lay Siberia; cold, forbidding, and virtually unknown. Journeys carried out in this region prior to Ivan's rule cost hundreds of men's lives and achieved little. But this cruel and ruthless ruler had been frustrated in his plans to expand to the west, and the vast tracts of the east looked tempting. The catalyst for expansion arrived in the form of a party of Cossacks, who came to Moscow in 1582 bearing 5,000 pelts, including those of beaver, fox, and bear. Clearly there were riches for the picking beyond the Urals. It fell to Yermak Timofeyevich to discover them on behalf of the Tsar.

Yermak was an outlaw, wanted by Ivan's government for piracy on the River Volga. He was also a Cossack, one of a famously free-spirited breed who lived in self-governing communities until falling under the jurisdiction of the Tsar in the 16th century. In fleeing from the Tsar's forces Yermak found himself in the extensive territories owned by the wealthy Stroganov family.

As it happened the Stroganovs were experiencing an unwelcome spate of incursions by Tartars from the far side of the Urals, led by the half blind and elderly chieftain Kuchum, allegedly a descendant of Genghis Khan, and the self-styled Emperor of Siberia. Tartars were the only politically organized group in Siberia capable of resistance. Other communities scattered around this mighty region of 4,800,000 square miles were isolated and ineffective. After winning permission from the Tsar to advance into Siberia, the Stroganov family employed Yermak for the purpose in the summer of 1579. By lending him men and muskets, the Stroganovs managed to mount an

Below: Siberia's Conquest by Yermak; 19th-century oil painting by Vassily Ivan Surikov.

expedition that not only stood to benefit them financially but also rid themselves of the troublesome Cossack at one go.

Mountains easily breached

The Urals, although largely uncharted, are only moderately high and proved no obstacle to Yermak and his 840 men. They relied greatly on river travel, building their own boats both before and beyond the peaks. Progress was swift, as the irate Kuchum noticed. Determined to stop Yermak's force, he installed chains across the River Tobol to sink their wooden craft and mounted an ambush. Yermak's intelligence was good for he took his men out of the boats and replaced them with bundles of sticks disguised in Cossack uniform. As Kuchum's men prepared to pounce the Cossacks attacked them from behind, annihilating the force.

Yermak was not always so lucky. In later battles his forces were badly depleted. But his superior weaponry assured him of ultimate victory. Eight weeks after leaving the Stroganovs he and his men marched into Sibir, Kuchum's capital, where they looted all available spoils and settled in for winter. Food was short but they received ample supplies from the local tribes who were opposed to Kuchum for his perpetual efforts to convert them to Islam.

In the spring Yermak sailed along the River Ob, which empties into the Arctic Ocean, delighted at the possibilities that still lay ahead. However, having experienced one Siberian winter where the temperatures drop below those of the North Pole, his men were keen to return home. He found himself trapped, unable to advance or retreat. Now he took one of his greatest gambles, by dispatching his trusted assistant Ivan Koltzo to the Tsar himself, bearing gifts and a letter imploring forgiveness for past misdemeanors and asking for new soldiers and finance to continue the mission. Ivan the Terrible was notoriously ill-tempered and irrational and, like Yermak, Koltzo was a wanted man. The chances of Ivan putting Koltzo to death and ordering the same for Yermak were high. But the gesture appealed to the Tsar's greedy nature and he issued cash, men… and amnesties.

Despite new resources, the Tartars remained unconquered. Yermak met his end in August 1584 during a surprise attack by Kuchum's men as he traveled down the Irtysh river. Oblivious to the coat of chainmail he wore as a gift from the Tsar, Yermak jumped into the water in a bid to escape the enemy and drowned. Tartars murdered Kuchum soon afterward.

Although Yermak had achieved much, the task was not yet done. Cossacks backed by Russian forces continued the thrust into Siberia. The mission attracted increased support when word about the fabulous furs of Siberia spread. By 1628 the Lerna River, which bisects Siberia, was in Russian hands. In 1639 Russians reached the Sea of Okhotsk on the Pacific Coast. The winners of this expansion were the settlers who traded from the new lands and the Russian government through collecting taxes there. The losers were the defenseless indigenous people who were slaughtered indiscriminately by the Cossacks in the 50-year expansion to the east.

Left: Ivan IV the Terrible became Tsar in name (under a regency) at the age of three and in fact from 1547. Despite an early enlightened policy toward Europe, his later reign was marked by cruelty and terror. His famous, unpredictable rages included the killing of his own son. Oil painting by Viktor Michailovich, 1897.

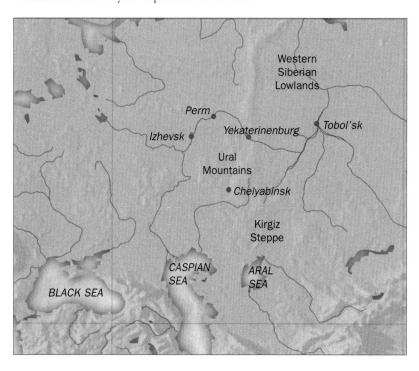

CHAPTER THREE

ASIA *from* 1600

B y the 17th century European knowledge about the Far East was increasing dramatically every decade. When Marco Polo wrote about his travels to Cathay there was little interest in developing contacts with a country so distant from Europe, and it was not until the 1500s, when the Portuguese traveled there by sea, that the economics of direct trade with China became viable.

India had a strong culture with Hinduism as its long-established religion. Early in the 16th century the Islamic Mughals invaded and imposed their faith on the people. Slowly but inexorably, India and the Far East were forcibly opened to trade by European colonial navies. In 1600 the English East India Company began importing spices and so encroached on Portuguese and Dutch possessions. Within 150 years the Company operated a monopoly in most of India that paved the way for British dominance of the subcontinent.

The interior of Arabia remained a mysterious and unexplored land right up to the 20th century. Likewise, Tibet successfully thwarted outsiders' attempts to visit its lands. Japan, on Asia's fringe, was under a series of feudal lords until 1639 when foreigners were expelled, and the country maintained its isolation for another 200 years.

Asia is the largest continent in the world, encompassing a third of the globe's dry land. Mighty plains, hostile deserts, wide rivers, and icy wastes—in fact, virtually every climatic environment on Earth—can be found somewhere within its boundaries. Exploring its reaches would mean mounting some of the longest and most arduous expeditions ever.

Travels in Asia		
Matteo Ricci	1577–1610	
Vitus Bering	1725–30	
Great Northern Expedition		
Nain Singh	1864–66	
Kishen Singh	1878–82	
Nikolai Przewalski	1870–88	
Francis Younghusband	from 1887	
Sven Hedin	1894–1906	
Alexandra David-Néel	1911–13	
	1917–23	
	1937	
Wilfred Thesiger	1946–47	
	1947–48	

Arctic Ocean

Barents Sea

Kara Sea

Laptev Sea

East Siberian Sea

Pevek

Bering Sea

SIBERIA

Okhotsk

Yakutsk

Sea of Okhotsk

Petropavlosk-Kamchatskiy

RUSSIA

changel

erm

Irkutsk

Ulan Bator

Vladivostok

L. Blakhash

Shenyang

Sea of Japan

JAPAN

MONGOLIA

Gobi Desert

Beijing

KOREA

Tokyo

Tashkent

Urümqi

Seoul

Kyoto

Kashi

Yellow Sea

Takla Makan Desert

Lanzhou

Nanjing

Kabul

Shanghai

Lahore

CHINA

East China Sea

TIBET

Chengdu

chi

Delhi

Lhasa

TAIWAN

Pacific Ocean

Great Indian Desert

Kathmandu

Hong Kong

INDIA

Varanasi

Macau

Philippine Sea

mbay

Calcutta

Hai Phong

BURMA

Bay of Bengal

PHILIPPINES

Goa

Rangoon

South China Sea

SIAM

Madras

Andaman Sea

CEYLON
(Sri-Lanka)

Gulf of Thailand

Saigon

Colombo

Malabar Coast

Indian Ocean

SUMATRA

Singapore

BORNEO

MATTEO RICCI

1552 to 1610

A Jesuit missionary who operated in China, Matteo Ricci had three crucial facets to his character: a deeply religious nature; the utmost respect for the Chinese; and a prodigious intellectual capacity that dazzled those he encountered. Not the first European to visit China, Matteo Ricci was certainly the most influential of his time.

Ricci was born in the Papal States to a pharmacist father and a devoutly religious mother. He was taught at home before being dispatched to Rome to study law. The philosophy of the Jesuits appealed to him and, by 1571, he determined to join its burgeoning membership. Six years later after extensive study of mathematics and astronomy his travels began. Ricci went first to Portugal to embark for India. His destination was the Portuguese colony of Goa on the Malabar Coast, but illness forced him to spend some time there. When he was sufficiently recovered Ricci was sent to China, where in the coastal cities foreigners were

Right: *Matteo Ricci in Beijing wearing the robes of a scholar and holding out a map of China. From a copper engraving by an unknown artist.*

treated with hostile suspicion. China had an enormous population even in the 16th century, and the possibilities of converting so many people to Christianity enticed many missionaries. But despite every effort to colonize China the Jesuits were halted before gaining a foothold on the mainland. The realization that it was going to be impossible to impose their will on this vast country through force dawned on them. Jesuits began to learn the Chinese languages, and Ricci also mastered the script.

He bided his time in Portuguese-held Macau with colleague Michele Ruggieri until 1583 when he was given permission to settle in Chao-ch'ing , the capital of Kwangtun province. In his book *History of the Introduction of Christianity in China* he explained the approach adopted by the Jesuits: "[we] tried to learn the language, literature, and etiquette of the Chinese, and to win their hearts and, by the example of their good lives, to move them in a way that they could not otherwise do because of insufficiency in speech and for lack of time."

To invite the interest of the Chinese, Ricci and Ruggieri filled their small mission with items from Europe. There were prisms, chiming clocks, and a selection of books. Most fascinating to the visiting Chinese was a map of the world, which illustrated other countries outside China, lands they never dreamed existed. Local officials asked the Jesuits to duplicate the map for them, and the result was a silk cloth measuring 12 feet by 6 feet illustrating Asia with its European promontory, known locally as the *Great Map of Ten Thousand Countries*. The Chinese, who through trade knew something about Europe, had copies of

Left: *The Great Wall of China at Mu-Tian-Yu.*

the map sent to Rome to help Europeans understand more about the Orient. In 1589 Ricci moved to Shao-chou, where he became close friends with a Confucian scholar, Chu T'ai-su, and through him met numerous high-ranking officials. Now Ricci wore the garb of a scholar, marking him out as one of the great minds of the age. His aim was to work in the Imperial City of Beijing but the Emperor Wan-li frustrated this ambition until 1601. However, word of Ricci's competence ultimately persuaded the Emperor to change his mind. By now another Jesuit, the Spaniard Diego Pantoja, accompanied him.

Cultural exchange

After the pair entered Beijing they become deeply involved with the academics of the city who assisted them in matters of translation and interpretation. Before his death in Beijing Ricci produced a number of books in Chinese. While he continued to expound the Catholic message, seeking similarities between Christian and Chinese literature, he acknowledged the importance of China's long-held traditions. He also taught the principles of mathematics to his Chinese companions who began to value his advice in numerous matters.

Ricci's observations of the Chinese way of life were enlightening to the west; he wrote: "…though they have a well-equipped army and navy that could easily conquer the neighboring nations, neither the king nor his people ever think of waging a war of aggression. They are quite content with what they have and are not ambitious of conquest. In this respect they are much different from the people of Europe who are frequently discontent with their own governments and covetous of what others enjoy."

VITUS BERING
1681 to 1741

Right: Vitus Bering was sent on a mission to discover the extent and peoples of Russia's vast northern and Siberian coasts for the Tsar.

Right: Tsar Peter I the Great, painting by Gotfried Schalken. The Tsar had his sights set on creating a new Russian land in North America by crossing the narrows between Siberia and Alaska.

Vitus Jonassen Bering is remembered as the mariner who discovered Alaska. A native of Denmark, he joined the service of Peter the Great (1672–1725) who was perplexed by the question of whether Asia was joined by a land bridge to North America. The Russian Emperor was already reveling in the wealth of furs from Siberia. The prospect of gaining colonial possessions in North America was enticing.

Peter created a powerful navy modeled on the great European fleets of the era, which he quickly used to chart the northern and eastern coastlines of Siberia. With his sights now set on America he charged Bering with the task of determining the geography of his far eastern lands. Peter the Great made his aims clear: "Once we have protected our Fatherland from enemies we should bring it glory through the arts and sciences. In our search for such a route we will be more successful than the Dutch and the English."

Bering was well qualified for the job. He learned to sail as a child and joined the Russian navy in 1703, soon rising to the rank of captain. He married a Russian and they had children. Accepting the challenge, Bering had little idea of the monumental job ahead.

The expedition he led set out from St. Petersburg, traveling overland to Okhotsk on the Siberian coast. There he constructed ships to take them onward to the Kamchatka Peninsula. It had already been an epic journey, taking more than two years to reach this point. Meanwhile the ambitious Tsar Peter had died, although his wife and successor, Catherine I, continued to sponsor the venture.

Skirting the Siberian coast Bering came across some land, which he named St. Lawrence Island. After that he entered a narrow strait. If fortune had smiled on Bering that day the weather would have been fine and clear and he would have realized he was within sight of land on both sides of his vessel, but unfortunately it was foggy. They had made it as far as the Diomede Islands, a chain that had already been discovered but which lay at the very limits of Russian maps. The goal now was to find out whether a bridge of land existed further north that linked the Asian and American continents.

At least one of Bering's officers, Aleksei Chirikov, urged him to sail on, but others were concerned at the prospect of wintering in such harsh conditions and Bering eventually sided with them and turned the ship around on August 16, 1728.

A better expedition

Bering survived the long journey home to St. Petersburg, arriving back in 1730, but Russia judged him harshly for returning without conclusive proof that there was no land bridge. Stung by the criticism, Bering suggested a further exploration, a massive undertaking involving a total of 10,000 men and 13 ships. Dubbed the Great Northern Expedition, it was the largest the world had seen, with four separate parties briefed to chart different sections of the Siberian coast. It took Bering no less than eight years to reach the Siberian coast at Okhotsk this time, laden with the equipment of his surveyors and scientists.

He sailed for Alaska from Kamchatka on June 4, 1741. German naturalist Georg Steller who traveled with Bering holds the honor of being the first European to step onto Alaskan soil. But Bering turned back rather than risk wintering in this uncharted land. Winter storms ultimately marooned his party in the Commander Islands, where Bering and 29 others suffered a slow death from scurvy and exposure. As they grew weaker and more defenseless, Bering and his comrades fell victim to wild animals, with Arctic foxes biting their frostbitten ears and noses as they tried to sleep. The animals so tormented the stricken Bering that he begged to be buried up to his neck in the ground before his death. A small band of survivors managed to hold out until the summer thaw, when they built a raft that got them back to Kamchatka.

Although the expedition claimed Bering's life, he was still criticized for his conduct. Steller complained that Bering would not take advice from anyone. But Bering's venture had given Russia a foothold in Alaska, which continued until 1867 when the United States purchased the region.

Bering was not the first Russian to travel through the Strait that now bears his name. It is now known that Semyon Ivanov Dezhnev (1605–72) made the journey decades earlier, but his endeavor was of little interest to a Russia that did not then have an interest in expansion beyond Siberia.

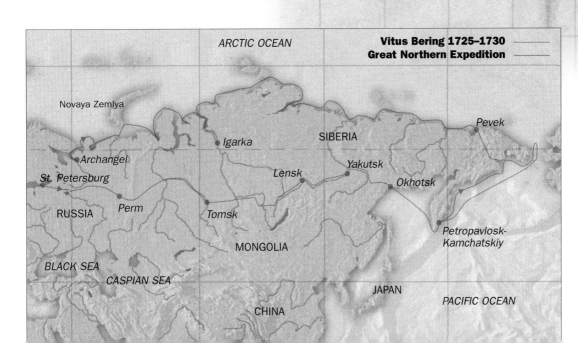

Above: *A detail from the map of Siberia drawn for Vitus Bering during the Great Northern Expedition showing Tibetan tribespeople.*

ARCTIC OCEAN

Vitus Bering 1725–1730
Great Northern Expedition

Novaya Zemlya

Igarka

SIBERIA

Pevek

Archangel

St. Petersburg

Lensk

Yakutsk

Okhotsk

RUSSIA   Perm

Tomsk

MONGOLIA

Petropavlosk-
Kamchatskiy

BLACK SEA

CASPIAN SEA

JAPAN

PACIFIC OCEAN

CHINA

NAIN *and* KISHEN SINGH

c1830 to c1882

1850 to 1921

Britain had a secure foothold in India by the middle of the 19th century. With the Great Trigonometrical Survey, which began in 1802, a generation of surveyors and cartographers had set to work on the subcontinent. Among them was George Everest (1790–1860), the Surveyor General from 1823, who went deep into the Himalayas, where the world's highest peak now bears his name. The most sensitive and arduous work, however, was carried out by a small group of Indian nationals who were able to maintain discretion and anonymity in regions that were hostile to the British.

By the latter half of the century the task of mapping India was largely complete, but there was a great gap in knowledge about Tibet and Nepal. The Tibetan border had been closed to Europeans since 1792. Lack of knowledge was so fundamental that even the whereabouts of its capital, Lhasa, was not accurately known.

At the time Tibet's strategic importance was inestimable. Britain, who had warred with Russia in the Crimea (1853–56), was concerned about Russian intentions. There was also much suspicion of China, which was effectively the sovereign power in Tibet and another potential

threat. This standoff between Britain, Russia, and China was referred to as "the Great Game."

Although Britain was prepared to take risks to learn more, attempts to infiltrate Tibet met with resistance, and the explorers William Moorcroft, Andrew Dalgleish, and George Hayward met violent deaths on the mountain paths, either from soldiers or from the bandits who infested the area. Captain Thomas George Montgomerie, of the Bengal Engineers, came up with a solution. He began a program of training Indians who, by passing themselves off as Buddhist monks or traders, could travel unhindered behind the borders. These men were spies, but their brief was to learn the geography of the country rather than engage in sabotage. If they were caught they would nevertheless face torture and death.

Montgomerie's plan

Montgomerie explained: "I noticed the natives of India passed freely between Ladakh and Yarkand in Chinese Turkestan, and it consequently occurred to me that it might be possible to make the exploration by that means. If a sharp enough man could be found, he would have no difficulty in carrying a few small instruments amongst his merchandise, and with their aid good service might be rendered to geography."

The instruments the spies carried were indeed ingeniously small and camouflaged to complement the men's disguise, in the form of

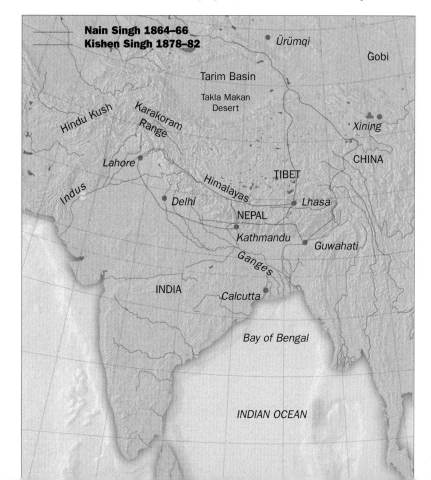

Nain Singh 1864–66
Kishen Singh 1878–82

Ürümqi

Gobi

Tarim Basin

Takla Makan Desert

Hindu Kush

Karakoram Range

Xining

CHINA

Lahore

Indus

TIBET

Himalayas

Delhi

Lhasa

NEPAL

Kathmandu

Guwahati

Ganges

INDIA

Calcutta

Bay of Bengal

INDIAN OCEAN

objects such as Buddhist rosaries and prayer wheels, used by every pilgrim. Each man's pace was measured and the total kept by slipping a bead around the rosary every hundredth pace, with a complete circuit of beads representing 10,000 paces. Consequently the men were restricted to walking on their missions. Only close inspection would reveal that the rosary had 100 beads instead of the correct 108 beads.

"I had noticed the frequent use made by Tibetans of the rosary and the prayer wheel, and consequently recommended [the spies] to carry both with them, especially as it was thought these ritualistic instruments could (with a little adaptation) form useful adjuncts in carrying out a route survey," Montgomerie said.

Thermometers were placed into hollowed walking sticks. Sextants, used for determining latitude, were dropped into the false bottoms of traveling chests. Mercury, necessary to use the sextant, was carried in a wax-sealed container, while inside the spies' clothes extra pockets were stitched. The custom-made instruments were produced in the workshops of British India, and for two years the spies were coached in their craft, trained to have a retentive memory, the ability to walk at high altitudes, and a geographer's eye.

The most famous of these spies was Nain Singh from northeast India who began his career in exploration working as a guide for a German expedition in the Himalayas. Each of his paces measured 33 inches, which meant 2,000 per mile. His records of distance later proved astonishingly accurate over long distances.

Singh's first mission was to Lhasa. He set out from Dehra Dun in January 1865, attaching himself to a merchant's caravan in order to slip through the border unnoticed. Then he walked through the region known as "the roof of the world." Since his route was circuitous it was not until January 1866 that Nain Singh reached Lhasa. Once there he was confronted with a test of his nerves. He was summoned to an audience with the Dalai Lama and if he did not go it would blow his cover. The months of training stood him in good stead, however, and no one suspected the humble man before the Lama was in fact a British spy.

To deduce the height of the Tibetan Plateau he plunged his thermometer into boiling water and compared the figure with that of boiling point at sea level. Reading the stars and charting the position of the sun, Nain Singh could then pinpoint the longitude of Lhasa so that its exact position would finally be known. Leaving Lhasa in April, Singh completed an 800-mile journey around the upper reaches of the Brahmaputra River, which bordered a Tibetan gold-mining area, before arriving back at Dehra Dun. He had taken 3,160,000 steps, each faithfully recorded.

Facing: Nain Singh's regular pacing made him an accurate spy for the British when it came to measuring out distances.

Below: The Potala Palace in Lhasa, Tibet, where Singh's cover was put to the test.

Word gets out

In 1873 Nain Singh and his cousin Kishen Singh (1850–1921) ventured into Chinese Turkestan, reaching the Takla Makan Desert. The following year they split up, with Kishen Singh exploring the Pamir region. Nain returned to join another mission scheduled to go into Lhasa, and then on to distant Beijing. At this time the British general supervising Nain Singh observed that the Indian was weary of long marches and anticipated "he may make one grand push if he fully understands that it is likely to be his last, and that he will get some position given him, or a pension."

Right: View of the Lhasa Valley from Ganden Monastery, Tibet.

By now his sight was failing, probably caused by too many instrument readings taken from the sun. Yet Nain Singh departed from India in July 1874, posing as a merchant and using sheep to carry baggage. Progress was slow and he arrived at Lhasa on November 18. However, rumors of a British spy approaching Lhasa somehow circulated. Realizing he was in imminent danger, Singh sent his findings back to India with two servants. He made good his escape two days after his arrival in Lhasa, on the pretext that he was going on a pilgrimage.

Ultimately he was detained inside Tibet for two months but finally arrived back in India in 1875. It was his last expedition, although he continued to train new recruits. His reward from the government was some land and revenue. In 1877 he was awarded the Royal Geographical Society's Gold Medal "for his great journeys and surveys in Tibet and along the Upper Brahmaputra, during which he determined the position of Lhasa and added largely to our knowledge of the map of Asia."

Continuing Singh's work

Kishen Singh's career continued, however. In 1878 he left India for a four-year trek encompassing Lhasa and western China. He was arrested twice, in China and Tibet, and was robbed but returned to India having traveled 3,000 miles on foot with details about land outside Chinese national borders that had never before been charted. Despite his triumph, there was no

happy ending for Kishen Singh. When he returned to his home he discovered his only son had died and that his family, having given up hope of seeing him again, had moved on.

Sadness also tinges the story of Kintup (1849–c.1914), another spy given the task of tossing 500 logs into the Yarlung Zangbo River in Tibet to prove that it was linked to the Brahmaptura River in India. Observers were to note the passage of the tagged logs downstream. His problems began when the official charged

1580s	1583	1600	1602	1603	1609	1610	1619
Yermak Timofeyevich explores beyond the Ural mountains for Russia	Matteo Ricci settles and teaches in China	English East India Company is founded	Dutch East India Company is founded	Persians capture Baghdad from the Ottomans	Dutch establish a trading post at Hirado, Japan	Matteo Ricci receives Imperial summons to Beijing	Dutch establish trading port of Batavia on island of Java

by the British to oversee the log operation sold Kintup, who was posing as his servant, into slavery. He did not escape from the slavers until March 1882, 18 months after he had left India. He found sanctuary in a monastery where once again his freedom was sorely restricted. Winning permission to go on a pilgrimage that summer, Kintup spent a month assembling the logs. Three months later he was permitted to go to Lhasa, ostensibly on a pilgrimage but in reality to send a letter to a colleague, warning

that his operation was about to get under way.

Kintup returned and committed the logs to the river at the rate of ten per day. He traveled down-river himself for 100 miles before heading west for home. Unfortunately, when he reached India in August 1884 he realized his letter had been lost. No one had observed the logs float down the Brahmaputra. His tremendous efforts had all been in vain, and it would be years before proof was finally made that the rivers were indeed connected.

1624	1624	1628	1638	1639	1639	1661	1690
Dutch establish trading post on Formosa (Taiwan)	Spanish traders are expelled from Japan	Russian colonists reach Lerna River in Siberia	Japan is closed to foreigners	English colonize Madras in India	Russians reach the Sea of Okhotsk on the Siberian Pacific coast	English found a colony in Bombay, India	English establish a colony in Calcutta, India

NIKOLAI PRZEWALSKI

1839 to 1888

Nikolai Mikhailovich Przewalski was a Russian soldier who forged his way through some of the loneliest land in the world. As a lasting tribute, the world's only surviving species of wild horse, a sturdy creature discovered by him in the Mongolian wilderness, was named after him.

His goal was to reach Lhasa and become the first European for decades to glimpse the imposing edifice of the Potala, the palace of the Dalai Lama, wedged box-like against slate-grey mountains. There was, of course, some competition between the major European powers over who would reach the Holy City first and Przewalski, financed by his government, had every reason to believe he would be triumphant. However, even after four attempts the closest he would get to Potala would be 150 miles.

That he had survived so long was a mystery to many. His journals record the chronic shortage of water that frequently blighted his expeditions: "Our situation was desperate. Only a few glasses of water were left, of which we took into our mouths just enough to moisten our parched tongues; our bodies seemed on fire, our heads swam, and we were close upon fainting." On this occasion he and his comrades were saved by the timely discovery of a well.

Przewalski knew that a few Europeans had already visited Lhasa. One was Thomas Manning, who posed as a Chinese doctor to slip through Tibetan security. He reached Lhasa in December 1811 to find the city outside the Potala something of a disappointment. It was "begrimed with smut and dirt…mean and gloomy," according to Manning who was ejected by the Tibetans after a year. French missionaries Evarist Huc and Joseph Gabet succeeded in entering Lhasa as part of a caravan from Beijing. They went undetected for less than two months. Afterward they wrote a highly improbable account entitled *Travels in Tartary, Thibet, and China*. Przewalski was both inspired and outraged by the book, which, at the very least, was guilty of being profoundly unscientific.

On his first expedition in 1870, Przewalski set off with three traveling companions from the Siberian city of Irkutsk, with Lhasa their stated destination. They went through Mongolia and sampled the privations of the Gobi Desert before they were forced to turn back. The second expedition began in the Chinese province of Xinjiang and the route was equally demanding. This time the Tien Shan mountains and the Takla Makan Desert blocked their path.

Przewalski was able to survey Lop Nur and some of the Astin Tagh mountain range before heading for home.

Death in the Himalayas

In 1879 he returned to the region once more. This time, just 170 miles from Lhasa, he encountered a considerable force of angry Tibetans convinced by Chinese rumor-mongers that he was planning to kidnap the Dalai Lama. Przewalski had a reputation for toughness but even he was unable to counter this group. Nevertheless, undeterred he set off for his fourth, and final, expedition in 1883, headed for the Tien Shan mountains. His dream came to a tragic end in the majestic surroundings of Issyk-Kul, the world's largest mountain lake in present-day Kyrgyzstan, where Przewalski drank infected water and died from typhoid. He was buried on its shores, a lofty 5,300 feet above sea level.

Before his death Przewalski was made a major general in the Russian army. His reputation among local people for strength of character was reinforced when he threatened to shoot servants in his Mongol caravan after they refused to continue in the face of harsh conditions. Rumors even abounded that he was a saint, on his way to see the Dalai Lama. In one incident he shot a Chinese peasant's aggressive dog after his own dog was attacked, saying: "if you let them kill your dog one day, they may try to kill you the next."

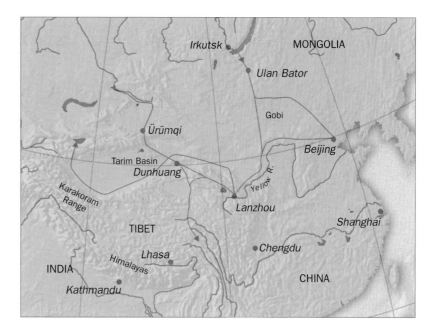

Below: The Yellow River is the main artery from China's east coast into the heartland toward Tibet, and many of the European explorers traveled along its banks.

FRANCIS YOUNGHUSBAND

1863 to 1942

Although Francis Younghusband was a keen geographer and a deeply religious man, he is chiefly remembered as an army commander who oversaw the carnage carried out in an ill-conceived British campaign that had fleeting benefits for the Empire.

Born in British India in the foothills of the Hindu Kush, Younghusband was the son of an army major, one of three who all followed their father into the army. He went to school in England and trained at the Royal Military Academy at Sandhurst.

He cut his teeth on expeditions in 1887 when he returned to India from Beijing by traveling overland across western China, notching up a number of firsts along the way. He covered a distance of 1,200 miles through the salt marshes and strewn rocks of the unrelenting Gobi Desert, going where no European had been before. He skirted the Takla Makan Desert shadowing the old Silk Road until he dropped south into India. Despite the harsh climate, he faithfully made important geographical notes that would be used to enhance future maps of the region.

As he neared British India, before him lay the Karakorum Mountains, the formidable border between China and present-day Pakistan. Lying between the Pamirs and the Himalayas the range includes K2, the second-highest mountain in the world. He crossed the range through the 19,000-foot high Mustagh Pass before coming down into Rawalpindi, seven months after setting off from China. No one had made such a trek before. Afterward he traveled to London to present his findings and,

at 24, became the youngest person elected to the Royal Geographical Society, which awarded him the Gold Medal for his "journey from Manchuria and Peking (Beijing) to Kashmir and especially for his route surveys and topographical notes."

Guarding the Empire

But geography was not Younghusband's primary purpose. His mission was one of reconnaissance in order to judge the likelihood of a Russian invasion of British India. For he was also a committed player in the game of military prowess that led to a second expedition in 1892 in the Pamir region in what is today Afghanistan. While he was there he encountered Russian troops who declared the territory had been annexed. Tension between Britain and Russia escalated.

The Dalai Lama refused to entertain official links with either vying country. Fear of Russian intentions grew until in 1904 it was decided to dispatch a mission to Lhasa to force British will upon Tibet. Younghusband, now a veteran of the mountain ranges north of India, led the expedition of 1,200 troops comprising British, Ghurka, and Indian soldiers across the mountain ranges. With them went 10,000 bearers and other support staff. The logistics of the operation alone were remarkable.

The men engaged in a few skirmishes until the stage was set for a major showdown on the high plains of Tibet. Opposing the British were 1,500 Tibetans armed with muskets and swords. Each carried a picture of the Dalai Lama, which they believed would shield them from injury. When the British machine guns opened up the lightly-armed Tibetans died in droves. The

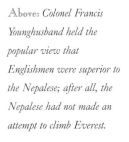

Above: *Colonel Francis Younghusband held the popular view that Englishmen were superior to the Nepalese; after all, the Nepalese had not made an attempt to climb Everest.*

Right: *Indian writing set c.1904 with painted cover depicting Colonel Younghusband on horseback, accompanied by a staff officer and interpreter.*

slaughter ended when British gunners finally took pity on their victims, but by then the death toll was an estimated 700. Younghusband conceded that it was "a terrible and ghastly business." A memorial to the excesses of the expedition now exists in Tibet's Khari La Pass. Eventually the Tibetans bowed to the inevitable and permitted Younghusband to enter Lhasa. He negotiated a hard-line deal with the spiritual leader, which rendered Tibet unable to make links with other countries and set out favorable trading conditions for Britain.

There followed an international outcry as the so-called "diplomatic mission" led by Younghusband was unveiled for what it was— an exercise in military annexation. Worse still, Tibet with its high plains and inaccessible passes was impossible for the British to defend and they pulled out entirely within just two years, rendering the slaughter even more pointless.

Nevertheless, Younghusband was intrigued by Tibet and developed a love of the Himalayan country. In 1921 a Tibetan concession permitted the occasional party of climbers to attempt the scaling Everest. With this in mind he coordinated a club linked to the Royal Geographical Society that would prepare expeditions for the eventual conquest of the summit. He envisaged "a steady continuity of effort over a number of years." In 1924 Younghusband vocalized a prevailing, racist view that Englishmen were better mountaineers than Sherpas, the local Nepalese mountaineers. Although Sherpas were accustomed to high altitudes they had not yet climbed Everest. "They have not even the desire to. They have not the spirit," Younghusband is quoted as saying. Despite this judgment, Sherpa Tenzing Norgay and Sir Edmund Hillary made the first successful ascent of Everest in 1953.

Above: West Face of Mount Everest. In spite of Younghusband's racist views it would be a Nepalese and an Englishmen who would finally conquer Everest together.

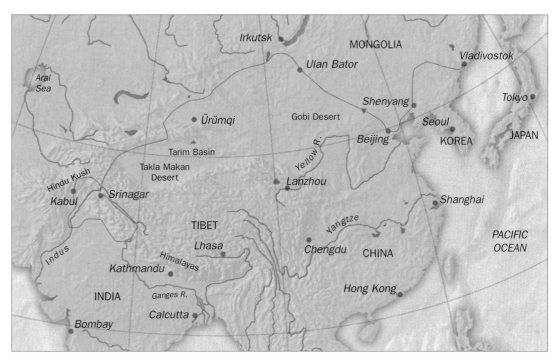

SVEN HEDIN

1865 to 1952

As an impressionable 15-year-old, Sven Hedin witnessed the return to Sweden of adventurer Nils Nordenskiold aboard the *Vega* (*see pages 142–143*). The nation went wild with delight and the celebrations transfixed the teenager. Hedin made up his mind then and there that he too would be a national hero and receive a welcome like Nordenskiold's.

His path to glory was not an easy one. Hedin explored the wastes of central Asia with its unpredictable weather and untamed terrain. Using his creditable skills as an artist, he committed hitherto unknown regions to the world map and also drew stunning panoramas to communicate the isolation and splendor of central Asia. His drawings were so accurate that in the last decade of the 20th century they were used to assist in geographically pinpointing satellite photographs of the area. Given that Hedin lost his sight in one eye in his 20s—it was restored by an operation when he was an elderly man—his achievements were astonishing.

Born in Stockholm, the son of the city's official architect, Hedin went to university before becoming a tutor in the city of Baku on the Caspian Sea. He seized the opportunity to travel around the region, usually on horseback, and mastered several languages as he traveled on through the Middle East. Afterward he wrote the popular travel book *A Journey Through Persia and Mesopotamia*.

Following a further spell at universities in Sweden and Germany studying geography and geology he was asked to act as interpreter for Sweden in the court of the Persian Shah, in Tehran in 1890. His spell as interpreter completed, Hedin received government funding for an expedition into central Asia. After visiting the Silk Road cities of Tashkent and Sarmarkand it became a grueling winter trek through the Pamirs and finally into Kashi,

1715	1723
Italian Jesuit Ippolito Desideri visits Lhasa	Russians capture Baku on the Caspian Sea from Persia

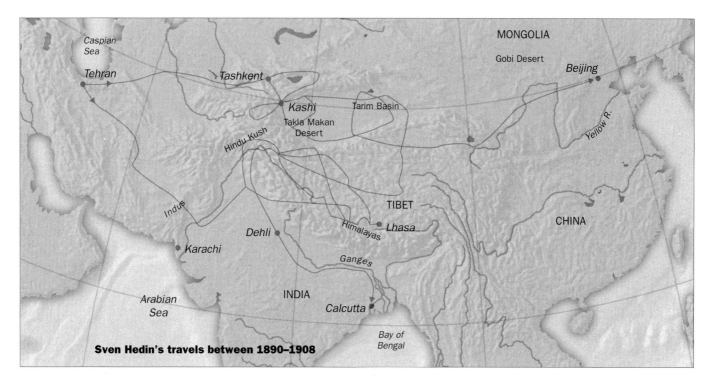

Sven Hedin's travels between 1890–1908

the westernmost city of China. By this time, his journey was considered pedestrian, but it gained Hedin valuable experience, and when the opportunity to cover similar territory arose again two years later, Hedin had no hesitation in going.

In 1894 he set off from Russian Turkestan with three porters. The going was tough as they went through the Pamirs but Hedin did not falter, earning him the respect of the Khirgiz tribesmen who accompanied him. His next aim was to tackle the Takla Makan Desert, an ambition that almost cost him his life. He brushed off the protestations of natives who insisted that evil spirits haunted the desert. But when the men became separated from their animals and then each other, they may well have pondered the warning.

Hedin, with one remaining porter and running critically low on supplies, hoped that they were nearing the River Khotans. The shifting sands made it impossible to maintain a sense of direction, and their efforts to drink the blood of a slaughtered sheep to alleviate their thirst came to nothing when the blood dried instantly in the heat. Hedin's companion finally collapsed in delirium, while Hedin himself stumbled on for a few yards and fell upon the riverbed he had been seeking—to find it dry. Luckily, Hedin found a pool nearby that had survived the drought, and he was able to save

both himself and the porter. In another of the parties a porter saved himself by following a camel that headed for water. The expedition lost two men and an unknown number of animals.

Back to full health, Hedin set off in 1895 for the Tarim He basin, mapping signs of the ancient town and waters of Lop Nur, known to the Chinese as the "Wandering Lake." Hedin correctly concluded that shifting sands caused the waters to move slowly across the landscape. After 1,300 miles Hedin traveled by a remote route to Beijing.

In 1899 he set off for Tibet, hoping to get to Lhasa but failing as so many had before. Yet the journey was not wasted for he discovered the ancient city of Lou-lan. A further expedition in 1906 took him to the Himalayas to trace the source of two of India's great rivers, the Indus and the Brahmaputra.

Although he returned to Sweden after this triumph—in 1902 he became the last person to receive a Swedish knighthood—he was lured back to Asia much later, in 1935, to map the Silk Road. Hedin was an admirable explorer with plenty of credits to his name and wrote numerous popular books. But in his old age during World War II he was an open sympathizer of the Nazis, a misjudgment that tarnished an otherwise great reputation.

Facing: Sven Hedin on expedition in Tibet. Hedin had no compunction in adopting the clothing and customs of the people whose lands he traveled through.

1728	1741	1770	1784	1794	1802	1825	1828
Vitus Bering discovers the Bering Strait between Siberia and Alaska	Bering sails to Alaska from Kamchatka peninsula in Siberia	British establish a trading post at Basra, Iraq	US merchant ships start trading with China	British capture the Seychelles from the French	British survey maps India	William Moorcroft lost in Bukhara following extensive travels in the region	Russian forces capture Tehran

ALEXANDRA DAVID-NÉEL

1868 to 1969

The purpose of Alexandra David-Néel's perilous expedition was the pursuit of religious fulfilment. French-born David-Néel became the first European woman to enter Lhasa, after enduring an awesome trek that exposed her to the dangers of attack, disease, and hypothermia. She was feted in some quarters for her achievement, but criticized in others for the lack of geographical data or useful information in her writings.

David-Néel was born in Paris but raised in Brussels, a wild child who was sent by her Calvinist father to an austere convent where he hoped her spirit would be tamed. As a teenager she became fascinated with mysticism and studied theosophy, Rosicrucianism, and spiritualism in London. An inheritance financed her first expedition in 1891 and she went as far as India, Sri Lanka, and the Himalayas. She returned to Paris and found work as a singer under the pseudonym Mademoiselle Myrial, a character invented by author Victor Hugo, who was a friend of her father's.

Right: In a world that was opening up to adventurous men, women were largely excluded, but the lure of far-away places drove the wild-spirited Alexandra David-Néel to travel to regions still unvisited by European explorers.

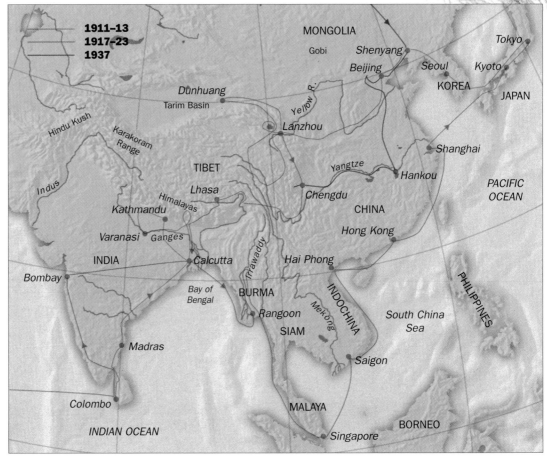

In 1900 she met French Railroad worker Philippe Néel, and when they married four years later so began one of the most unorthodox unions in history. Finding the confines of matrimony a strain, David-Néel toured the world financed by her husband, never to return to him. Despite the separation, they corresponded in affectionate terms with surprising regularity. With Philippe's death in 1941, David-Néel said she had lost her best friend.

A fourteen-year odyssey

After departing from her husband in 1911 David-Néel made an unorthodox move, to Sikkim where she met the visiting Dalai Lama and lived in seclusion in a cave. She also encountered 15-year-old Aphur Yongden, who became her adopted son and a Lama. By 1916 she had entered Tibet at the invitation of the high ranking Panchen Lama. The British were nervous about a French woman wandering through this vital buffer state at will and forcibly ejected her from her cave at Sikkim.

In the company of Yongden, she visited Japan, China, and then secretly returned to Tibet to find refuge at the Buddhist monastery in Kumbum on its border. Here she translated rare manuscripts relating to the Tibetan mystics into French and English. Since many of these manuscripts were later destroyed or lost, her translations were vital to posterity.

In 1921 she set out again with Yongden, intent on reaching Lhasa. The journey took three years, mostly spent outside the boundaries of Tibet, which illustrates the nature of the region's hostile territory. The hazards included

wild animals, robbers, and suspicious government officials. The inhabitants of one region they traveled through were said to be cannibals. To protect herself against the bitter weather she practiced *tumo* breathing, a psychic art that helps yogis to keep warm. Likewise she employed *lung-gom-pas*, a method of trance that enables speedy, seemingly effortless movement. Famously, one of their meals was a soup made from boiling water and pieces of leather hacked from their shoes. She disguised herself as a peasant by dying her hair and skin with ink and wearing rags. Her Tibetan was so polished by this time that it did not arouse suspicion.

They finally penetrated Lhasa in February 1924 and explored it for two months, even touring the Potala (the palace of the Dalai Lama), which was open as part of a public celebration. David-Néel was thrilled by her achievement but also frustrated—bound by her disguise in peasant garb, she was unable to explore literary or intellectual avenues.

By May 1925 she had returned to France. Already an accomplished writer, the descriptions of her escapades in Tibet made compelling reading. The government sponsored her to visit China to conduct further studies in Buddhism. She returned to France as World War II drew to a close and lived in Digne in southern France, where Yongden died in 1955 after years of alcohol abuse.

David-Néel's journey across mountains and high plateaus was a personal and spiritual one, but through her writings western readers gained their first glimpses of a region that is still one of the most mysterious places on Earth.

Above: *The power of the lands she traveled through affected David-Néel profoundly, heightening her own developed affinity for mysticism.*

FREYA STARK
1893 to 1993

The beautifully crafted literature of travel writer Dame Freya Stark brought the enigma of Arabia into the conscious thinking of readers all over the world. Unlike the travel writers of later years who viewed their chosen destinations from the windows of coaches and retired into luxury hotel rooms to pen their blinkered observations, Stark spent years living among Arabs and traveled throughout the remotest regions of the peninsula.

Not surprisingly, this unusual woman had a most unorthodox start in life. She was born in Paris, where both her parents were studying art, and visited England and Italy at an early age, so she was no stranger to travel. As a girl in Italy she worked in a friend's carpet factory and was badly scarred in an accident. A talented linguist, she went on to study literature at a London university. At the outbreak of World War I she worked first as a censor in London, then as a nurse tending the wounded from the Italian frontline.

As a child she was fascinated by the tales in the *Arabian Nights*, having received a copy for her ninth birthday. After the armistice ended World War I, she decided to visit Arabia and see its mysterious customs at first-hand and embarked on a course at the School of Oriental and African Studies in London to learn Arabic. Armed with the language, she went to work as a writer on the *Baghdad Times*, at the invitation of the Iraqi Prime Minister. Even at this early stage she eschewed the usual accommodation reserved for westerners and chose instead to live among the residents of the city; an unusual move at the time.

Living in Arab society

Soon she yearned to explore beyond Baghdad. Initially following routes used by the crusaders centuries before, she traveled deep into the Middle East, visiting the regions that are now Syria, Iran, Kuwait, Arabia, and Yemen. Her triumphs were numerous. She was the first European woman to set foot in many parts of Arabia. Her home was a Bedu tent or a roadside shack. She learned local customs and ceremonies, and became fluent in Arabic.

The Assassins, outlaws who dogged the crusaders and traded in hashish, became an interest. She researched their history and, in 1931, mapped the region they dominated on behalf of the Royal Geographical Society and discovered a previously unknown castle in the process. In 1937 she accompanied Dr. Getrude Caton-Thompson and Elinor Gardner in the first archeological excavations in Yemen, which yielded the Moon Temple of Hureidha dating from the 5th century BC. Sometimes she worked alongside Britons Doreen and Harold Ingrams, who became famous for their efforts to promote individual liberties and welfare in Yemen.

In 1942 she was awarded a medal by the Royal Geographical Society for her "travels in the East and account of them." Although she spent most of her life as a single woman, she married historian Steward Perowne in 1947, but

Facing: Freya Stark at work on a book in 1957 while she was living in Asola. Italy.

Right: Never content to be on the fringe of the Arab world, Freya Stark traveled deep into the desert and shared the loneliness of the Bedouin tribes.

the union lasted only five years. A year later she took a trip that she felt was far more difficult than anything she had experienced in all her previous travels. She crossed the Atlantic by ship, suffering not only seasickness but also appendicitis. Afterward she said it inspired "a philosophic and placid acceptance of any other trial."

Following another round of travel in the Middle East she turned her attentions to Turkey, visiting the country often. When she wearied of expeditions she retreated to Cyprus. Even at the advanced age of 77 her adventures were not over—she crossed the Himalayas, which she felt were her "last terrestrial footsteps to infinity."

In total she wrote more than 30 books as well as two tomes of essays, an autobiography stretching to four volumes, and a further eight volumes of letters. Ironically for a woman who suffered frequent bouts of poor health and often traveled under conditions of extreme hardship, she lived to be 100.

WILFRED THESIGER
b1910

The world's emptiest desert lies in Arabia, where giant dunes lie shoulder to shoulder over an area of 250,000 square miles. Rain is a rare visitor and peak temperatures reach more than 122°F. The Arabic term for the area is

Above: *Wilfred Thesiger, wearing Bedu clothing, in the Empty Quarter, 1948.*

Rub'al Khali, or "Empty Quarter."

Wilfred Thesiger traversed it not once but twice, the only man ever to do so. Hunger, extreme thirst, and the constant threat of ambush were occupational hazards for this extraordinary man who was a cartographer, medic, hunter, and

writer. His affection for the Arabian desert and its people were his prime motivation for exploring the region: "I went to southern Arabia only just in time. Others will go there to study geology and archeology…even to study the Arabs themselves, but they will move about in cars and will keep in touch with the outside world by wireless. They will bring back results far more interesting than mine but they will never know the spirit of the land or the greatness of the Arabs."

Thesiger was raised in a privileged environment. He was born in Addis Ababa in Ethiopia, where his father was a British government representative. Links between the future ruler Haile Selassie and Thesiger senior were so strong that the Englishman looked after the African's young son Asfa Wossen while his famous father was embroiled in civil strife. The families maintained close links thereafter.

Thesiger junior returned to Africa at age 24, after schooling at Eton and Oxford, and began his career as an explorer. His aim was to discover the route of the Awash River. To do so he had to run the gauntlet of the feared Danakil, who wore the testicles of their victims on a belt, and whose leader had declared a hatred of westerners. Duly Thesiger met the warriors. "The knowledge that somewhere in this neighborhood three previous expeditions had been exterminated, that we were far beyond any hope of assistance, that even our whereabouts was unknown, I found wholly satisfactory," he wrote later.

The Empty Quarter

He and his men were fortunate to escape with their lives. Later, as a district commissioner in the Sudanese political service, he devoted his time to exploration of the Tibesti Mountains and to game hunting. Then came World War II and Thesiger fought in Africa, the Middle East, and latterly with the newly-formed elite Special Air Service.

After the conflict he got a job with the

1863	1854	1860	1862	1866–8	1867	1870s	1872
Schliemann begins archeological search to prove existence of Troy	US naval gunships force Japan to open up to trade	Russia founds the port of Vladivostok	France annexes southern Vietnam	Marie-Joseph Garnier leads Mekong River Expedition in Cambodia	Ferdinand von Richthofen follows the course of the Yangtze River	Nikolai Przewalski explores central Asia	Ney Elias returns overland from China to Europe

1946–47
1947–48

Jerusalem

Basra

Cairo

Riyadh

Abu Dhabi

SAUDI ARABIA

EGYPT

Mecca

Jeddah

RED SEA

Mirbat

Al Mukallà

INDIAN
OCEAN

Middle East Anti-Locust Unit and used the opportunity to explore the Empty Quarter. The threats he faced were substantial, ranging from dehydration to dysentery, sandstorm to assassination. Nevertheless, Thesiger rose to the challenge in the late 1940s. By now he had adopted the lifestyle of the Bedu tribesmen, whose abiding comradeship moved him deeply. He shared their urge to wander but did so with map-making in mind, knowing that before his efforts almost nothing was known about the interior of this mighty dustbowl. He testified that "no man can emerge from the desert unchanged."

From 1951 Thesiger lived with the Marsh Arabs of southern Iraq, paddling to their settlements in primitive canoes. Although untrained, he administered basic health care, which undoubtedly saved countless lives. During this time he met Frank Steele, vice-consul in Basra. Ordinarily Thesiger preferred to travel alone but he made an exception with Steele.

Together, Thesiger and Steele traveled to Lake Rudolf in Africa in a great camel trek and slept in the open air. It was a profound experience: "Few other sights have made a greater impact on me. I saw the lake spread out beneath me, stretching toward the Ethiopian frontier where it ended 150 miles away. We had come a long way from Kula Mawe on foot and now felt a sense of achievement."

Thesiger continued to live in Africa until he retired to Britain at the age of 88. His best-remembered book remains *Arabian Sands*, obligatory for any serious desert traveler. Like Freya Stark, Thesiger had the utmost respect for the Africans and Arabs he met, particularly the Bedu (or Bedouins, as they are commonly misnamed). The impact of western technology and its encroachment on desert culture was a source of immense regret to him: "I realize that the maps I made helped others with more material aims to visit and corrupt a people whose spirit once lit the desert like a flame," he said.

Above: "No man can emerge from the desert unchanged," wrote Thesiger after spending years wandering the Empty Quarter in the company of Bedu tribesmen.

1875	1885	1889	1891	1900	1906–8	1906–42	1908
Nain Singh returns to India after exploring Tibet	Anglo-Russian dispute over Afghanistan leads to exploration of the region	Germany begins work on the Berlin-Baghdad railroad	Alexandra David-Néel makes first visit to the Himalayas	Wilhelm Filchner begins journeys in Pamir	Sven Hedin travels in Tibet	Sir Marc Stein carries out archeological exploration in Central Asia	Oil is discovered in Persia (Iran)

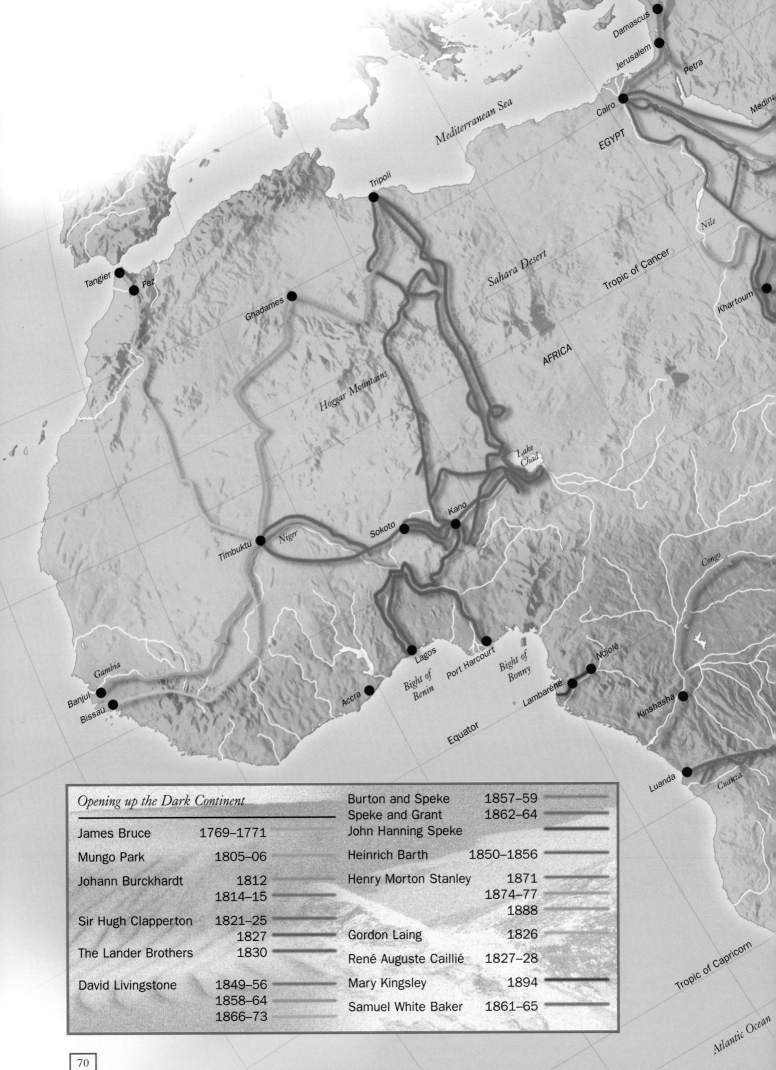

Damascus

Jerusalem

Petra

Medin...

Cairo

EGYPT

Mediterranean Sea

Nile

Tripoli

Sahara Desert

Tropic of Cancer

Ghadames

AFRICA

Khartoum

Tangier

Fez

Hoggar Mountains

Lake Chad

Kano

Timbuktu

Niger

Sokoto

Congo

Gambia

Lagos

Port Harcourt

Bight of Bonny

Ndjolé

Banjul

Bight of Benin

Lambaréné

Kinshasha

Bissau

Accra

Equator

Luanda

Cuanza

Tropic of Capricorn

Atlantic Ocean

Opening up the Dark Continent

James Bruce	1769–1771
Mungo Park	1805–06
Johann Burckhardt	1812
	1814–15
Sir Hugh Clapperton	1821–25
	1827
The Lander Brothers	1830
David Livingstone	1849–56
	1858–64
	1866–73

Burton and Speke	1857–59
Speke and Grant	1862–64
John Hanning Speke	
Heinrich Barth	1850–1856
Henry Morton Stanley	1871
	1874–77
	1888
Gordon Laing	1826
René Auguste Caillié	1827–28
Mary Kingsley	1894
Samuel White Baker	1861–65

CHAPTER FOUR

AFRICA *from* 1600

Impenetrable vegetation, deadly tropical diseases, hostile tribes, and dangerous wildlife meant that Africa was the last continent to be fully explored by outsiders. Centuries after North and South America had been colonized, Africa had only been penetrated a few miles inland by European and Muslim slave traders.

An estimated ten million Africans were captured and transported as slaves to the new colonies in the Americas, a trade that was partly achieved by exchanging guns, ironware, cloth, and food with local chieftans. Consequently the coastal ports through which this inhumane business was processed became wealthy and expanded. When European public opinion turned against the slave trade, numerous well-intentioned missionaries and explorers came to the shores of Africa determined to stamp it out. Conflict between slave traders and explorers hindered the progress of expeditions on numerous occasions.

Because of the risks and the questionable rewards of travel in the interior, only the most dedicated and determined would enter. Those who survived often returned with strange ailments that would kill them years later. Still, the challenge of exploration lured an increasing number of adventurers, many of them sponsored by their governments or by large organizations such as the Royal Geographical Society, to map and chart Africa in preparation for colonizing the continent.

European governments, fearful of what their rivals were up to, continued to pump money into exploration with a view to expanding their colonial territories. The Conference of Berlin in 1884 may have helped to settle outstanding claims in Africa and establish a protocol for future colonizing the continent, but it also prolonged the suffering of a continent and its people.

JAMES BRUCE
1730 to 1794

In 1770 James Bruce claimed to have found the source of the Nile. He was not the first to make the claim—Jesuits led by Father Pedro Paez had done so in 1615. Ungraciously he dismissed the Jesuits as liars.

Finding the source of the Nile was a centuries-old European dream, and much controversy raged around anyone who asserted to have discovered it. But it was Bruce who was dismissed as a liar when he returned to England to publish the account of his time in Africa. Most of what he wrote was probably true, but his bombastic, arrogant manner made people sceptical. Ironically it was his bluff and bluster that helped keep him alive in the interior of Africa.

Bruce was born in Scotland but raised in England. After meeting and marrying his wife he joined her family's wine merchants' business, but when she died within a year, Bruce consoled himself by traveling to Spain and Portugal, where he learned the Iberian languages and Arabic. In 1758 the inheritance he received following his father's death meant that Bruce could commit himself to exploration. Briefly, he served as the British Consul in Algiers before a spell of archeological excavation in Greece and Syria. Then he prepared to chart the Blue Nile.

His expedition set out from Cairo and sailed down the Red Sea to Abyssinia (Ethiopia). Robbers who chanced upon Bruce were held at bay by the fearsome sight of his bright red hair and by his pistol and bluster. Bruce stayed in Abyssinia's capital of Gondar for months, enjoying what was by all accounts an indulgent and excessive lifestyle. When he realized it was customary for local chieftains to offer esteemed guests the services of a sister or daughter, Bruce took full advantage. He favorably impressed the Abyssinian ruler through his actions to curtail a smallpox epidemic afflicting the city. Bruce had only basic training in medicine but he used it with gusto. His inoculation program saved the life of the regent's sick son. In so doing he struck up an enduring sexual relationship with the ruler's wife, Ozoro Esther.

A dangerous country

As he became more involved in internal disputes, he witnessed the practice among warriors of collecting the testicles of enemies and hurling them like rose-petals at their triumphant leader. While the sexual freedom of Gondar suited the promiscuous Bruce, the culture of cruelty did not. Bloodshed was rife in Abyssinia, often administered at the behest of the ruler and for the slightest offense.

Bruce was keen to resume his quest for the source of the Blue Nile. On November 4, 1770, he reported: "We saw immediately below us the Nile itself, strangely diminished in size and now only a brook that had scarcely water to turn a mill. I could not satiate myself with the sight, revolving in my mind all those classical prophecies that had given the Nile up to perpetual obscurity and concealment."

As a measure of the self-importance he felt he went on: "Though a mere private Briton I triumphed here, in my own mind, over kings and their armies."

Above: *James Bruce's bluff and arrogant manner did not endear him to his own people, but it served him well in the outback of the Abyssinian desert.*

1415	1416	1421	1433	1433	1433	1445	1445
Portuguese capture Ceuta on the Mediterranean coast of Morocco	Portuguese explorers reach Cape Bojador on North African Atlantic coast	Chinese ships establish direct contact with Arab East African ports	Chinese make final voyage to East Africa	Chinese emperor forbids any further trans-ocean voyages	Timbuktu is captured by desert nomads	Portuguese reach Cape Verde on the west coast of Africa	African slaves are sold for the first time in Portugal

He returned to Gondar and remained there for a year before setting off for home. His adventures were numerous but the gory spectacle of a royal wedding feast stands out among them. The custom was to serve raw beef carved from a live animal, so the muscles still twitched as it was being served. Nubile women fed the choicest cuts to men before tucking in themselves. The unfortunate cow died slowly in front of the diners, whose thoughts turned from food to sex, and an orgy ensued.

Leaving the savagery and sex behind, Bruce made his way northward, braving a 20-day desert trip en route to Cairo. Although he was well-received in France, he was deemed a liar in Britain. Retiring to his estate in Scotland, he married a second time, but once again was quickly widowed. Bruce himself died following a fall down a stairwell, but not before he had written *Travels to Discover the Source of the Nile*, published in five volumes. Despite initial public scorn it was ultimately hailed as an epic of African travel.

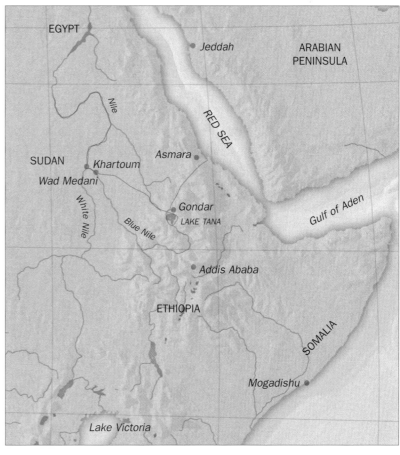

1469	1498	1561	1595	1613	1626	1652	1688
Portuguese explorers cross the equator while voyaging down African coast	Vasco da Gama circumnavigates Africa and sails on to India	Portuguese voyage up the River Zambezi	Dutch establish a trading post on Guinea coast	Jesuit Pedro Paez visits source of Blue Nile	French settlers and traders establish a colony on Madagascar	Dutch settlers found the colony of Capetown in South Africa	French Huguenots arrive in South Africa

MUNGO PARK
1771
to
1806

Right: The young Mungo Park dreamed of exploring Africa.

Below: From the edges of the Sahara to the Atlantic Ocean, the River Niger flows through desert sands, sparse savannah, and tropical rainforest. 18th-century explorers were simply not equipped for the dangers of hostile natives and rampant disease they encountered on its banks.

For Mungo Park, Africa's River Niger became an obsession, and he was ultimately to die exploring its delta. The lure of Africa in general and the Niger in particular was ever-powerful. Park once confided: "I would rather brave Africa and all its horrors than wear out my life in long and toilsome rides over the hills of Scotland."

His father was a farmer, but Park had other ambitions. He trained at Edinburgh University as a surgeon and went on to join the East India Company as a ship's doctor. He first came to the notice of the African Association—formed to promote exploration—through scientific observations published following a trip to Sumatra. Park was allocated the task of surveying the mysterious Niger. No one knew where it originated, which way it flowed, or where it met the sea.

He arrived on Africa's west coast in July

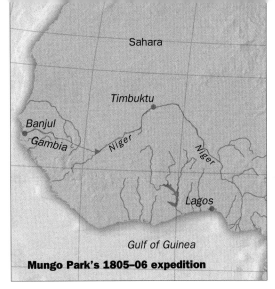

Mungo Park's 1805–06 expedition

1795 and headed up the previously mapped Gambia River. Afterward he went on horseback over unknown territory trying to find the Niger. He fell ill, fortunately in the proximity of a friendly tribe, and stayed with them for several months to recuperate.

However, most of the indigenous people he encountered were hostile, at war with each other and with strangers. They did not welcome a white face and were not hesitant in meting out death or maiming. Park was held prisoner by a group of aggressive Muslims who threatened to take out his eyes and cut off his hands. Although Park escaped after a few weeks of captivity he suffered nightmares about the experience for years after.

On July 20, 1796 he reached the Niger. "…I saw with infinite pleasure the object of my mission—the long-sought-for majestic Niger, glittering in the morning sun, as broad as the Thames at Westminster and flowing slowly to the east."

Triumphant but out of supplies, Park went downstream for six days until he was forced to abandon his expedition through lack of provisions. As he made slow progress to Gambia—where he had been given up for dead—Park was in grave danger of dying from disease or ambush.

Memoirs for a curious public

At home he was hailed a hero. His book *Travels in the Interior Districts of Africa* was a big success. In it he gave fascinating insights into African life as he saw it in his 30-month odyssey. Park was fascinated by the tribeswomen he met—on one occasion he was even allowed to converse with Moorish women in their tents. "All these ladies were remarkably corpulent, which is considered here as the highest mark of beauty. They were very inquisitive and examined my hair and skin with great attention; but affected to consider me as a sort of inferior being to themselves, and would knit their brows, and seemed to shudder when they looked at the whiteness of my skin."

Once, a party of women presented themselves at his hut with a view to establishing whether Christians were routinely circumcized. Park escaped the embarrassment by making a joke of it. When staying with friendly tribes, he was fed and nurtured by local women. Some went so far as to make up a song about him that began: "Oh pity the white man, no mother has he!"

Park married and acquired a country estate in Scotland but, like many explorers, he found it difficult to settle. By 1805 he was preparing another expedition to plot the Niger's course, with more cash, more men, and extra provisions. This time disease took a terrible toll, reducing the party to a quarter of its numbers by the time they reached the Niger.

On November 17, 1805 he wrote to a patron in England declaring: "It is my intention to keep to the middle of the river and make the best use I can of winds and currents till I reach the termination of this mysterious stream." He wrote to his wife on the same day, pledging to come home soon. Sadly he was never seen again.

His family and colleagues believed him captive in Africa. Tragically, his son disappeared in the region 20 years later while looking for his lost father. The truth, according to the sole survivor of the venture, who was tracked down much later, was that he was attacked by a tribe and drowned while trying to escape. He was mourned as a pioneering explorer, and the notes from his last journey were published posthumously.

Below: Provisions and potable water were often in short supply. This scene of Mungo Park sharing water with cattle is from the Rev. Isaac Taylor's Scenes of Africa, *published in 1824.*

JOHANN BURCKHARDT
1784 *to* 1820

In the early 19th century, many explorers were dispatched to Africa to explore the River Niger, crucial to Europe's exploitation of the continent. Johann Burckhardt was one such individual, but his love of the Middle East meant that he never actually reached his intended goal.

Although Burckhardt was born in Switzerland, his education took place in Germany and England. While he was in England he approached the African Association with a view to mounting an expedition. The Association founder, Sir Joseph Banks (1743–1820), the veteran naturalist who accompanied James Cook on his voyages, asked Burckhardt to explore the Niger. Given that the area was Arab-dominated, Banks suggested that the young Swiss should get some Arabic under his belt. With the tenacity and strength of will that appears characteristic of the adventurous breed, Burckhardt put in great efforts to become fluent. He absorbed himself in the study of the language and the culture for four years before departing for the Middle East. Burckhardt visited Syria in three successive years and then set up base in Cairo from 1812, where he converted to Islam.

Feeling that there were gaps in his

Above: *Johann Burckhardt longed to explore the River Niger, but his years of preparation extended so much that he never made the trip.*

understanding of the Arab world, Burckhardt further delayed his trip to the Niger in order to polish his cultural and linguistic skills, and during this period the forbidden holy cities of Islam became a major preoccupation for him.

Burckhardt joined a caravan setting off from Cairo to cross the Sahara, and then made his way through Jordan on a route he instinctively believed would take him to the ancient city of Petra. His suspicions were correct. He emerged from a narrow ravine to see the 60-foot grand face of the *Khazneh*, or "Treasury," looming in front of him. Behind, lay the remains of Petra, a once-thriving trading center established about 300 BC by the nomadic Nabataean tribe.

The Romans took control of Petra in AD 106, leaving their mark in the architecture of the temples and tombs. The city fell into decline when sea routes became more greatly favored for trade. Muslims took over from the Christians in the seventh century and its temples were converted to mosques. By the time of Burckhardt's arrival, two millennia of desert winds, rain, and several earthquakes had taken a toll but the find was still outstanding. No European had set eyes on Petra for centuries.

Abu Simbel rediscovered

Burckhardt went back to Cairo, where once again his stated aim to explore the Niger was postponed, this time for the lack of a caravan heading in the right direction. Not wishing to waste any opportunity, Burckhardt departed Cairo in 1813 on a donkey and followed the Nile south to examine the desert region above Aswan. Another remarkable historical find presented itself and Burckhardt became the first European to see the temple of Ramesses II at Abu Simbel, built by the ancient Egyptian civilization that had dominated the area 30 centuries earlier.

His adoption of Islam inspired confidence and friendship in Muslims, not least the Viceroy of Egypt who helped him achieve another goal. Burckhardt longed to visit Mecca, the religious city in Arabia closed to non-Muslims. He had too much respect for Islam to go in disguise. Fortunately the Viceroy permitted him to be

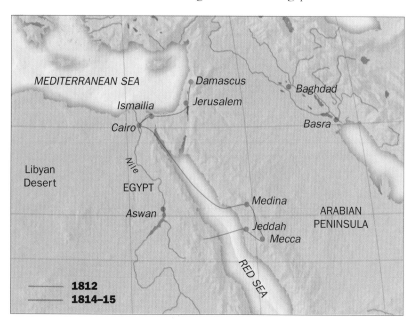

MEDITERRANEAN SEA

Damascus

Baghdad

Ismailia

Jerusalem

Cairo

Basra

Libyan Desert

Nile

EGYPT

Medina

ARABIAN PENINSULA

Aswan

Jeddah

Mecca

RED SEA

— 1812
— 1814–15

declared a Muslim so he could enter the city and visit the Kabbah and the tomb of Mohammed quite openly. When he returned to Egypt in 1816 he recorded his experiences and published books. He still had every intention of fulfilling his obligation to the African Association to explore the Niger, but he contracted dysentery and died in Cairo.

Burckhardt is remembered as much for his meticulous preparation as for his expeditions. His study of Islam rendered him as intellectually competent in his knowledge of the Koran as any academic. His writings never enjoyed popular appeal, being dull and analytical in nature, but were of tremendous practical assistance to subsequent generations of travelers.

Sir HUGH CLAPPERTON *and* RICHARD LANDER

1788 to 1827

1804 to 1834

Right: Hugh Clapperton was one of the first Europeans to sight Lake Chad and to prove that the River Niger was not, as widely believed, a tributary of the Nile.

Another 19th-century explorer who met an early death, Hugh Clapperton covered thousands of miles in a life that ended before he could celebrate his 40th birthday. The challenge of African exploration then fell to his servant, Richard Lander, who achieved greatness in his own right before dying on the continent at the tragically young age of 30.

One of 21 children, Hugh Clapperton was a seafaring Scot who joined the Royal Navy at the age of 13 and rose to the rank of captain. In 1821 he was selected by the British Colonial Office for an expedition to journey south across the unknown African interior from Tripoli on the north coast to Lake Chad. The aim was to discover whether the River Niger ran through Bornu, which is in present-day Nigeria, and it involved a trek through the Sahara Desert. Clapperton was in the company of Dr. Walter Oudney, the expedition leader, and army major Dixon Denham (1786–1828).

Relations between the three men quickly

broke down when both Oudney and Denham claimed the post of leader. Clapperton sided with Oudney and remained with him while Denham frequently organized solo forays. Despite their rivalry, in February 1823 they became the first Europeans to see Lake Chad and then to establish that the Niger turned to run south rather than east. This put paid to the long-held theory that the Niger was a tributary of the Nile.

Clapperton and Oudney decided to explore to the west. Oudney died along the way, killed by some tropical disease. Clapperton continued, hoping to find the source of the Nile. His plans were halted at Sokoto where the local chieftain, a notorious slave trader, had banned expeditions from passing. Although Clapperton was vehemently against slave trading, he stayed long enough to make important observations about the customs he witnessed.

Returning to England in 1825, Clapperton made arrangements for his travel notes to be published before setting out once more for Africa. This proved particularly crucial because the journals of Dixon Denham, which were

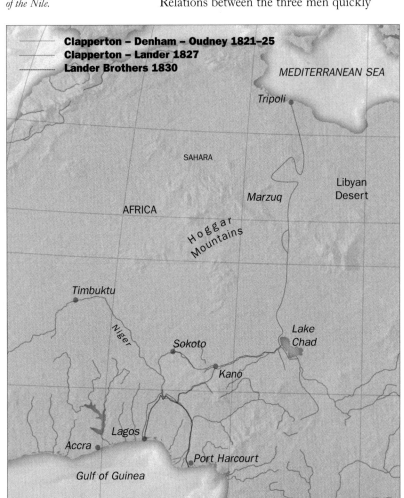

Clapperton – Denham – Oudney 1821–25
Clapperton – Lander 1827
Lander Brothers 1830

MEDITERRANEAN SEA

Tripoli

SAHARA

Marzuq

Libyan Desert

AFRICA

Hoggar Mountains

Timbuktu

Niger

Sokoto

Lake Chad

Kano

Lagos

Accra

Port Harcourt

Gulf of Guinea

published in 1826, claimed that he alone made the courageous journey north to south (Denham also died of fever in Africa at only 42).

This time Clapperton took as his servant Richard Lemon Lander, the son of a Cornish innkeeper. As a servant to gentlemen he

developed a taste for travel and had already been to the West Indies and southern Africa before joining Clapperton. With Clapperton, Lander made his way into the hazardous interior of western Africa, carrying a bugle on which he would often play the popular and apt ditty *Over the Hills and Far Away*. He came out alone after Clapperton—already weakened from illnesses previously sustained in Africa—died at Sokoto. Grief-stricken at the loss of his master and friend, Lander came home to England armed with Clapperton's papers, which he duly had published.

Tracing the Niger

Lander was also keen to return to Africa on this unfinished business of geographical exploration. He won a grant from the government and, in the company of his brother John, set out in 1830 to determine the path of the Niger.

They began almost from the point where Mungo Park had lost his life a quarter of a century earlier, at Bussa. Both men dressed Turkish-style and wore hats with enormous brims, causing some hilarity among the local people. Exploring up and then downstream in uncharted waters to the river's delta, their work came to an abrupt end when they were taken hostage by men from the Ibo tribe. A slave trader eventually paid the necessary ransom. This put Richard Lander in the ignominious position of having to row in a 40-paddle slaver's canoe to find British help, while his brother remained hostage in the clutches of the slave traders. Finally the pair returned to England, and together they wrote three volumes titled *Journal of an Expedition to Explore the Course and Termination of the Niger*. Lander received the first gold medal ever issued by the newly formed Royal Geographical Society in 1832. His commendation read: "For important services in determining the course and termination of the Niger." He returned to Africa on what was to be his final expedition, this time paid by a private firm to lead a trading mission up the Niger. His boat came under attack from hostile natives armed with swords and muskets, which they had acquired from slave traders. The expedition returned to the coast and crossed to the island of Fernando Po (Bioko), where he died from his wounds.

Left: Valet and friend to Hugh Clapperton, Richard Lander became an explorer in his own right after Clapperton's death in West Africa, and won a medal for his expedition to the mouth of the River Niger.

Below: Although the market for black slaves was fueled by western needs in the new American colonies, it was the emirs of the northern Niger who benefitted from selling people of neighboring tribes to the white man. After the long trek to the coast slaves were boarded at ports like Lagos.

DAVID LIVINGSTONE

1813 to 1873

Right: David Livingstone from an engraving of c.1870. Livingstone explored more of Africa than any other, but he never lost sight of his primary mission, to end slavery and bring Christianity to Africans.

Facing: The first white man to see the majesty of the great falls on the Zambesi, which he named after Queen Victoria. Lithograph published in 1866.

Below: Livingstone's steamer Ma-Robert on the Zambesi. From The Life and Explorations of David Livingstone, c.1878.

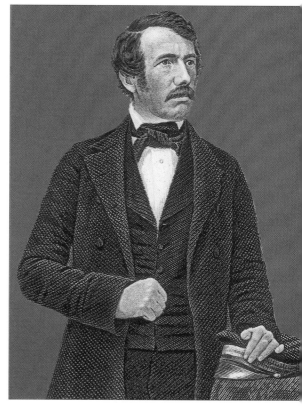

Revered as one of the greatest explorers ever, David Livingstone traveled an estimated 29,000 miles in Africa, explored about a million square miles, and was the first white man to cross the continent from west to east. However, Livingstone never lost sight of his original reason for visiting Africa: to spread the Christian message. For many, though, the most enduring image is his meeting with fellow explorer Stanley.

David Livingstone was one of five children born to poor but devout parents living in tiny accommodation in Blantyre, Scotland. Like other children he was dispatched to the local mill to work a 14-hour day from the age of ten. The young Livingstone was determined to carve a new life for himself and, with his first week's wages, he purchased a book on Latin grammar, which he studied late at night. Through hard work and determination he saved enough money to attend medical school, where he also studied theology. In 1838 Livingstone contacted the London Missionary Society. He was later ordained and, by 1841, had joined a medical mission, called Kuruman, in South Africa run by a fellow Scot Robert Moffat.

Once there, he met Moffat's daughter Mary and his resolutions to remain a bachelor and devote himself entirely to religion came under threat. Still, he longed to go off into the unknown and set up Christian centers of his own. He made several trips north in search of possible sites. On one such trip he was attacked by a lion, and he later recalled how the big cat crunched the bones of his left arm to splinters and left 11 puncture wounds. He never regained full use of the limb.

He returned to Kuruman to be nursed back to health. In 1845 he and Mary were married by Moffat, and the couple soon had children. Unwilling to be separated from her husband, Mary joined Livingstone on his subsequent expeditions. In 1849 they crossed the Kalahari Desert, never before visited by Europeans, and saw Lake Ngami (the achievement won him a financial award from the Royal Geographical Society with which he bought himself a chronometer to help fix latitude). Two years

later they were the first whites to set eyes on the huge Zambesi river. Livingstone kept copious notes and data, which greatly impressed the Royal Geographical Society.

Personal tragedy strikes

But the expeditions called for enormous physical endurance. Their one-month-old daughter died, almost certainly due to the hardships of the environment. In 1852 Livingstone took his wife and children to Cape Town and put them on board a ship bound for England. With his family gone, Livingstone made friendships with local Africans for whom, unlike many of his contemporaries, he had great respect. Livingstone referred to the slave trade as "this open sore of the world," and he worked relentlessly to end the practice, which by this era had been outlawed in Britain and many other nations but still continued in some countries. He was horrified at the way abused bodies of young slaves were abandoned where they dropped, through exhaustion or illness. It was his avowed aim to open up new trade routes, either overland or by river, to undermine those in use by slave traders and force them out of business.

Unlike other explorers Livingstone treated the Africans who accompanied him on expeditions as colleagues rather than porters. Following a difficult trek from Linyanti in central Africa to Luanda on the west coast, Livingstone elected to stay with his men rather than accept a passage aboard a British frigate, despite suffering fever, malaria, dysentery, and starvation. Ironically, it was Portuguese slave traders who ultimately helped him, but because of their presence Livingstone could not be sure that his men would be able to return to Linyanti as free men. He convalesced before going back to central Africa, then departed for the east coast and the Indian Ocean. En route he discovered the enormous waterfalls on the Zambesi, which he named Victoria after the British queen. It was the only English name he had ever picked for an African landmark.

The expedition ended when he arrived at the east coast on May 20, 1856, where he awaited a ship bound for England. The reunion with his family was joyful but the call of Africa left Livingstone unsettled.

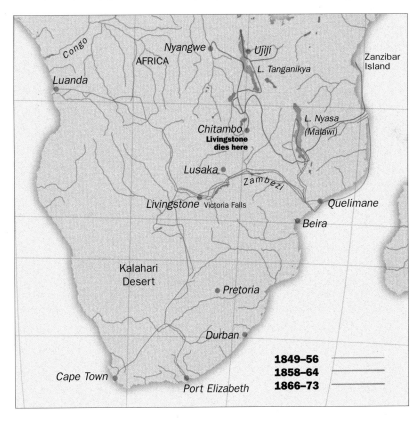

Below: On one trip Livingstone was attacked by a lion that splintered his left arm and left him severely wounded. He was saved by his faithful African porters. From a book illustration of the 1880s.

Livingstone's luck runs out

By March 1858 he was on his way back with a grant from the British government to record the geographical, mineral, and agricultural resources of central and eastern Africa. With him were his brother Charles, the artist Thomas Baines, and four other Europeans.

Until now Livingstone had been accustomed to traveling as a lone European. The flaws in his abilities to lead a team quickly became apparent and friction ensued. To compound matters, the boat they used for river travel proved unsuitable, and Livingstone's habit of freeing slaves he encountered riled the local Portuguese. Constantly at odds with the slave traders, his personal safety became increasingly at risk.

Events soon turned to tragedy. In 1858 Mary returned to Africa to be reunited with her husband, only to succumb to a fever that had dogged her for several years. She died in 1862 aged only 41, after which Livingstone was racked with guilt and self-doubt about the risks he had put her through. By 1863 the expedition was stopped, having failed to live up to expectations.

Livingstone returned to Britain for what would be his last visit to his homeland. This time he received Royal Geographical Society

1717	1770	1786	1806	1811	1815	1819	1817
Dutch begin importing slaves to Cape Colony, South Africa	James Bruce maps source of Blue Nile	Botanist Francis Masson makes fourth journey into southern Africa	Mungo Park dies at Bussa Rapids	William Burchell begins travels in southern Africa	Revolt by Afrikaaners is suppressed by British troops in South Africa	Zulu tribe establish control of Natal province in South Africa	Johann Burckhardt dies of dysentery after visiting Mecca

money and private sponsorship, with a brief to discover the sources of the Nile, Congo, and Zambesi rivers. He embarked on the venture in 1866 and disappeared for years. The lack of contact prompted four rescue missions from Britain in addition to the successful one led by Henry Morton Stanley in 1871. Livingstone, believing his work unfinished, refused to return with Stanley. While many had considered Livingstone frosty, Stanley warmed to the aging explorer; "I was converted by him although he had not tried to do it," he wrote.

Livingstone busied himself at Lake Nyasa and Lake Tanganikya, heading north as far as the village of Nyangwe on the Lualaba river. He was puzzled by the question of why the Nile river flooded seasonally, and he put much research into trying to discover the reason. His energy was astonishing, despite the illnesses he suffered. "I have drunk water swarming with insects, thick with mud and putrid with rhinoceros urine and buffalo dung, and no stinted draughts of it either."

A painful end

Once again he was plagued with misfortune when opportunistic Africans stole his possessions and incoming supplies and left him destitute. His crisis deepened as the instruments that enabled him to calculate his position failed. Of the 60 men who set out on the expedition, only 11 survived. For the first time Livingstone became lost in the dense jungle. By April 10 he knew that death was imminent. "I am pale, bloodless, and weak from bleeding profusely ever since March 31 last. An artery gives off a copious stream, and takes away my strength. Oh, how I long to be permitted by the Over Power to finish my work."

Within three weeks of writing this he was dead. He was discovered in his hut, on his knees in prayer. His companions buried his heart beneath a mulva tree beside Lake Tanganikya. At considerable personal effort and risk they took his embalmed body to Zanzibar on the coast where it was shipped back to England. Livingstone was buried in Westminster Abbey.

The Christian missions he established did not endure, but he paved the way for other missionaries to succeed, and although his efforts to end the slave trade proved ineffective, he inspired popular hostility toward it. Livingstone's contribution to mapping Africa was immense, the benefits of which were felt for decades afterward.

Facing: "Dr. Livingstone, I presume?" The historic meeting between Stanley and Livingstone at Ujiji, November 10, 1871. From a sketch supplied by Stanley.

Below: Livingstone writing his journal. Engraving after a drawing by Stanley, published in 1874.

Sir RICHARD BURTON *and* JOHN HANNING SPEKE

1821 to 1890

1827 to 1864

A great geographical mystery tantalized the Victorians. Much was known about the Nile and there was increasing awareness of the great Egyptian civilization that once flourished on its banks. Now the public wanted to know from where the waters of the mighty Nile rose. It was known that the source must lie in deepest Africa, a region as yet unexplored by Europeans. Curiosity and the quest to know the mysteries of Africa were a powerful incentive for explorers to rise to the challenge. Whoever solved the conundrum of the Nile would bask in glory and public acclaim.

Two men—with drastically different characters—accepted the huge personal risks involved. Sir Richard Francis Burton was regarded by some as the greatest thinker of his generation. He mastered 30 languages and was a noted anthropologist. His partner, John Hanning Speke, was broody, abrupt, and more inclined to shoot local tribesmen than communicate with them. The fundamental desire they shared to find the source of the Nile ultimately destroyed them both.

They met in India where they both served in the army, and first traveled to Africa together in 1855, two years after Burton had come to public attention for entering Mecca disguised as a pilgrim. This first African mission was aborted, however, when an attack by local Somalis left Burton with a spear wound in his jaw and Speke was forced to flee for his life.

The following year they returned to Africa, Burton having visited the Crimea between times. Departing from the east coast trading center of Bagamoyo on June 27, 1857, they traveled with 130 men and 30 mules, bearing scientific instruments and basic furniture among other items, determined to locate a slug-shaped lake which tribesmen and coastal missionaries spoke of. Neither knew whether the goods they carried, including cloth, beads, and wire, were enough to bribe local tribes into cooperation—or if the ammunition they carried would be sufficient to keep hostile natives at bay. Both knew they would almost certainly contract serious tropical diseases. Like most men at the time, they were imperialists, but while Burton reveled in African cultures, Speke reviled them. Burton confessed to his journal that he had a "brimful of enthusiasm" about the prospects ahead.

Two sources

Their initial destination was Tabora, an Arab trade depot some 600 miles from the coast. Not surprisingly, illness struck them both before they even reached Tabora. Speke suffered a violent malarial fever, which left him delirious. While listening to Speke's semi-conscious ramblings Burton became aware that Speke held a deep grudge against him. It is thought that the malaria left Speke with permanent brain

Below: As an orientalist, Richard Burton often adopted local dress to disguise himself. This picture was painted c.1853.

damage. Burton, meanwhile, suffered a gradual paralysis, which left him unable to walk for almost a year. The strain in their relationship was beginning to show.

When they reached Tabora there was unexpected news. There was not one lake in the vicinity, as expected, but two. But which was the source of the Nile? They considered Lake Tanganikya as the most likely, and headed west for its shore. By the time they reached the lake Burton appeared to be on the brink of death. He later wrote: "I developed a queer conviction of divided identity, never ceasing to be two persons who generally thwarted and opposed each other." At night both explorers suffered from frightening hallucinations as they tried to sleep in the nocturnal environment of the jungle.

Speke began to suffer from an eye condition that left him unable to see the lakes and rivers they visited properly. The explorers attempted to recuperate on the shores of lake Tanganikya before moving on. They used two giant canoes to search around the lake for the source of the Nile. Burton sat slumped in the stern but, despite his illness, he was determined to strive onward. Only when the native boatmen refused to paddle into the territory of cannibals did the mission come to a halt. They returned to Tabor having found a river leading from the lake, but

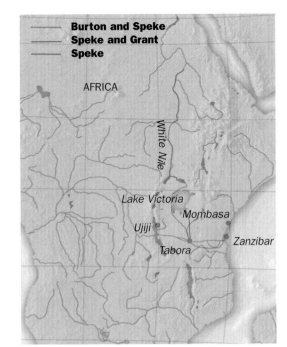

unable to determine whether it was the Nile.

Speke then struck out alone for the second, northerly lake while Burton stayed in Tabora to arrange supplies and extra finance for the expedition. Thus Speke alone saw the splendid waters that he named Lake Victoria for the English Queen. Speke was convinced that this was where the Nile rose. To celebrate he shot some wild birds and then returned to Burton triumphant. But he came back with no convincing proof that his assumptions were correct.

Below: A Sesse canoe on Lake Victoria, named by Speke. Burton and Speke used native canoes to search for the source of the Nile.

Burton sidelined

Burton and Speke had made a pledge to each other to reveal nothing to the public in England about their expedition unless they were both available. But Speke was the first to return home in 1859 by two weeks. When the ailing Burton reached England he discovered that Speke had already cornered all the credit for their joint enterprise. He had convinced the Royal Geographical Society that the Nile's source was probably Lake Victoria, and succeeded in securing money for a further expedition. Speke's motives have been scrutinized since. While he was indeed the first to see Lake Victoria, only the most ignoble would suggest that Burton's flair for languages, organization, and diplomacy had played no part in the expedition's success.

Speke's duplicity meant that Burton did not receive funding to join further expeditions. Indeed, he became sidelined, despite his protests. Speke returned to Africa in 1860, this time in the company of James Augustus Grant (1827–92). They labored up the coast of Lake Victoria, passed some time in a tribal community and found a main tributary of the Nile. However, the absence of Burton with his geographical knowledge meant that Speke's survey of the area was too poor to be considered conclusive.

The Nile debate

When Speke returned home his outspoken claims offended the Royal Geographical Society and in 1864 it was decided to settle the Nile row by holding a public hearing. The society asked Speke, Burton, and Livingstone, among others, to debate the matter. But Speke would not be able to attend. The day before the debate Burton confronted his erstwhile companion, their first meeting for five years. In Burton's account of the event, he said: "I saw him at 1.30p.m. and at 4p.m. he was dead. The charitable say that he shot himself. The uncharitable say that I shot him."

Despite the obvious implications, it is likely that Speke died from self-inflicted gunshot wounds. Speke may have been concerned he would be out-argued by the intellectually able Burton and that humiliation would follow. Two opposing tributes to Speke enhance the ambiguities about his character. James Grant wrote: "Captain Speke was pure-minded, honorable, regardless of self and self-

Below: John Hanning Speke (right) and Augustus Grant. Together they finally discovered the main source of the Nile.

denying, with a mind always aiming at great things and above every littleness." Burton, however, wrote: "[He] was uncommonly hard to manage… He ever held, not only that he had done his best on all occasions but that no living man could do better."

Because of Speke's untimely demise, the debate never was canceled, but 20 years later Burton conceded that Speke's discoveries were valid. After the Nile debacle, Burton failed to secure a place in the public's affections and turned to drink for solace, but his career continued in diverse ways. He married Isabel Arundell and together they traveled the world when he became a British government consul. They went to Fernando Po in Africa, Brazil, Damascus, and Trieste while finding time to make two personal visits to Iceland and an expedition to Egypt.

Burton suffered cholera, pneumonia, and hepatitis on his later travels, in addition to surviving a desert ambush in which he faced 300 men. He eventually died in the comfortable environs of Trieste, by then a well-known writer. One of his most famous translations was the *Kama Sutra*, published in 1883. Two years later he published his stories based on *Arabian Nights*. He was extremely forthright about sex and studied erotica from the east, which led to criticism in some sections of Victorian society. Less controversially, he was famous for his books on swordsmanship and falconry. His wife Isabel

burned many of her husband's papers after his death, destroying just about everything that had not already been published.

Although he was a remarkable man Burton was not buried in Westminster Abbey as one might have expected, but in a small cemetery in Mortlake, West London. Respecting her husband's wishes, Isabel had the tomb built in the shape of a Bedu tent and included a window because he disliked the dark.

Above: *A view of the Nile from an engraving made in the late 19th century. For decades the source of the great river had remained a mystery to explorers.*

Below: *Reverse of the medal commemorating Speke and Grant's expedition to discover the source of the Nile.*

Big GAME HUNTERS

When white men made their first hunting forays into Africa, the continent's south and east were teeming with wildlife. However, the heads and hides of Africa's finest animals became prized trophies among the wealthy, who indulged themselves in the latest and most fashionable recreation—big game hunting. Many were experienced hunters from India whose dedication to the sport helped to decimate the wildlife of two continents.

Of course, the ecological disasters of the 20th century could not have been foreseen by Victorian hunters. There existed a general assumption that the game population was inexhaustible. Often the explorers who pioneered new routes across Africa were also interested in hunting. Most went armed with the latest weaponry, not only for their own defense but also for bagging a kill. Traditionally, big game hunters were pictured either on canvas or in photographs with their guns and an animal skin at their feet.

Hunting was an obsession for John Hanning Speke as his journals reveal: "I found myself at once in view of the Nile on one hand and the Asua river on the other… The bed of the Asua seemed very large, but, being far off, was not very distinct. Nor did I care to go and see it then, for at that moment, straight in front of me, five buffaloes, five giraffes, two eland, and sundry other antelopes, were too strong a temptation." In fact, he regretted that hunting was not his sole purpose in visiting Africa: "A rich variety of small birds, as often

For European and American hunters, the vast untouched tracts of Africa represented an all-year-around open season and the challenge of taking trophies from the largest of land beasts.

happened, made me wish I had come on a shooting rather than on a long exploring expedition."

A clash of cultures

The arrival of big game hunters inevitably gave tribesmen access to firearms. Speke witnessed for himself the kind of pitfalls that could happen after presenting a young king with a gun: "The king now loaded one of the carbines I had given him with his own hands and, giving it full-cock to a page, told him to go out and shoot a man in the outer court." Speke did not attempt to counsel the king on the sanctity of human life but he and other westerners must be considered complicit in the many deaths that resulted from introducing 19th-century weapons to African tribal societies.

Arab traders also inspired the widespread slaughter of game—particularly elephant and rhino. Ivory was always in demand in the marketplace and commanded a good price. Arab ivory merchants had beaten Europeans to the most fruitful hunting grounds, and a kind of cold war was waged between Arab and western ivory hunters as the two cultures attempted to dominate the market.

Joseph Thomson mounted two expeditions in the lands lying east of Lake Tanganikya between 1879 and 1883. A keen game hunter himself, he was enthralled by the conspicuous range of wildlife he encountered: "Turn in whatever direction you please, [game animals] are to be seen in astonishing numbers, and so rarely hunted that unconcernedly they stand and stare at us, within gunshot." The Thomson gazelle is named for this hunter, first seen by him as he traveled through what are today protected national parks.

Major areas for big game hunting in the 19th century

SAHARA

West African savannah

AFRICA

Upper Nile

Kenya

Tanzania

ATLANTIC OCEAN

Zimbabwe

KALAHARI

South Africa

INDIAN OCEAN

Below: A group of 19th-century white hunters pose proudly behind their trophy

HEINRICH BARTH

1821 to 1865

The heavy death toll exacted by tropical diseases such as malaria during exploration of the River Niger halted European expeditions for a spell. Indeed, the forested coastal regions of West Africa became known as the "white man's grave," an epithet still in common parlance as recently as the 1950s. In the mid-19th century it was hoped that a pause in exploration would allow medical knowledge to find cures for the devastating illnesses. Alas, as is still often the case today, expectations exceeded the pace of development. Quinine was not used until 1854, and the transmission of malaria by the mosquito wasn't understood for a further 50 years. A saying of the time was:

> "Beware and take care of the Bight of Benin
> For one that comes out there are forty goes in."

German scholar Heinrich Barth got out of the Niger region alive but, like many others, died later as a result of sickness contracted in Africa. Barth was an academic genius, excelling at languages, history, geography, and archeology, but he failed to appreciate the value of social skills. A loner since childhood, he appeared unable to strike up convivial relations with others. Perhaps that is what made him so suited to a career in exploration.

Barth developed a taste for travel when his father sent him on a European tour after he distinguished himself at the University of Berlin. The tour included North Africa and Barth was intrigued to know what lay behind the continent's bustling northern coastal ports. When his post in Berlin as a lecturer on North Africa ended, Barth seized the opportunity to join a mission going deep into the continent. The British government sponsored the Mixed Scientific and Commercial Expedition of 1850, which was led by James Richardson, and included two other Germans, Adolf Overweg and Eduard Vogel. The expedition was to travel from Tripoli through the Sahara Desert to the city of Kano, now in northern Nigeria.

Among the shifting sands of the Sahara Barth found riches from a bygone age. As he trekked further south the well-documented Roman amphitheaters gave way to less-known human artifacts. In the Hoggar Mountains Barth saw astonishing cave paintings featuring animals such as giraffes and hippopotami. The earliest dated back to 8500 BC, while the most recent was AD 1000. It was conclusive proof that the region had not always been a desert. The receding Ice Age had created a temperate climate that lasted for millennia. As conditions slowly became too arid to maintain a large population, humans left the area. Some went to the banks of the Nile and became the first Egyptians.

Dissent and death

Despite such heartening discoveries, relations were not cordial between Barth and Richardson. Overweg cast his lot with Barth and the pair

Right: Barth, second from right, and the other members of the troubled Central Africa expedition of 1850: James Richardson, left, Adolf Overweg, second left. Eduard Vogel on the right teamed up with Barth after the original group had split due to dissent, and Richardson and Overweg had perished.

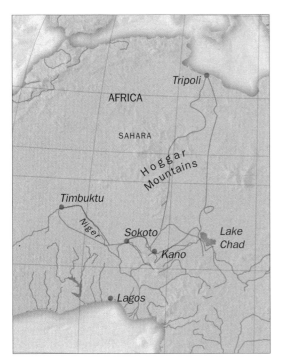

for Zanzibar but was redirected by London toward Timbuktu. The trip was arduous, with gangs of bandits posing the greatest threat. Nevertheless, he reached his goal on September 7, 1853. He remained there for eight months before returning to Kuka.

From tribesmen he learned that he had been given up as lost and that another explorer, Eduard Vogel, was in Africa trying to trace his last known movements. Barth met Vogel and they traveled together for a short while before Barth set out for Tripoli and England. In 1856 he received a gold medal from the Royal Geographical Society for his "extensive explorations in central Africa, his excursions about Lake Chad, and his perilous journey to Timbuktu."

In his final years Barth wrote several books describing his travels to a public thirsty for knowledge about the "Dark Continent." It was not until several decades after his death, however, that explorers would take note of the true worth of his pioneering work.

Below: The Great Mosque at Timbuktu, founded in 1325, is the oldest south of the Sahara.

traveled apart from their appointed leader. After negotiating a safe passage with the local Tuareg tribe the trio decided to take separate paths, agreeing to meet in Kuka. Richardson succumbed to malaria and never reached Kuka.

Barth went via Kano, which captivated him. He spent a month there, observing its inhabitants and geography and drawing affectionate sketches depicting its daily life. Onward he went, to Kuka and beyond, investigating the upper Benue River and the Shari River. But the run of good luck ended with the death of Overweg on September 27, 1852, also a victim of malaria.

Barth had been preparing to head

HENRY MORTON STANLEY

1840 to 1904

I t is impossible to speak the name of Henry Morton Stanley without affixing in the same breath his most famous words: "Dr Livingstone, I presume." Stanley uttered this phrase when he encountered the missing jungle explorer, David Livingstone on November 10, 1871. The words became so well-known that Stanley bitterly regretted ever having said them. And it is for this expedition alone, in which he searched for Livingstone throughout East Africa, that Stanley is best remembered, although he did in fact lead many journeys into the unknown.

Stanley was born John Rowlands into a life of extreme poverty in Denbigh, Wales. At the age of five he found himself in St. Asaph's workhouse where he was educated and developed a love of books. Confusion surrounds his adolescence, not least because his own memoirs appear to be somewhat embroidered. But it is known that at 18 he worked his passage to America where he was employed by a cotton merchant, Henry Hope Stanley, whose name he took. Stanley joined the Confederate army during the American Civil War. After his capture at the battle of Shiloh, Stanley appears to have enlisted in the Union army but was invalided out of service. Convinced that his future lay in America, Stanley won citizenship and became a

Right: Despite his many successful forays into what was then regarded as the "Dark Continent," Stanley was not highly regarded by contemporary explorers because he was a journalist rather than a member of a respected geographical institute.

newspaper correspondent.

As a journalist he traveled widely across America, Ethiopia, Asia, and Europe. In 1869 James Gordon Brown, the publisher of the *New York Herald*, dispatched Stanley to find David Livingstone, a Scottish missionary who was obsessed with finding the source of the Nile. Livingstone was reputed to be wandering lost in Africa's interior.

In 1871 Stanley finally reached the coast of Africa. The expedition was substantial, with about 2,000 men. They split into five groups and made tracks toward Livingstone's last known destination. Finally he encountered Livingstone at Ujiji, an Arab trading post on the shores of Lake Tanganikya. He reported the meeting thus:

"I would have run to him, only I

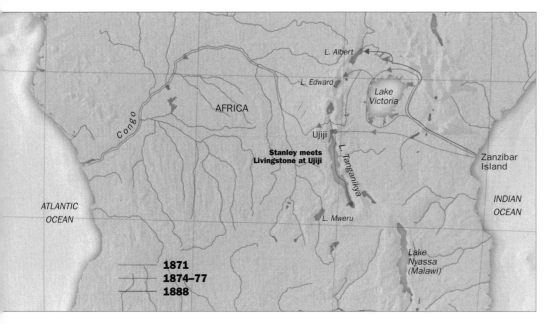

was a coward in the presence of such a job, would have embraced him, only, he being an Englishman [he was in fact a Scot], I did not know how he would receive me, so I did what cowardice and false pride suggested was the best thing—walked deliberately to him, took off my hat and said: 'Dr Livingstone, I presume?' "

As Stanley had suspected, Livingstone was determined to stay in Africa. Nevertheless the pair struck up a friendship which was both unexpected and fulfilling. Stanley left Livingstone in the jungle, where he perished shortly afterward. On hearing the news of his associate's death, Stanley returned once more to East Africa to chart the hidden waterways. He became the third westerner to cross Africa, traveling from the Indian Ocean to the Atlantic between 1874–77. The trip was richly financed but grueling. Out of the four westerners who had started the expedition, Stanley was the only one to survive. And about 70 percent of the black porters died as a result of Stanley's ruthless determination.

His next mission was to colonize the Congo on behalf of King Leopold II of Belgium. Again Stanley drove other members of his expedition to their limit. His endeavors in the Congo started a scramble among the European nations to establish African colonies.

On his final trip to Africa, Stanley was the people's choice to go to the aid of the stranded Eduard Schnitzer, also known as Emin Pasha, a German botanist who had longstanding links with the continent. Stanley chose a roundabout route to reach Schnitzer on the bank of Lake Albert in 1888. Once more he found a man devoted to his work in Africa and who was thoroughly unhappy to be rescued.

Stanley returned to England and married at the age of 49. He regained his British citizenship, won a seat in parliament, and was knighted in 1899. Although the world at large knew him as the "Congo king," Stanley had to fight hard to win the respect of other explorers—probably because of his robust win-at-all-costs attitude, and the fact that he was employed by newspapers rather than by one of the respected geographic organizations.

MYSTERIES *of the* SAHARA

Above: *Inspired by stories of Robinson Crusoe, Frenchman René-Auguste Caillié determined on a life of adventure, and became the first European to enter fabled Timbuktu and live to return and tell the tale.*

Facing: *Alexander Gordon Laing beat Caillié to Timbuktu, but was killed on his return journey. For all pan-Sahara adventurers, the feared Tuareg, nomads of the deep desert, were the greatest threat.*

In arid North Africa, the world's largest desert smothers millions of square miles of land. The Sahara stretches for some 3,200 miles from the Atlantic to the Red Sea, and a thousand miles south. Between 1000 BC and AD 1600, African kingdoms maintained trade routes across the Sahara. Caravans transported salt, leather, gold, and slaves. The success of trading links largely depended on the cooperation of the Tuareg people, nomads who are experts in surviving the Sahara's climate.

While they tolerated or participated in the trade between Africans and Arabs they were hostile to Europeans, fearing their intentions for the region. The center of Tuareg territory was Timbuktu. In its heyday in the 15th century Timbuktu was a wealthy commercial center with a tradition of religious scholarship. But after Moroccan invaders moved in at the end of the 16th century the city's peace and stability was threatened. It declined in importance, trade moved elsewhere, and the riches once associated with Timbuktu evaporated.

Europeans were somewhat deluded about Timbuktu in the 19th century. Since no European had survived a return journey to the city, which was jealously guarded, it was thought that Timbuktu was a mystical city with mighty gold reserves. The desire to explore it was so immense that the Geographical Society of Paris put up a 10,000 franc prize to the first European to enter the city. The winner was René-Auguste Caillié.

As a child, Caillié (1799–1838) read the adventure classic *Robinson Crusoe* and determined to embark on a life of travel and adventure. He came from a poor family but seized the opportunity to take part in an expedition to Senegal when he was just 16. Caillié spent some years in Africa, living as a Muslim, before setting off for Timbuktu. He left in 1827 from the west coast, posing as an Arab. Headgear shielded his pale face and a copy of the Koran hid his expedition notes. He had no weapons.

Although his progress was impeded by illness Caillié eventually entered the city unchallenged in April 1828. Timbuktu was by now a shabby shadow of its former self with earth-built houses dotted over a sandy plain. Caillié was crushed to find no treasures or architectural glories. Two weeks later he left Timbuktu in a trader's caravan that crossed the Sahara to the north African coast. He was forced to beg for food and water. Back in Europe, despite some

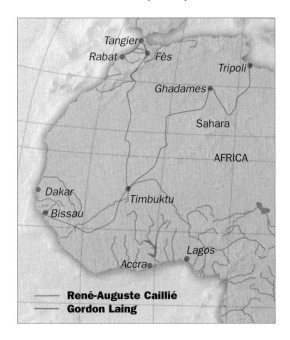

skepticism about his story he was awarded the cash prize and published a book about his experiences.

A deadly journey

Caillié was not in fact the first European to visit Timbuktu, but he was the first to live to tell the tale. In 1826 Edinburgh-born Alexander Gordon Laing (1793–1826) is known to have reached Timbuktu. The British army officer had a brief to develop trade and discourage slavery. A savage attack on the way to Timbuktu left his three black porters dead while he himself was seriously injured. Still he continued on and stayed in the city for two days before heading for home. Doubtless he experienced the same disappointment as Caillié at the realities of Timbuktu. We will never know for sure because Laing was killed on his return journey and his notes were destroyed.

It is possible that Robert Adams, an American sailor shipwrecked off the coast of

West Africa in 1810 and taken prisoner by
Arabs, beat both Laing and Caillié. By his own
account he was in Timbuktu for several months.
But his descriptions of a drab city failed to fit in
with the fables that abounded at that time in
America and Europe. Although the African
Committee gave him some credence, his
adventures published in 1816 were widely
believed to be fabricated.

A later victim of the unpredictable desert
dwellers was the Dutch heiress and explorer
Alexandrine Tinne (1835–69). Unlucky in love,
Tinne left her home in The Hague and went to
Africa, hiring a fleet of boats in Cairo to carry
herself, her mother and aunt, scientists and
servants with the intention of sailing to the
Nile's source. When the river became
unnavigable she struck out overland in central
Africa, exploring between the Congo and the
Nile rivers. She had hoped to meet John
Hanning Speke but was forced to return to
Cairo alone, her mother, aunt and most of the
scientists having died of malaria. In 1869 she
tried to become the first European woman to
cross the Sahara, but on her way to a Tuareg
camp she was robbed and killed by her guides.

MARY KINGSLEY

1862 to 1900

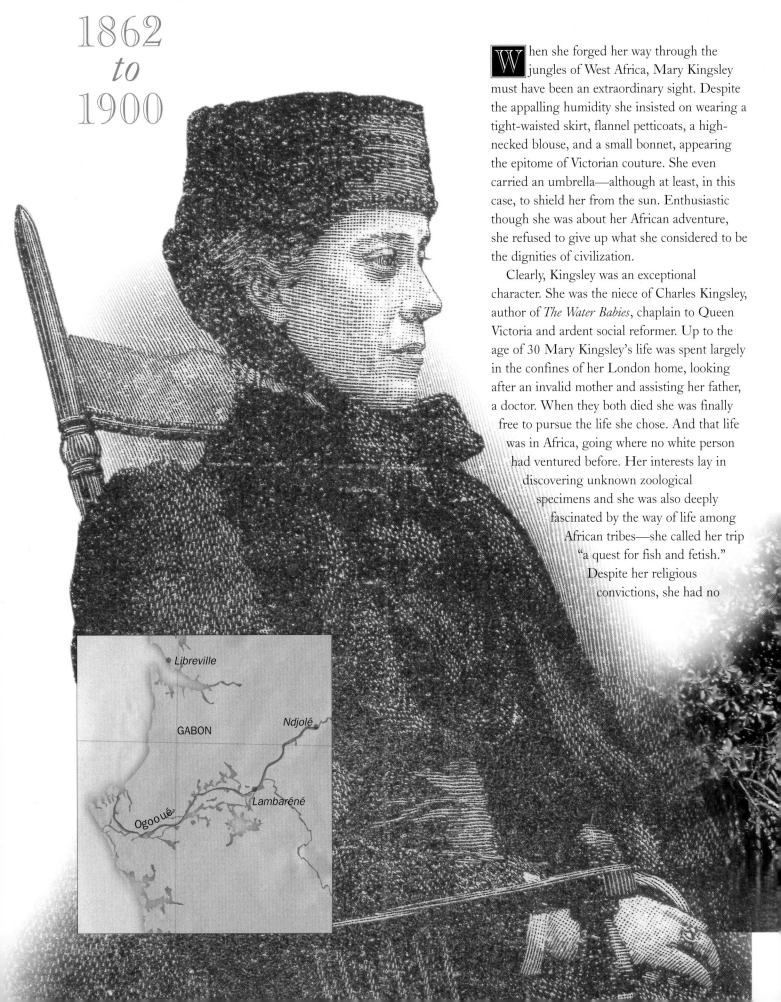

When she forged her way through the jungles of West Africa, Mary Kingsley must have been an extraordinary sight. Despite the appalling humidity she insisted on wearing a tight-waisted skirt, flannel petticoats, a high-necked blouse, and a small bonnet, appearing the epitome of Victorian couture. She even carried an umbrella—although at least, in this case, to shield her from the sun. Enthusiastic though she was about her African adventure, she refused to give up what she considered to be the dignities of civilization.

Clearly, Kingsley was an exceptional character. She was the niece of Charles Kingsley, author of *The Water Babies*, chaplain to Queen Victoria and ardent social reformer. Up to the age of 30 Mary Kingsley's life was spent largely in the confines of her London home, looking after an invalid mother and assisting her father, a doctor. When they both died she was finally free to pursue the life she chose. And that life was in Africa, going where no white person had ventured before. Her interests lay in discovering unknown zoological specimens and she was also deeply fascinated by the way of life among African tribes—she called her trip "a quest for fish and fetish." Despite her religious convictions, she had no

Libreville

GABON

Ndjolé

Lambaréné

Ogooué

desire to change the faith of those she met and respected tribal traditions.

This respect proved to be her passport to success. She made two expeditions to Africa. The first, in 1893, took her from Calabar in present-day Nigeria, inland first toward the River Niger and then veering south toward the Congo. She returned to England the following year. Finding it impossible to settle, she set off again within months. This time she focused on Cameroon and Gabon, traveling first by paddle steamer then by canoe over rapids, into a deeply forested area notorious for its cannibals. Kingsley discovered the virtues of posing as a trader. Tribes readily accepted her if she offered items including fishhooks, tobacco, and cloth. Although she never married, in order to side-step difficult questioning by local people, Kingsley claimed she was looking for a long-lost husband. Her expeditions contained a catalog of alarming incidents. Once she tumbled into an elephant trap—a giant pit disguised with foliage. The voluminous swathes of her skirts saved her from serious injury. On another occasion she slipped and fell from a high path through the roof of a hut. It was the first time its occupants had seen a white woman, and their alarm at this unexpected visitor dropping in must have been great!

Surviving great danger

Undaunted by accounts of cannibals in Gabon, Kingsley entered villages where the residents—the appropriately named Fang people—were known to feast on human flesh. She stayed in one chief's hut, surrounded by the remains of people he had eaten. Wherever she went she earned immense respect from the local populace not least because she was prepared to take part in local customs. She also carried ointments and medicines for the tribespeople. Her guides, inspired by her altruism, enabled her to complete her expeditions.

Her second expedition lasted almost one year. Before her return to Britain in 1895 she climbed Mount Cameroon, at 13,350 feet the region's tallest peak. She brought home with her 65 species of freshwater fish, seven of which were previously unknown and now take their generic names from her. During her time in England she wrote three books: *Travels in West Africa*, *West African Study* and *The Story of West Africa*, which were illuminating guides to life in Gabon. She planned a further trip to this same region of Africa in 1899 but, following the outbreak of the Boer War in South Africa, changed her plans. Instead, she went to Cape Town where she worked as a nurse caring for Boer prisoners of war. At the age of only 38 she contracted typhoid fever and died.

Facing:*Victorian couture in the jungle—Mary Kingsley saw no reason to lower her standards when going among the tribespeople of Africa.*

Below: *In her travels through West Africa, Kingsley encountered the ubiquitous mangrove swamps lining the river banks. At the time no one knew that this was the habitat of malarial mosquitoes.*

The AKELEYS

1860
to
1926

1875
to
1970

1878
to
1966

Right: Carl and Mary Akeley started by preserving dead animals and then moved to keeping them alive and preserving their habitats.

As the 20th century dawned there was a change in the character of expeditions setting off from the western world into Africa. Since most of the major geographical questions had now been answered a fascination with the continent's abundant wildlife began. Ultimately it would lead to the birth of numerous worthy conservation projects, but at the beginning of the century it meant collecting specimens for transport to Europe or America. The fate for many captured animals was the indignity of taxidermy.

One of the pioneers of modern taxidermy—the art of stuffing and mounting animals—was Carl Akeley. A talented sculptor, photographer, explorer, and naturalist, he was dissatisfied with using straw or wood shavings as stuffing. With a keen eye for the original shape of the living animal, he used wood, wire, or even bone to mimic animal limbs. To reproduce tendons and muscles he added clay. When the figure was complete he made a cast and fitted the animal skin over it. Akeley was equally concerned about the painted

backdrops placed behind the inanimate animal. With precise detail he linked it to a particular location.

His art helped to create one of the most dramatic museum displays of its time. The Akeley Hall of African Mammals at the American Museum of Natural History vividly recreates 28 scenes straight from the jungles and the plains. One even shows the place where

Right: By the start of the 20th century the depredations of white hunters had begun to threaten the gorilla population of Africa. Carl Akeley was among the first naturalists to campaign for a gorilla sanctury.

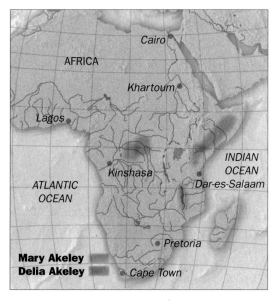

Mary Akeley
Delia Akeley

1850	1854	1863–6	1864	1865	1868	1869	1871
Francis Galton and Charles Andersson land at Walvis Bay to explore inland	William Baikie leads Niger expedition	Georg Schweinfurth explores from Red Sea to Nile	Samuel White Baker names Lake Albert	Gerhard Rohlfs is first European to travel from Tripoli to Lagos	Gustav Nichtigal begins explorations of Chad and Sudan	Alexandrine Tinne murdered by Tuareg	Henry Morton Stanley meets David Livingstone

Akeley was buried following his death in 1926 during a collecting expedition in Africa. The Akeley Hall at the museum was not finished until a decade after his death and became the kind of exhibition that other museums around the world aspired to.

Akeley married twice and each of his wives continued collecting specimens for museums long after his premature death. His first wife, Delia Denning Akeley worked as an assistant to Akeley before marrying him in 1902. Together they went to Kenya in 1905 and spent 18 months gathering exhibits for Chicago's Field Museum. Delia herself shot two elephants during this time. They returned on a collecting mission again, this time in 1909 on behalf of the American Museum of Natural History. Much of the responsibility for the expedition fell to Delia, since Carl was stricken with sickness. She still found time to observe the behavior of baboon colonies, unwittingly starting something of a trend among women explorers.

Although Akeley and Delia divorced in 1923 she continued to visit Africa. She won commissions in her own right to seek out valuable exhibition material. Accordingly she canoed down the Tana River in Kenya, spending ten weeks studying wildlife in the environment. After this she crossed the Somali Desert. Having fulfilled her obligations to the Brooklyn Museum of Arts and Sciences, she determined to find the much-rumored pygmies of the Belgian Congo. Delia expected to find them ill-nourished, believing this to be the reason behind their short stature (even the men's average height was less than 5 foot), but in fact she discovered a healthy people. She stayed with them for several months, during which time they showed her how they hunted with bows and arrows, nets, and spears.

Another trip to the Congo region was aborted due to adverse weather. Delia wrote magazine features and two books about her experiences.

Akeley's second wife, Mary had already proved to be the adventurous type. As a single woman she made a series of journeys through the wilds of Canada, studying some of the Indian tribes of the country, as well as

undertaking some climbing in the Canadian Rockies. After their marriage in 1924, Mary and Akeley were determined to furnish the American Museum of Natural History with a Great African Hall. With this ambition in mind they set off to the Belgian Congo in 1926. Their particular interest was in gorillas. In 1921 Carl Akeley had led an expedition to the Virunga Volcano and was struck by these majestic animals. The risk that the gorillas could become extinct was already clear by that time, and he campaigned for a sanctuary to be established in Africa for them.

Following Akeley's death in the Congo, Mary completed the task they had set out to undertake and continued to explore Tanganikya and Kenya, providing new and enlightening maps on these areas. She continued to highlight the dangers facing traditional cultures in Africa as well as animal habitats through books and photographs.

By the time of her final visit to Africa in 1952 the era of taxidermy was coming to an end. In 1960 Jane Goodall established a camp on the banks of Lake Tanganikya to observe the behavior of chimpanzees. This approach, coupled with the use of TV cameras, brought Africa into the homes of people across the world.

Above: African tribes had always hunted from necessity, but the European demand for ivory in the 19th century meant that elephants came under threat of attack for less noble purposes.

Below: Carl Akeley was also interested in the natural habitats of the animals he collected, and recreated them as backgrounds to his displays. These rhinoceroses, like the other illustrations on these two pages, are from a book published in 1875.

SAMUEL WHITE BAKER

1821 to 1893

Samuel White Baker was perhaps the most eccentric explorer of the 19th century. He was also one of the most widely traveled, having visited not only Africa but also Syria, India, Japan, the United States, and Cyprus.

Baker's complex personality remains a riddle. He loathed the slave trade but still thought little of the Africans he encountered, insensitively branding them "savages." Armed for combat, he also carried a full Scottish highland attire on his travels in Africa with which to make a favorable impression on tribesmen. (This was a technique used some 15 years previously by Francis Galton and Charles Andersson in southern Africa. They rendered potentially hostile natives speechless after dressing in the garb of the English huntsman.)

Most sensationally of all, he bought his fiancée Florence from a slave auction in Bulgaria. Together they traveled through unknown territory in Africa, although they were as yet unmarried. When they finally wed back in London after their African odyssey, Queen Victoria was so shocked by the scandal that, while she knighted Baker, she refused to receive Florence at court.

Baker and Florence set out from Cairo in April 1861 determined to find the source of the Nile, and unaware of the progress made by Speke and Grant. For a year they surveyed rivers in Ethiopia, gaining valuable experience, before descending, via Khartoum, to the trading post of Gondokoro. Plans to find the source of the Nile from there were thwarted when they ran into Speke and Grant returning victorious from Lake Victoria.

Fresh challenges

On hearing their news, Baker was both elated and crushed. "Does not one leaf of the laurel remain for me?" he asked. In reply Speke and Grant made it clear that there was still glory to be had in defining the various sources of the Nile, and that there was a significant lake hitherto unexplored in the vicinity of Lake Victoria which clearly had a bearing on the issue. They passed over vital maps before departing, exhausted, for the north coast and home.

Right: *Baker's expedition carried dismantled steamships across the Sudan's desert, in readiness for the exploration of equatorial Africa's rivers and lakes.*

Baker and Florence set out with renewed purpose. But in their path lay hostile slave traders and sufficient hardships to prompt their previously loyal porters and troops to mutiny. More than once Baker was forced to question the worth of his expedition, particularly when he saw Florence close to death with fever. Commoro, chief of the Latooka tribe, asked him: "Suppose you get to the great lake, what will you do with it? What will be the good of it?

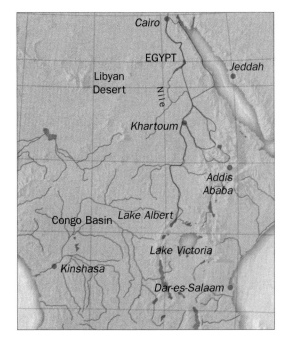

If you find that the large river flows from it, what then?"

Still they continued until, on March 14, 1864, they finally found the lake. Baker recorded their emotions on achieving their goal: "The glory of our prize burst suddenly upon me! There, like a sea of quicksilver, lay far beneath the grand expanse of water—a boundless sea horizon on the south and south-west, glittering in the noonday sun; and on the west, at 50 or 60 miles' distance, blue mountains rose from the bosom of the lake to a height of about 7,000 feet. It is impossible to describe the triumph of that moment; here was the reward for all our labor—for the years of tenacity with which we had toiled through Africa. England had won the sources of the Nile!"

The greatness of the moment affected him, and he named the Lake for Queen Victoria's husband Albert who had died in 1861. His maps of the area proved beyond question that Lake Albert was indeed one of the sources of the Nile. The splendid waterfall, which graced this early stretch of the Nile, he named for Sir Roderick Murchison, president of the Royal Geographical Society.

On his return to England Baker gave a typically humble version of events: "I claim no honor as the discoverer of a source, for I believe the mighty Nile may have a thousand sources. The birthplace of the river lies among the great chain of lakes bosomed among the mountain ranges of Equatorial Africa… I wish only to lay before the world this simple and straightforward narrative of my expedition for the benefit of geographical science, trusting that nearly five years in Central Africa may have been of service in determining the great basin of the Nile."

The PYRAMIDS *and* ANCIENT EGYPT *Revealed*

The pyramids at Giza are the sole survivors of the original Seven Wonders of the World. Centuries of expeditions slowly shed light on their secrets and now every schoolchild knows that they are the funerary monuments built for Pharaohs Khufu, Khafre, and Menkaure between 2600 and 2500 BC. All were robbed of their treasures in antiquity, but the buildings remain astonishing and mysterious feats of engineering.

While Islamic scholars of the Middle Ages debated the extent of the treasure that they knew must once have been stored in the pyramids, the buildings' purpose was unknown to Europeans for centuries. Until the late 16th century they were thought to have been grain storage houses. The first European to attempt a scientific analysis of the pyramids was Italian Prospero Alpino who, in 1582, visited Egypt and measured the height and perimeter of the pyramid of Khufu. While he correctly concluded that pyramids were the tombs of kings he also insisted, wrongly, that the Sphinx was hollow.

No other expedition made notable advances until Napoleon Bonaparte invaded Egypt in 1798 and assigned a team of scientists and mathematicians to study the pyramids. Bonaparte himself conducted some of the operation. His mathematician Gaspare Monge estimated that all the blocks from the three pyramids of Giza could be used to make a 10-foot-high, 1-foot-thick wall around France.

It wasn't until 1925 that a burial chamber (thought to have been the final resting place of Queen Hetepheres) was discovered at the bottom of a 98-foot shaft inside Khufu's pyramid, by American Egyptologist George Reisner. And in 1954 a further incredible discovery was made by Egyptian archeologist Kamal el-Mallakh. A dismantled boat was unearthed in a giant pit at the south side of Khufu's pyramid (also called the Great Pyramid). Disassembled into many pieces, it measured 141 feet in length when it was put together.

In pharaonic times, the prominence of the pyramids meant that they very quickly succumbed to grave robbers. To protect their tombs and those of their ancestors the pharaohs searched for new burial grounds. Their solution

Above: One of the most famous faces in the world— the short-lived and little-known pharaoh Tutankhamun became world famous through the work of Egyptologist Howard Carter.

Right: The Pyramids of Giza were a tourist attraction as long ago as the early Victorian era. This contemporary engraving shows Egyptians helping a European touring party to scale the blocks of Khufu's Great Pyramid

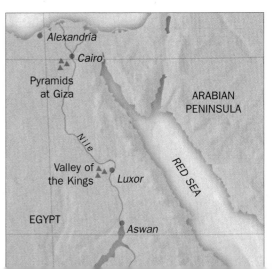

was a new royal cemetery at Thebes, hundreds of miles south of Giza. Between about 1580 BC and 1085 BC tombs were dug out of the limestone cliffs, and temples were constructed below. Today we know it as the Valley of the Kings.

Carter's discovery

It was here that Tutankhamun's grave was discovered, miraculously untouched while tombs all around had been plundered. The expedition that discovered it is now one of the most famous of all time. The men behind the find were Howard Carter (1874–1939), an English archeologist and former Inspector of the Egyptian Antiquities Service, and Lord Carnarvon, an enthusiastic amateur Egyptologist.

With Carnarvon's money and Carter's expertise the pair claimed credit for finding numerous noblemen's tombs close to the Valley of the Kings at Thebes. All the time, Carter harbored ambitions to uncover the tomb of Tutankhamun, the king who ruled for less than ten years and who died before his 19th birthday.

From 1917 Carnarvon financed Carter in excavations around the Valley of the Kings, all of which were fruitless. Losing faith in the project by 1922, the aristocrat had to be persuaded by Carter to try just one more season of digging. Within three days, the team discovered a series of steps cut out of rock leading to a sealed entrance. Carter curbed his urge to immediately enter and waited for his sponsor to make the

journey from Cairo to Luxor. What followed was surely the greatest event of their lives.

Behind the doorway was a rubble-filled corridor leading to a further door. Carter made an observation hole and looked into an annex filled with gilded furniture, including beds, chests and chairs, unused for more than 3,000 years. Beyond was an even more breathtaking scene. The burial chamber was almost filled with an enormous gilded shrine, one of four, which housed the sarcophagus.

By dint of bad luck Carnarvon did not live to witness the revelations of the shrine. The coffin was not opened until 1925, nearly two years after his death from an infected mosquito bite. Although he had always suffered from ill health his death came as a surprise. Superstitious stories about a curse quickly spread. But if a curse existed it bypassed Carter who spent years overseeing the emptying of the tomb and cataloging artifacts. He lived until he was 65 and died a peaceful death. His discovery in the Valley of the Kings left one little-known pharaoh of ancient times as the most famous face in the modern world.

Above: The Pyramids of Giza and the Sphinx are set dramatically against the background of a dust storm in this engraving from the last half of the 19th century.

Below: Howard Carter (kneeling) examines the inscriptions on the doors of the fourth shrine, evidence that they were about to discover the sarcophagus of Tutankhamun in 1922.

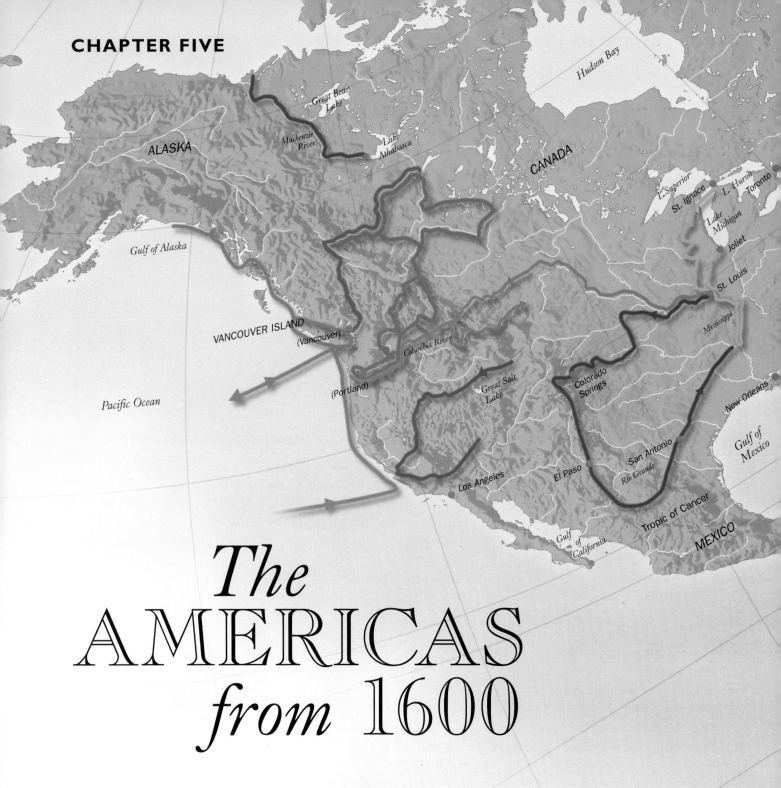

CHAPTER FIVE

The AMERICAS from 1600

hen the Americas were discovered in the 15th century none of the early explorers could guess just how far these rich, virgin lands extended. There were plenty of people ready and willing to find out, attracted by the possibilities of discovering untold riches.

The initial rush to find gold and other sources of instant wealth slowly succumbed to a more methodical approach to colonization. The abundance of exploitable land, which was in increasingly short supply in a heavily-populated Europe, attracted fur traders, cattle farmers, and crop growers. South America, with its thick rain forests, proved impossible to open fully for colonization but North America, with its grassy plains and temperate climate was less arduous.

The frontier, for ever being pushed back, remained uppermost in North American mentality. After the American Revolution, the culture of the Wild West developed, which speeded expansion. William F. Cody, alias

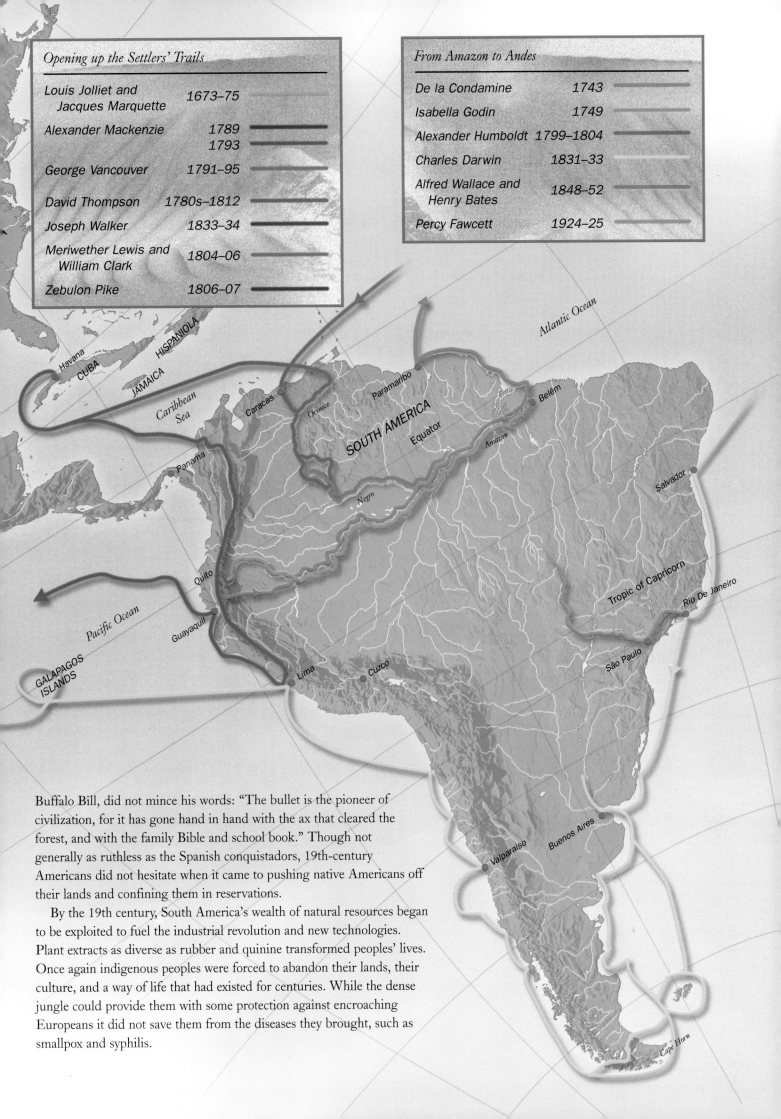

Buffalo Bill, did not mince his words: "The bullet is the pioneer of civilization, for it has gone hand in hand with the ax that cleared the forest, and with the family Bible and school book." Though not generally as ruthless as the Spanish conquistadors, 19th-century Americans did not hesitate when it came to pushing native Americans off their lands and confining them in reservations.

By the 19th century, South America's wealth of natural resources began to be exploited to fuel the industrial revolution and new technologies. Plant extracts as diverse as rubber and quinine transformed peoples' lives. Once again indigenous peoples were forced to abandon their lands, their culture, and a way of life that had existed for centuries. While the dense jungle could provide them with some protection against encroaching Europeans it did not save them from the diseases they brought, such as smallpox and syphilis.

LOUIS JOLLIET *and*
JACQUES MARQUETTE

1645
to
1700

1637
to
1675

Right: Louis Jolliet had intended a religious life but turned instead to exploration. In addition to finding the Mississippi Jolliet and Marquette were the first white men to see the land on which today Chicago stands, and a suburb of the city is named after Jolliet. From a watercolor painting after a statue.

For more than a century after Columbus landed in the New World, Spain kept a stranglehold on its interests in North America. With the late entrance of France and England into the colonial land-grab, the two new powers pushed their frontiers south and west in an effort to gain more territory, inevitably to the detriment of the Spanish.

While France had carved itself a slice of the New World in the early 16th century there was little urgency about its ambitions, primarily due to lack of finances. It took a visionary like Samuel de Champlain (c.1567–1635), the founder of Quebec, to put France on the map in the Americas. He did so in a series of expeditions down the St. Lawrence river and then went overland as far as Lake Ontario and Lake Huron. Despite a perpetual battle against the French authorities' disinterest in exploration of the region, de Champlain continued to stake France's claim whenever he could. Following his death Louis Jolliet adopted the same cause. Jolliet was born in Quebec, and was undoubtedly raised on stories of heroism centered on de Champlain. At any rate, Jolliet, a gifted musician, changed his mind about devoting himself to religion in 1667. Instead he went to France to learn the latest in cartographic techniques.

When he returned to Canada he teamed up with his brother Adrien, who had started a fur-trading business, and together they planned an expedition into the wilderness to expand trade. Their enterprise was thwarted by Adrien's sudden death in 1670. Two years later Jolliet was asked by the governor of Quebec to lead an expedition, not least to assess the mineral wealth of the area near the Great Lakes. Among the people Jolliet chose to join his party were his remaining brother Zacharie and Father Jacques Marquette, a Jesuit priest who lived among Huron Indians.

They had heard about a large river south of Canada—the Mississippi—but did not know if it flowed south into Spanish territory in the Gulf of Mexico or west, into the Pacific. If the latter was true they believed it could be a short cut to China and all the trading potential it held. Despite high hopes for the expedition there was no money forthcoming to finance it. Jolliet had to pay himself and hope to recoup the costs in trading opportunities along the way.

On May 17, 1673 Jolliet, Marquette, and five others set off in canoes from the Mission of St. Ignace at Michillimakinac, on the north bank of Lake Michigan. They paddled around the shoreline until they entered the Fox river in Green Bay. Local Indians, translated by Marquette, warned of the perils of proceeding—not only were the Mississippi

inhabitants barbarous and cruel but monsters lurked in the waterway, they said. Regardless, Jolliet continued and joined the waters of the Mississippi on June 17, 1673. The Indians they met were friendly, and the only monsters they encountered were painted on cliffs. For 1,000 miles they traveled down the river, charting its twists and bends to make the first map of the Mississippi.

Disaster strikes

By July they entered lands controlled by hostile Indians and knew also that they were nearing territory belonging to Spain. Regretfully they decided to turn back rather than "deliver ourselves to the Spaniards of Florida." Although they had not reached the mouth of the Mississippi as they had hoped to, they established beyond doubt that it led into the Gulf of Mexico.

Disaster struck as they made the tortuous journey back to Canada. A canoe containing Jolliet's notes and his map capsized in the Lachine Rapids. Three men drowned and Jolliet himself was lucky to survive. "I was rescued after four hours in the water, by fishermen who never usually went to that spot, and who would not have been there if the Holy Virgin had not accorded me that favor…nothing remains to me but my life."

Marquette, weak with dysentery, preached to 2,000 Indians on the Illinois river over Easter 1675. He died shortly afterward. His notes

were the only surviving records of the Mississippi venture. In fact, doubt still remains as to whether the published versions were actually his or were written by a colleague who embellished them with recollections from Jolliet.

As for Jolliet, he was somewhat sidelined by the French authorities after his return because they were disappointed at the few immediately exploitable results of his trip. He began his own fur-trading company and worked with some success until 1679 when the French governor turned to him once more, this time asking Jolliet to head a spying mission against the English encamped in Hudson Bay. Jolliet continued to make maps and explored the Labrador coastline before his disappearance during a trip in 1700.

Above: With the aid of friendly Indians, Jolliet and Marquette discover the Mississippi.

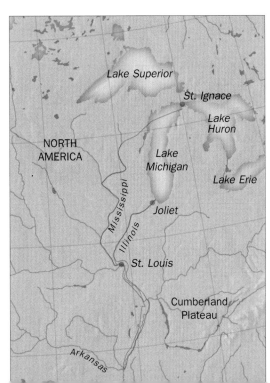

CHARLES MARIE *de la* CONDAMINE

1701 to 1774

The first man to sail down the River Amazon was Francisco de Orellana (1511–46), who in 1540 ran the gauntlet of hostile natives during an epic voyage spanning some 3,000 miles. With a legend of warrior women, the Amazonians, uppermost in his mind, it was de Orellana who coined the mighty river's name. Another 200 years passed before the first scientist, Charles Marie de la Condamine, visited the region, and he too navigated the unmapped river.

A fastidious French aristocrat with an analytical mind, de la Condamine was dispatched to South America with a brief to resolve one of the scientific puzzles of the day; Sir Isaac Newton had claimed the world bulged at the equator and was flatter at the Poles, while French astronomer Giovanni Cassini theorized that the opposite was true.

De la Condamine's mission was fraught with difficulties. He and his party were in Spanish territory and the Spaniards were wary of strangers on their shores. The group's doctor was killed by an angry mob; a botanist reportedly went mad when a servant rubbished specimens he had been collecting; one man died from malaria; another fell from scaffolding. De la Condamine and astronomer Pierre Bouguer clashed regularly. In a final insult, news reached the party that an expedition sent north by France with the same brief had conclusively proved that Newton's theories were correct.

After spending eight difficult years in South America trying to complete his mission, de la Condamine decided to finish his time there by

Above: *Charles Marie de la Condamine navigated the Amazon to prove a scientific theory but returned with more valuable discoveries, such as latex and quinine.*

navigating the Amazon from the Andes in the west to the Atlantic coast in the east. Pedro Maldonado, a Spanish colonial official, accompanied him on the expedition. Traveling in hollow log canoes measuring 44 feet and piloted by local Indians, the pair covered an astonishing 2,600 miles along the Amazon between July 23 and September 19, 1743.

Despite de la Condamine's dependence on native skills and manpower, he had nothing positive to say about the Indians of South America: "They are all gluttons to the point of voracity, when they have something with which to satisfy it; but sober when obliged by necessity to be so—they can do without anything and appear to want nothing… Enemies of work, indifferent to all motives of glory, honor, or gratitude. Solely concerned with the immediate object and always influenced by it; without care for the future, incapable of foresight or reflection." Rank ingratitude, then, from a man who feasted on the triumph of his trip.

De la Condamine was spellbound by the environs of the Amazon: "I found myself in a new world, separated from all human intercourse, on a freshwater sea, surrounded by a maze of lakes, rivers, and canals, and penetrating in every direction the gloom of an immense forest." Among his discoveries were the incredible properties of latex, the shock given by electric eels, quinine, exotic fruits, and many unknown species of plant. He also brought back to Europe the drug curare. De la Condamine drew maps as he traveled and explored at least some of the Amazon's tributaries.

Jean Godin and Isabella

On reaching the ocean he turned north and made his way up the coast to find a port for passage back to France. He returned in 1745, a decade after setting out on his original expedition, and published his memoirs. However, even greater stories of human endeavor were to come from his colleague on the expedition, Jean Godin des Odonais, and his wife Isabella.

Godin had also resolved to travel down the Amazon before returning to France, but he ran into difficulties and remained in the western part of Amazonia. In 1749 Isabella set off from the east coast in search of her husband, along with a large party of relatives and servants; two brothers, a 12-year-old nephew, three Frenchmen, an African servant, three maids, and 31 Indian helpers. Disaster struck early on when they discovered a village that had been deserted following a smallpox epidemic. The Indians in Isabella's party fled. Soon the party split, with two going ahead for help while Isabella and her family remained in the jungle. For 25 days they waited before setting off on foot in desperation. One by one the members of the party perished, and only Isabella survived. Alone and facing almost certain death through starvation and disease, she was fortunate to run into a group of friendly natives. Given up for dead by her family, she survived to continue the journey up the Amazon and was ultimately reunited with her husband. Her death-defying story was published across the world.

Above: *The tractless jungle of the Amazon basin. The many splits and oxbow lakes made early navigation a difficult process.*

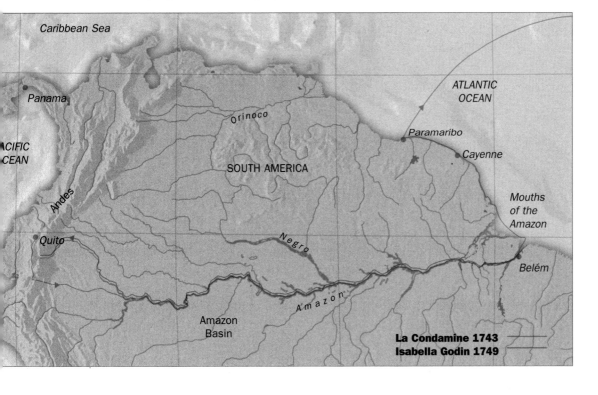

ALEXANDER MACKENZIE

1764 to 1820

Scots-born Alexander Mackenzie was one of numerous explorers who searched for the elusive northwest passage through the American continent. Unlike many of his contemporaries, he survived to tell the tale of his journey. By the age of 15 Mackenzie had moved from his home in Stornoway, in the Scottish Hebrides, to New York and then, to escape the American Revolution, to Montreal. It was there that he joined a small fur-trading company called Finlay, Gregory & Company that was taken over by the larger Northwest Company. He soon rose to prominence in the firm and, by 1788, he was in charge of the Lake Athabasca region.

His headquarters was situated at Fort Chipewyan, a trading post recently built by his cousin Roderick Mackenzie. The region had just been opened up for fur traders by trapper Peter Pond (1740–1807) who had made basic maps of the waterways and was convinced the large river adjoining the Great Slave Lake north of Lake Athabasca flowed to the Pacific Ocean.

Mackenzie enthusiastically embraced the idea and planned his first expedition. By June 1789 he was ready to depart, in the company of four French Canadians, two of their wives, an Indian guide called "English Chief," and two of his wives. Within a few days there was a setback. The Great Slave Lake was still ice-bound and they were held up as they tried to cross it.

They located the mouth of the river and set off, encouraged by the fact that its course ran in a westerly, or sometimes southwesterly, direction. They came within sight of the Rocky Mountains and were certain they would soon be breaching the peaks, but their hopes were dashed when they found that the river veered away from the mountain range and swung northward. By July 13, 1789 Mackenzie and his party had found to their dismay that the river opened up into a delta that flowed into the Beaufort Sea—part of the Arctic ocean—and not into the Pacific as they had hoped. Mackenzie named it "Disappointment River," reflecting his mood. That he had traveled some 3,000 miles in just 100 days along a route never before taken was of little comfort. Only later was it called Mackenzie River in honor of the explorer who first charted its course.

Preparing for success

In 1791 Mackenzie left for England, determined to learn more of the explorers' art. For a year he studied astronomy and cartography, and when he returned he brought with him the latest navigation instruments. By the following year plans for a second expedition were well advanced. This time the party included a second in command, Alexander Mackay, six French Canadians, and two Indian guides, as well as Mackenzie's faithful dog.

They set out from a fort on the Peace River, which heads west from Lake Athabasca, on May 9, 1793 in a 26-foot birch bark canoe, custom made to Mackenzie's specifications. The first difficulties they encountered were in the notorious rapids of the Peace River canyon. Laboriously they towed or carried the canoe and its contents down the treacherous stretch where, of course, no riverside paths existed.

When the waterway divided Mackenzie and his party chose to follow a section of the Fraser river until it became almost impassable. On July 4 the party unanimously agreed to abandon the

Above: *Having left his name on a river that refused to do what he wanted of it, Alexander Mackenzie helped open up British Columbia by negotiating the torturous rapids of many Canadian rivers that descended from the Rocky Mountains to the Pacific Ocean.*

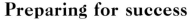

1607	1608	1608–28	1609	1613	1616	1616	1632
Jamestown, first English settlement in Americas is established in Virginia	Samuel de Champlain founds Quebec	Etienne Brule explores the Great Lakes	Henry Hudson sails up Hudson River	Dutch set up a trading post on Manhattan island	Sir Walter Raleigh arrives at Orinoco River in search of gold	English explorer William Baffin discovers Baffin Bay in Canada	English colony of Maryland is established

canoe and go overland to reach the coast. The arduous journey ended on July 19 when they reached the coast of what is today British Columbia where the Dean Channel meets the sea. Mackenzie wrote the following account: "I now mixed up some vermilion in melted grease, and inscribed, in large characters, on the southeast face of the rock on which we had slept last night, this brief memorial: 'Alexander Mackenzie, from Canada, by land, the twenty-second of July, one thousand seven hundred and ninety three'."

Although the route he used would be completely impractical for trade, Mackenzie had crossed the continent overland using the most northerly route yet. King George III knighted him in 1801. As an employee of the Northwest Company he was concerned that his discoveries would create fierce competition between it and the Hudson Bay Company, and he initiated talks that would ultimately lead to their amalgamation.

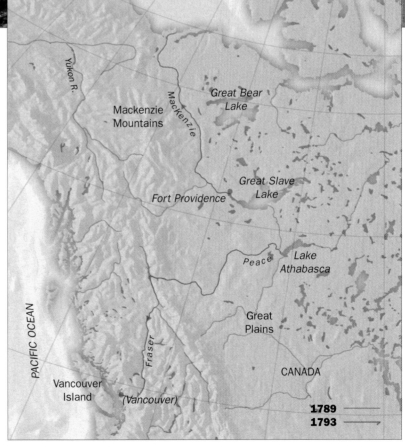

1634	1648	1654	1655	1660	1667	1671	1673
Jean Nicollet reaches Lake Michigan	Simon Dezhnev sails through Bering Strait (not proved)	Portuguese expel the Dutch from Brazil	French capture the island of Haiti from Spain	Father Claude Allouez explores the Great Lakes	Bahamas are added to the English colony of Carolina	Jesuit Charles Albanel establishes fur trading routes around Hudson Bay	Louis Jolliet and Jacques Marquette explore the Mississippi

Baron ALEXANDER *von* HUMBOLDT

1769 to 1859

A scientist, botanist, naturalist, and meteorologist, Humboldt devoted himself to all these subjects and still had energy to spare. His vast capacity for knowledge and exploration coupled with virtually relentless enthusiasm earned him the fashionable title of the age, "Universal Man."

Born in Berlin in the same year as Napoleon, Humboldt's desire to travel was fueled by the writings of Charles marie de la Condamine. He showed an awesome intellect from an early age, mastering French, English, Spanish, and Russian. He and his brother Wilhelm, a distinguished scholar and statesman who went on to found Berlin University, were friends of the writers Goethe and Schiller.

Before starting his career as an explorer he was an inspector for the mining industry and traveled extensively around Europe. Plans to join various expeditions ended in disappointment until the wealthy Humboldt teamed up with Aimé Bonpland, a Frenchman with a yearning to see South America. Together they sought permission from the Spanish king to explore his dominions in South America and this was duly granted. On July 16, 1799 they arrived on the continent to commence a five-year expedition that would double the world's knowledge about South America.

For the first nine months Humboldt and Bonpland explored the Orinoco river basin by canoe, finally discovering that it was linked to the Amazon river system. The electric fish Humboldt encountered fascinated him. The *gymnoti* were notoriously difficult to catch or observe since they buried themselves in the riverbed. "I cannot remember ever having received a more terrible shock," he wrote, after treading on one.

Further up the Orinoco insects became a problem. Gnats and mosquitoes had a particular affinity for the humid air, the stagnant waters, and the fertile soil. The torment caused by the insects during months of travel included stomach complaints, fever, thirst, and even depression. "It is not the dangers of navigating in small boats, the savage Indians, or the serpents, crocodiles, or jaguars that make Spaniards dread a voyage on the Orinoco; it is, as they say

with simplicity 'El sudar y las moscas' ('the perspiration and the flies'),'" Humboldt noted.

Conflict and suspicion

Like other travelers of the era, they were dependent on the Jesuit brothers already established in remote regions for food and other supplies. One of the missionaries, Father Bernado Zea, attached himself to the expedition, proving vital to its success with his working knowledge of the region. Still, the Spanish, who were relentlessly suspicious of newcomers, jealously guarded their territory. "How can anyone believe that you have come to be bitten by mosquitoes and measure lands that are not your own?" one settler had asked.

Space inside the canoes was scarce because most was given up for the scientific instruments they carried and the specimens they collected. By the end of their initial nine-month expedition Humboldt was traveling with a veritable menagerie and had gathered 12,000 plants. During their years in the region, Humboldt and Bonpland also traveled to Cuba and overland through what is now Colombia, Ecuador, and Peru, collecting data and specimens on a daily basis. Humboldt believed his greatest achievement had been to scale Ecuador's giant volcano Chimborazo which he believed was the highest point on earth. Although he did not reach the summit he climbed to 19,300 feet, higher than anyone before him.

By the time their adventures in South America drew to a close they had traveled 6,000 miles and collected some 60,000 plants. When they finally decided to return to Europe they were feted for their achievements. Ultimately Humboldt turned his numerous notebooks into no less than 30 book volumes, the last of which was not published until he was 65.

Although politics prevented his traveling after this expedition (he was suspected of being a spy), nevertheless he visited Siberia, still for the most part unknown to Europeans. Humboldt lived to the ripe old age of 90, becoming the grand old man of exploration in his era.

Above: *Humboldt and Bonpland on the Orinoco, from an 1877 engraving.*

Facing: *Alexander Humboldt noting specimens.*

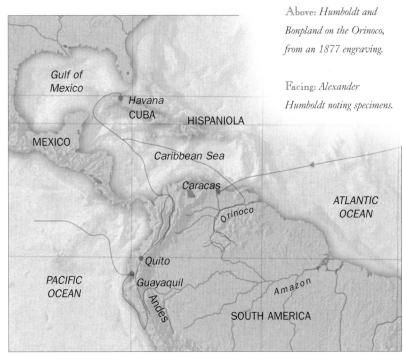

GEORGE VANCOUVER

1758 to 1798

Early in his life George Vancouver found glory alongside the legendary explorer James Cook—and almost lost his life with him. Later he became famous in his own right as a guiding light in the history of Canadian exploration. At the age of 13 George Vancouver joined the British navy. Within two years he was accompanying explorer James Cook on his

discoveries to be made and this view was supported by the British Admiralty. Consequently, in 1790 Vancouver was promoted to commander of HMS *Discovery* and sent to map the Pacific coast of North America. It was shoreline Vancouver had already seen in the company of James Cook but the possibility of finding a northwest passage slicing through the Canadian arctic was tantalizing; it would have allowed more direct trade routes between Britain and China.

European rivalry

In addition to charting the coastline he had a tricky political issue to resolve. The Spanish loosely governed a great deal of west coast territory including Nootka Sound in present-day British Columbia. It was here that a trading dispute sprang up when Spanish ships captured the centers established by British fur traders. The Spanish were already concerned about rumors of Russian expansionism in the region and had acted in haste. Conflict loomed until the Nootka Sound Convention of 1790 was drawn up, which offered reparations to the

Above: *Captain George Vancouver, probably by Abboth, now in London's National Portrait Gallery.*

trailblazing 1772–75 voyage around the globe. He was a midshipman on the third voyage, which ended in Cook's death on Hawaii in 1780. The day before Cook was killed in a violent exchange with natives Vancouver was also attacked. He survived and returned to England with the remaining crew and afterward worked principally in the Caribbean.

Cook had explored much of the Pacific Ocean, but Vancouver felt there must be more

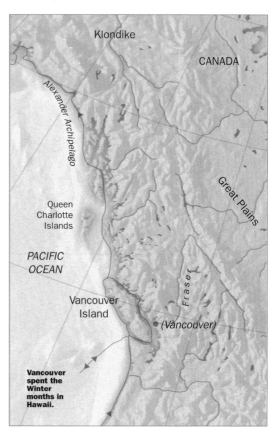

British and also ended Spanish exclusivity in the region. Now Vancouver had the task of enforcing the terms of the Convention.

The *Discovery* sailed on April 1, 1791 along with another ship, the *Chatham*, under the command of William Broughton. Plotting a course via the Cape of Good Hope, New Zealand, and Tahiti, Vancouver wintered in Hawaii, aiming to complete the work begun by Cook, before heading on the final leg to what is now California. He began his task of charting the coastline above San Francisco, bypassing the mouth of the Columbia River in doing so. Even when an American ship's captain told him about a great river in the vicinity, Vancouver doubted its existence. Consequently the captain, Robert Gray, embarked on exploration of the river himself. On May 12, 1792 he became the first explorer to sail up the river. He traded with Indians, mapped the river for 20 miles, and named it "Columbia" after his ship. By the time Vancouver had second thoughts and dispatched Broughton to search for the river, it had already been claimed by the U.S.A.

There were, however, other accomplishments to be made. By August 1792 he had circumnavigated the place that now bears his name, Vancouver Island, using a number of small boats from the *Discovery* and the *Chatham*

because the waters around the island were too shallow for the ships. The next destination was Nootka Sound where Vancouver met Juan Francisco de la Bodega Y Quadra, the Spanish official, to discuss the terms of the 1790 Convention. They could not agree on the practical application of the Convention, but in the process of disagreeing they discovered a mutual respect and friendship that would last the rest of their lives.

Both men agreed to seek clarification from their governments about their agreements and Vancouver returned to Hawaii for the winter months to undertake more surveying work. He returned to the west coast of North America in May 1793, going as far north as Alaska and south again to below San Francisco. He wintered once more in Hawaii and carried out more work on the American coast before heading home for England around Cape Horn. He arrived in the Thames on October 20, 1795, a veteran of some 65,000 miles in the *Discovery* and no less than 10,000 miles in the ship's small boats. His circumnavigation of the globe had contributed greatly to fulfilling the cartographer's dream of a complete world map, while dreams of a northwest passage—which mariners had sought for three centuries—were finally put to rest.

Above: A large mural in Oregon's state capitol rotunda at Salem depicts Captain Robert Gray near the mouth of the Columbia when he discovered the "River of the West" in 1792.

DAVID THOMPSON

1770 to 1857

Below: A selection of surveying equipment from the late 18th century. With items like these, men such as David Thompson mapped the North American continent. These actually belonged to Sir John Franklin (pages 140–141) whose ill-fated expedition perished in the Arctic wastes.

David Thompson has no lakes or mountain ranges named after him. Few people today have even heard of him, yet it was Thompson who mapped tracts of Canada and was undoubtedly one of the world's greatest geographers. Thompson was born into poverty in London, England and was educated at Grey Coat Charity School in Westminster where he showed a prodigious talent in mathematics. At 14 he became an apprentice clerk with the Hudson Bay Company, and it was this minor post that brought him to the New World in September 1784. Within two years he had changed his desk job for a hands-on role as hunter and explorer. In Canada's unexplored territories Indians were seen as a commercial ally rather than an enemy. Accordingly, Thompson spent the winter of 1787 with the Peigan Indian tribe, learning their language and culture.

In 1788, still employed by the Hudson Bay Company, his leg was shattered in an accident. The break was so bad that he was unable to walk for eight months and then he was compelled to use crutches. He spent his convalescence productively, learning the skills of surveying and being trained how to read the stars by Philip Turnor, the company's astronomer. From that point on he maintained meticulous charts and tables (his measurements were so fine that today's satellite surveys have shown his maps to be accurate to within a mile).

For several years Thompson surveyed the Saskatchewan river and Lake Manitoba. It became obvious that his priorities were map-making rather than fur-trading, which was not how the Hudson Bay Company viewed his role. By 1797 Thompson had switched allegiances and joined the rival Northwest Company. During his first year he traveled more than 4,000 miles while mapping the new nation of Canada and established trading posts as he went.

He still found time to marry, his wife Charlotte Small being of mixed European and Indian parentage. They were married for more than 60 years and had 13 children. Thompson was a pious man who, despite the hardships of

exploration and the pressures of business, adhered strictly to his own principles. He refused to trade alcohol with Indians, believing it to be harmful. He would read the Bible aloud to the illiterate among his travelers. Alongside his own devout faith he maintained respect for the spiritual beliefs of the native tribes.

In a setback to his work, a party financed by John Jacob Astor beat Thompson to the mouth of the Columbia river by sailing around Cape Horn to Canada's west coast, and one of Astor's men, Robert Stuart, discovered the South Pass through the Rockies, a key section of which would become the Oregon Trail. Nevertheless, Thompson charted the Columbia and its tributaries. He accurately pinpointed the 49th parallel, the newly declared border between the U.S.A. and the British territory that would one day become Canada, and established trading centers to the benefit of the Northwest Company. The challenge of finding an accessible route over the Rockies was still uppermost in North American minds, and ultimately Thompson found his way through, using what is now known as the Athabasca Pass.

The surveyor's art

He became an object of speculation among his fellow travelers: "Both Canadians and Indians often inquired of me why I observed the sun, and sometimes the moon, in the daytime, and passed whole nights with my instruments looking at the moon and stars. I told them it was to determine the distance and direction from the place I observed to other places; neither the Canadians nor the Indians believed me, for both argued that if what I said was truth, I ought to look to the ground, and over it, not to the stars… neither argument, nor ridicule, had any effect and I had to leave them to their own opinions…" Like many other explorers who relied on taking readings from the sun, Thompson was almost blind in old age.

In 1812 Thompson settled in Montreal and spent two years producing a large, detailed map of western Canada. He set out on later expeditions, but his sound advice to the authorities was largely ignored and the accolades which he might reasonably have expected were never heaped upon him. It was left for Thompson himself to provide the relevant tribute to his achievements, which he did eloquently after writing 77 volumes of journals:

"Thus I have fully completed the survey of this part of North America from sea to sea, and by almost innumerable astronomical observations have determined the positions of the mountains, lakes, and rivers, and other remarkable places of the northern part of this continent; the maps of all of which have been drawn, and laid down in geographical position, being now the work of 27 years."

Above: By the end of his career Thompson claimed to have determined the position of every mountain and every lake in the regions he charted.

JOSEPH WALKER
1798 to 1876

I magine California as a land clothed in redwood trees, with fertile valleys, soaring eagles, and miles of unspoiled wilderness where cities like Los Angeles and San Francisco now stand. This is just how Joseph Walker found the region after a strenuous hike through the Sierra Nevada. California was Spanish territory but remained unexploited. The natural barriers around it included the Rocky Mountains, the Sierra Nevada, and the Mojave Desert; all mean and inhospitable terrain. Intrepid churchmen had made their way along the coast, building missions as they went. Prospectors from Spain followed them, still searching for El Dorado, the city of gold. Indians in the vicinity were, on the whole, peaceful.

Other Europeans who desired to go there could only do so by sailing around Cape Horn in South America and up past the Spanish territories of Central America. A rough passage was guaranteed, so few braved the journey. As a consequence of this coastal migration, knowledge of the Rockies was limited.

One American had already reached California by an overland route. Jedediah Strong Smith (1798–1831) and his men endured desperate conditions when they crossed the treacherous Mojave Desert. In fact, Smith used the same route twice, losing 25 men to hostile Indians in the process. Smith himself was killed by Comanche during another expedition. His sorry tale was hardly an inspiration for others, although he did contribute hugely to the Fremont-Gibbs-Smith map, which was for decades the most authoritative of the American West. Despite Smith's achievements, Walker still had his work cut out for him.

Little is known of Walker's early life, although he was probably born in Virginia and raised in Tennessee. He was part of the expedition that surveyed and mapped the Santa Fe Trail from Missouri to New Mexico in 1819. French-born Pedro Vial (c.1750–1814) had already done much of the legwork, setting out from Santa Fe on May 21, 1792 at the behest of New Mexico's Spanish authorities in order to open up a new route to Missouri and Illinois. Along the way Indians captured Vial and two comrades. After six weeks of imprisonment a French-speaking Indian intervened to secure their freedom. They continued along the Kansas and Missouri rivers and arrived in St. Louis on October 3. Twenty seven years later it was left to the team, which included Walker, to map and survey the Santa Fe Trail that would take settlers south and west.

Onward to the Pacific coast

In 1831 Walker met Benjamin Bonneville (1796–1878), an accomplished soldier turned trapper. At least, that is what he claimed to be. In retrospect it seems probable that Bonneville was a U.S.A. government spy since he was little interested in the fur trade but greatly interested in the activities of the British and the local Indians, and with the mineral deposits and the natural history of the region. He became a laughing stock among other trappers when he built a fort at the Green River, since its location made it useless as a base for the purposes of gathering furs. It was, however, an excellent observation post.

Bonneville did not secure new territory for America or add to the new nation's geographical

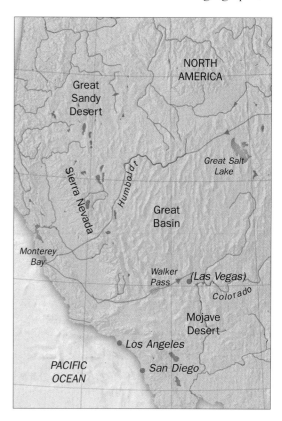

knowledge. However, he did supply the War Department with one of the most detailed intelligence reports written during the era. And it was Bonneville who dispatched his field commander Walker to explore west of the Great Salt Lake. Heading a party of 60, Walker left Bonneville's fort on August 20, 1833. The mission was a tough one, particularly when it came to crossing the Sierra Nevada. Scaling the peaks was no easy task and the horses they took now became more of a hindrance than a help. However, all the hardships were forgotten when they first caught a glimpse of the scenic Yosemite Valley, now a national park.

Between mountains and sea the delights of virgin terrain awaited them. The vistas were stunning and the wildlife so abundant that they believed they had found America's "Promised Land." Before turning back Walker and his party went to Monterey on the coast where they struck up cordial relations with the Mexican government officials who held it.

When they finally decided to head for home, in January 1834, Walker was keen to find a fresh route without the rigors of mountaineering for which they were ill-equipped. They followed the Sierra Nevada to its most southerly point where they trekked through a comparatively low-lying route now called the Walker Pass. It was this that would become the prescribed trail for settlers and miners following the 1848 gold rush. Walker led his party to a rendezvous with other mountainmen. Hungry, thirsty, and exhausted, the members of the Walker party were at least all alive. Walker returned to California with early settlers and eventually died there.

Facing: A land clothed in giant redwod trees is how Joseph Walker found California after crossing the Sierra Nevada.

Below: The Promised Land—Upper and Lower Falls in Yosemite Valley.

CHARLES DARWIN
1809 to 1882

*A*lthough he sparked one of the greatest controversies of the century, Charles Darwin (1809–82) was not a contentious character. He had a comfortable upbringing and, before graduating from Cambridge University, planned to live a quiet life as an English country parson. His university years were to change his aspirations, however, and the course of history.

Although not a scholar, he distinguished himself as a passionate naturalist and was accordingly nurtured by one Cambridge professor, John Stevens Henslow, who taught him the value of keeping meticulous notes and making keen observations. Through Henslow Darwin was able to secure the unpaid job of naturalist aboard HMS *Beagle*, a ship setting off to survey the coast of South America.

The sights he saw and the specimens he found during five years of roaming around the continent led him to question everything he had ever believed in. He challenged the conventional wisdom on The Creation as contained in the Bible, causing uproar among religious fundamentalists with his evolutionary theories. The debate on Darwinism, as his findings became known, continues even today.

Right: Charles Darwin in 1840. Watercolor after the portrait by George Richmond.

Above: Darwin's Galapagos finches drawn during the voyage of the Beagle. *The birds' adaption to their different environments began to confirm his theories on "transmutation" of the species.*

Voyage of the Beagle

Immediately the ship left port in December 1831 Darwin suffered the misery of seasickness. He never managed to shake off the affliction but nothing could persuade him to abandon the voyage. While the expedition was, in essence, sea-borne the *Beagle* was in port for lengthy periods, during which time Darwin would go ashore to study the local habitat and its species.

He was spellbound by what he found, as this excerpt from his journal reveals: "The day has passed delightfully; delight is, however, a weak term to express the feelings of a naturalist who, for the first time, has wandered by myself in a Brazilian forest. The elegance of the grasses, the novelty of the parasitical plants, the beauty of the flowers, the glossy green of the foliage, but above all the general luxuriance of the vegetation, filled me with admiration."

The next day he wrote: "I can only add raptures to the former raptures… I collected a great number of brilliantly colored flowers, enough to make a florist go wild… The air is deliciously cool and soft; full of enjoyment, one fervently desires to live in retirement in this new and grander world…"

At one point he discovered the bones of prehistoric animals, similar species to those

roaming in South America today only much larger. Darwin began to wonder if the existing animals were descendants of those living millions of years ago who had adapted to survive.

His most famous port of call was the Galapagos Islands, in the Pacific Ocean off the coast of Ecuador. Darwin was staggered to find 15 varieties of finch—all similar but nevertheless distinct species—living on the islands. Each variety had a beak suited to obtaining the food available in its environment, so the large ground finch had a strong beak for breaking nuts and seeds while the warbler finch had a long beak suitable for catching insects. All differed to the species known on the mainland. To Darwin it appeared that the birds best-suited to their habitat survived while others died out.

In Chile he discovered fossilized seashells some 12,000 feet above sea level. Clearly the contours of the earth had undergone a radical change. Echoing the opinions of many geologists, Darwin suggested that the land had buckled upward over great periods of time, taking the seashells with it. When Darwin witnessed the effects of a major earthquake in Chile he realized how volatile the planet could be, and this reinforced his views.

By now Darwin was beginning to seriously question one of the cornerstones of the Bible, that earth and all living things were made by God in six days. He confided in his journal: "In July opened first notebook on Transmutation of Species. Had been greatly struck from about the month of previous March on character of South American fossils and species on Galapagos Archipelago. These facts (especially the latter) are the origin of all my views."

Above: The Beagle *laid up ashore for cleaning near the River Santa Cruz.*

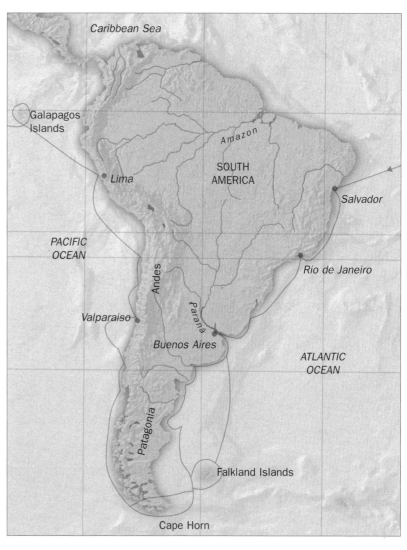

Science and Christianity

On board the *Beagle* Darwin shared quarters with the Captain, Robert Fitzroy. The pile of plant and animal specimens that grew on the ship began to try Fitzroy's patience, but worse still were the unorthodox views being formulated by Darwin. Fitzroy was among many who were deeply offended with the theories formulated by Darwin. Like most Victorians, Fitzroy was appalled at the notion that human beings could be part of the animal kingdom.

Few people, scientists or otherwise, contradicted the accepted beliefs. One who had done so was Darwin's own grandfather, Erasmus Darwin, who had written papers that suggested the possibility of evolution. Another belonged to Sir Charles Lyell who argued in his book *Principles of Geology* that the earth's surface was constantly changing and had done so for millions of years. The first volume of Lyell's book had just been published when Darwin set off on the *Beagle* and he took a copy with him to South America. Darwin had two further volumes sent out to him after they were published. In 1838 he read an essay by British economist Thomas Robert Malthus which echoed his own views on competition and survival.

He pondered on his ideas surrounding natural selection for a number of years, refining strands and aspects. A reserved individual, Darwin had no desire to stir up a hornets' nest with outrageous and hasty argument.

1682	1699	1718	1718	1723	1726	1741	1743
René-Robert La Salle explores Mississippi	French colonize Louisiana	Spanish establish settlement of Pensacola in Florida	French found the port of New Orleans in Louisiana	Death of Jesuit Samuel Fritz who established 50 settlements along the Amazon	Pierre La Verendrye establishes fur trading posts in the Canadian West	Vitus Bering dies, having sighted Alaska	Charles Marie de la Condamine navigates the Amazon River

Left: *Despite the controversy Darwin stirred up among Christians, who felt he was attacking the very basis of faith, the evolutionist was buried with honors in Westminster Abbey in May 1862.*

Consequently, his first published work when he returned from the trip to South America was the interesting but unproblematic *Journal of Researches*, which appeared in 1839. In the same year he married his cousin Emma Wedgwood (both were grandchildren of the pottery firm founder Josiah Wedgwood). His work on evolution was withheld even longer because Darwin had no wish to upset his devoutly Christian wife.

It was not until 1856 that Darwin began work on a book expounding the theories of natural selection. Publication was preempted by the findings of naturalist Alfred Russel Wallace in Malaysia on a similar theme (*see page 132*). In 1858 Charles Lyell arranged for Darwin and Wallace to unveil their work at the Linnaean Society in London. Only after this event did Darwin get on with completing his defining work, *On the Origin of Species by Means of Natural Selection*. When it was published in November 1859 the first edition sold out within a day. Darwin had taken great care to omit his most controversial theories, those relating to humans. Only much later in *The Descent of Man* did he argue that humans evolved from a common ancestor shared with the apes.

The issue was brought sharply into public focus in 1860 in a debate at Oxford University. Darwin's views were argued for by Thomas Henry Huxley (1825–95), the biologist and philosopher who coined the term agnostic to describe his own beliefs. In opposition, defending the Bible, was Bishop Samuel Wilberforce.

Despite his achievements, there were still many holes in Darwin's arguments. How did the variations in species originate and how were they passed down the generations? Science could not provide answers to these questions until the following century. Nevertheless, Darwin's reputation as a respected scientist was complete. Evolutionary theories would be elaborated on long after Darwin's death, sometimes in ways that would have appalled him, such as the now discredited racial theories of the Nazis. Darwin's interest remained in the peaceful progress of the world, his beliefs summed up as follows: "How much more powerful than man is Nature herself."

1748	1769	1770	1787	1789–94	1791	1792	1793
Thomas Walker discovers Cumberland Gap	Juan Hernandez escorts Spanish colonists from Mexico to California	Samuel Hearne makes first overland trip to Arctic Ocean for Hudson's Bay Co	Peter Pond reaches Lake Athabasca	Alessandro Malaspina heads scientific expedition to South America	George Vancouver sets out for northwest America on survey expedition	Robert Gray sails up Columbia River	Alexander MacKenzie reaches the Pacific coast of Canada overland

DANIEL BOONE

1734 to 1820

Daniel Boone was a pivotal figure in the exploration of the West. His life story has become fogged by romantic myth and, contrary to widespread belief, he was not responsible for discovering either Kentucky or the Appalachian mountain pass known as the Cumberland Gap. Perhaps his greatest practical contribution to the settlers' advance was to carve out the so-called Wilderness Road between the Carolinas and the West. This opened up the rich farmland beyond the Appalachians—the central Kentucky bluegrass region.

Boone was born into an English Quaker family in Berks County, near present-day Reading, Pennsylvania, on November 2, 1734. He had little formal education but enjoyed an idyllic childhood, exploring and hunting in the forests around his home. By the time his family moved from their isolated log cabin to a Yadkin

Right: A frontiersman through and through, Daniel Boone carved out a Kentucky bluegrass empire for thousands of settlers and opened up the way across the Mississippi into Missouri.

River settlement in North Carolina, Boone had developed the essential skills of a frontiersman and the eye of a marksman. In 1755, two years after the move, he found himself fighting for the British under General Edward Braddock in

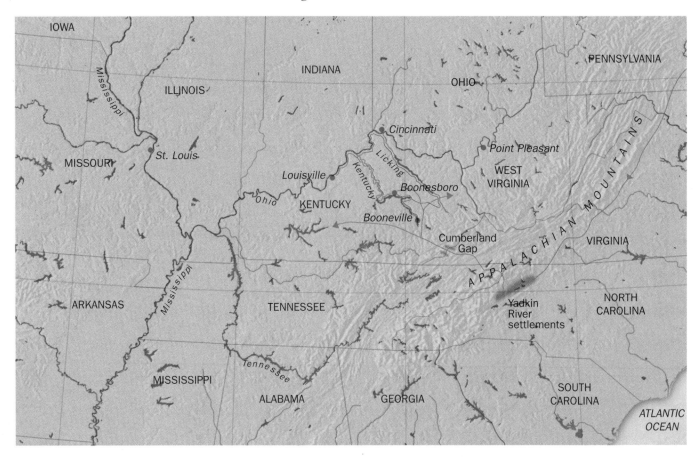

1799	1799	1803	1805–6	1807	1818	1820	1833
Baron Alexander von Humboldt leads five year expedition to South America	Daniel Boone leads pioneers and settlers to Missouri	William Clark and Meriwether Lewis begin overland expedition to Pacific	Zebulon Pike searches for source of Mississippi	David Thompson establishes trading post on Columbia River	Donald McKenzie explores Snake River	Stephen Long sets out to explore the Platte and Arkansas	Joseph Walker discovers Yosemite Valley, now a US National Park

what became known as the French and Indian Wars. The following year he returned to marry Rebecca Bryan and settled down for almost a decade to farm and hunt the land.

In the late 1760s however, Boone grew increasingly restless. He made several forays around the Yadkin region and in the winter of 1767–8 pushed across the Appalachians in an attempt to reach bluegrass country. While this foray proved a failure, it sharpened Boone's curiosity and he needed little persuading to make a second attempt. When one of his closest friends, fellow war veteran John Findley, visited the family's cabin in 1769 seeking a skilled woodsman to guide him across the Appalachians, Boone offered his services. Together with four other men, he and Findley negotiated the Cumberland Gap and discovered a hunter's paradise teeming with buffalo and wild turkey and offering a vast acreage of fertile farmland.

One by one the small party began to drift back east, although Boone stayed for almost two years, wandering alone along the Licking and Kentucky river valleys and tracing the Ohio as far as the falls near modern-day Louisville. He lived by hunting and trapping and amassed some valuable furs to bring back to his family. Unfortunately he was robbed by a band of Cherokee Indians on the trek home and returned with only his memories. His tales of the land of plenty across the mountains were, however, enough to convince seven families, including his own, to resettle there and the party set off through the Cumberland Gap in 1773. Again they fell victim to an Indian raiding party and this time Boone's son and five others lost their lives. Reluctantly, the pioneers retraced their steps.

In the meantime, the lure of bluegrass country was getting ever stronger. In 1775 a land-hungry Carolina trading company acquired some Cherokee territory through the terms of a dubious treaty and hired a gang of 28 men to mark a trail—the Wilderness Road—across the mountains. Boone was appointed as the company's agent and was instrumental in supervising the construction of the first non-Indian settlement in Kentucky. His fort and collection of crude log cabins became known as Boonesboro and before the year was out his family had settled there with him.

Pioneer hardship

What may seem to a modern reader a great adventure was in fact a daily struggle to survive, but through his skills and leadership Boone became a cult figurehead for settlers all over the newly independent United States. Stories were told of how he rescued three girls, including his daughter, from kidnap by Shawnee warriors, survived capture by the same tribe (whose elders admired his hunting prowess), and even became an adopted son of Chief Blackfish. When he discovered that the Shawnee were planning a renewed attack on Boonesboro he managed to warn his people, prepared reinforcements, and organized a spirited defense. After nine days of fighting the Shawnee finally gave up.

From a legal standpoint, however, Boone discovered that he could not sustain his claim on surrounding lands and was forced to move on, first to Boone's Station, Kentucky and later to Mount Pleasant, West Virginia. In 1799 he again headed west, leading hundreds of settlers to new homes in Missouri.

Below: Daniel Boone died on September 26, 1820 near St. Louis, Missouri while at the home of his son Nathan. In 1854 his remains and those of his wife were removed to their beloved Kentucky.

1840s	1849–64	1859	1863	1871	1912	1925	1988
John Fremont maps Northwest	Richard Spruce collects plants in South America	Charles Darwin publishes *On the Origin of Species by Means of Natural Selection*	Henry Bates publishes *The Naturalist on the River Amazon*	Edward Whymper publishes *Travels Amongst the Great Andes of the Equator*	Hiram Bingham discovers Machu Picchu	Percy Fawcett vanishes in Mato Grosso	Death of artist Margaret Mee who made 15 canoe trips up the Amazon

MERIWETHER LEWIS
and WILLIAM CLARK

1774
to
1809

1770
to
1838

In 1803 America's third president, Thomas Jefferson, pulled off the most spectacular land deal ever. He bought 828,000 square miles of territory from Napoleon Bonaparte of France, who needed money to pursue his wars in Europe, for $15,000,000. The deal, which was called the "Louisiana Purchase," more than doubled United States' territory at a stroke. Jefferson knew that America would have access to enormous commercial wealth if it could exploit the riches of the interior. Before the land sale he governed approximately 5.3 million people, two thirds of whom lived within 50 miles of the Atlantic coast. Following the deal, he needed to prove that it was possible to unite an entire continent under one government.

Jefferson's determination to expand westward is illustrated by the fact that even before the Louisiana Purchase, an expedition to open up new overland routes had been planned. Jefferson had commanded his secretary, Meriwether Lewis, to gather together a team and equip it for exploration. Lewis chose William Clark (1770–1838) as his co-leader. Both were Virginia-born and served in the army but there the similarities ended. Lewis was humorless, gruff, and prone to melancholy. He was favored by Jefferson because of his republican beliefs, although the President noted too that Lewis was "brave, prudent, habituated to the woods and familiar with Indian manners and character."

Clark, on the other hand, was far more optimistic and easygoing. He was the talented cartographer, while Lewis kept the more accurate journal. Clark made excellent progress with the Indians they encountered, while Lewis used his powers of observation to record the flora and fauna along the route. Most importantly, they maintained respect for one another.

Negotiating the Rockies

Once the Louisiana Purchase had been sealed, the expedition was no longer a covert mission but a scientific one, charged with finding routes across the wilderness between the Mississippi and the Pacific, negotiating with Indian tribes, scaling mountains, navigating rivers, and bringing back as much information as possible for assessment in the east. Lewis and Clark recruited 36 others to join the party: four army sergeants, 24 privates, and a further eight non-military personnel. French-Canadian fur trapper, Toussaint Charbonneau was among the civilians and Sacagawea, his Shoshone Indian wife, not only cared for a baby son, Jean Baptiste, but also proved her worth as interpreter and pacifier.

Jefferson persuaded Congress to invest $2,500 in the expedition, which Lewis used to buy compasses, a chronometer, a telescope, thermometers, two sextants, and other measuring

Right: *Described as humorless and gruff, Meriwether Lewis cuts a surprisingly dandyfied figure in this engraving.*

implements. Included in the supplies were hatchets, saws, mosquito curtains, soap, soup, salt, and writing paper. They also hauled with them gifts for Indians, including silk ribbons, tobacco, mirrors, and 33 lbs. of beads.

The expedition set off from St. Louis in 1804, going up the Missouri in canoes before wintering in the Mandan villages. The Rockies were a formidable barrier but Sacagawea helped them negotiate a route to the Columbia, and by November 1805 they were in sight of the Pacific. On the coast they built a log cabin for winter accommodation and scavenged the surrounding countryside for survival.

In March 1806 they split up for the return journey. Clark followed the Yellowstone while Lewis went via the Great Falls and was attacked by Blackfoot Indians who tried to steal his guns and horses. He and his men fled. Lewis and Clark united again before returning to St. Louis 28 months after their departure. They dispatched the following message to Jefferson: "In obedience to your orders we have penetrated the continent of North America to the Pacific Ocean and sufficiently explored the interior of the country to affirm with confidence that we have discovered the most practicable route which does exist across the continent by means of the navigable branches of the Missouri and Columbia rivers."

While the easy trail Jefferson had been hoping for was not found, the mission was an overwhelming success. Sergeant Charles Floyd, one of nine recruited from Kentucky, was the only fatality, from a burst appendix, and there had been remarkably little armed conflict.

Although Lewis and Clark were rewarded for their efforts only Clark prospered He became Superintendent of Indian Affairs in Upper Louisiana, began a fur-trading company, and was finally made governor of Missouri. Lewis became governor of Upper Louisiana but found the post fraught with difficulties and became increasingly addicted to alcohol. In 1809 his body was found bearing two gunshot wounds; he had apparently committed suicide. Clark, who had married and had a son named the boy Meriwether Lewis Clark in honor of his partner.

Above: *Quaintly called* A Canoe striking on a Tree. *this illustration from* Journal of Voyages *by Peter Gass, published in 1812, shows Meriwether Lewis and William Clark suffering a mishap on their expedition.*

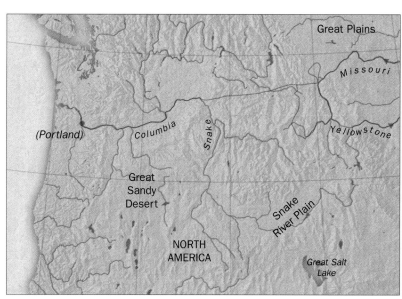

ZEBULON MONTGOMERY PIKE

1779 to 1813

Right: Like a great many before him, Zebulon Pike combined exploration with spying and his activities resulted in being imprisoned by the Spanish.

When William Clark made it to the Pacific he announced in his journal: "We now discover that we have found the most practicable and navigable passage across the continent of North America." In fact, this was not so, and the route they had followed would rarely be used by settlers. One of the men determined to open an easier route through the Rockies was Zebulon Montgomery Pike.

Pike was already a seasoned explorer, having led an expedition in 1805 to discover the source of the Mississippi. An army lieutenant, he led 20 men more than 2,000 miles from St. Louis to Leech Lake, Minnesota, which he wrongly identified as the river's source. The consummate explorer, he attempted to make a claim on the northern lands for the United States and, to ease the way, he also opened negotiations with Indian tribes in the region.

The following year he turned his attentions to the Southwest. Like Clark and Lewis, he had the backing of President Jefferson. Ostensibly his mission involved the tracking of the Red and Arkansas rivers. In reality he was also evaluating Spanish power in the region and the distribution of natural resources.

Pike's Peak

As he made his way through the Front Range of the Rockies he came across the 14,000-foot mountain now known as Pike's Peak close by present-day Colorado Springs. Pike attempted to climb the mountain but was defeated by a November storm. Later the explorer predicted that "no one will ever reach the summit." In fact Dr Edwin James reached the summit just 14 years after Pike had failed. The first woman, Julia Archibald, achieved an ascent in 1858. Today it is possible to get to the top by funicular, by car (negotiating 156 hairpin bends), or on horseback or foot on a 13-mile trail.

Pike and his party then turned south into New Mexico, which was Spanish territory. The Spanish duly arrested him, and his dubious protestations of being lost were unsurprisingly treated with scorn. In part, Pike was being used as a political pawn by his superiors to test the resolve of the Spanish in keeping Americans out of their territories. Pike and his colleagues were

Right: Pike's Peak today.

escorted across Texas and into Louisiana, still making valuable mental notes all the while about the potential of the region for the U.S.A. On July 1, 1807 the Americans were released and Pike headed for home to make his enlightening report. His intelligence helped pave the way for Stephen F. Austin to establish the first U.S.A. settlement in Texas in 1821. However, Pike's description of the lands lying east of the Rockies effectively put the brakes on settlement for a generation. He called it "the Great American Desert," an opinion echoed by Major Steven Long when he led an expedition west in 1819.

Pike stayed in the army and became a brigadier general. During the war of 1812 he directed an assault on the town of York (now Toronto, Canada) and was killed as a result of a gunpowder explosion.

After Pike and Long came John Charles Fremont (1813–90), an accomplished cartographer. However, historians have since pointed out that Fremont did little frontier work. He put down on paper what previous settlers or trappers had already discovered but left unmapped. Like many other explorers of America's West, Fremont was taken aback by the beauty of the continent's interior. In Colorado he recorded how he and his party first came within sight of the mountains: "Here again a view of the most romantic beauty met our eyes. It

seemed as if, from the vast expanse of uninteresting prairie we had passed over, nature had collected all her beauties together in one chosen place."

It was Fremont's work that paved the way for settlers, who began arriving in increasing numbers in the western regions from the mid-1840s. Fremont himself made a fortune in the Gold Rush, which had inspired many to head west. As America's West opened up, it marked an end to the era when only trappers and mountainmen had dominated the region.

Above: Windy Point on Pike's Peak. This photograph of the 1880s shows that Pike's Peak had already become an attraction for visitors, who could walk or ride to the top of the mountain that had defeated Pike himself.

EDWARD WHYMPER

1840 to 1911

Before climbing in the Andes Edward Whymper had already made his name as a mountaineer. In 1865 he had been among the first to conquer the Matterhorn in the Alps. He emerged as both hero and villain because in the descent four of the party plunged to their deaths, despite Whymper's efforts to save them.

The tragedy—for which he was heavily criticized—left its mark on Whymper.

Above: The young Whymper was drawn to the Alps and the challenge of climbing the "impossible" east face of the Matterhorn.

Afterward he issued the following advice to assist subsequent generations of climbers: "Climb if you will but remember that courage and strength are nought without prudence, and that a momentary negligence may destroy the happiness of a lifetime. Do nothing in haste, look well to each step; and from the beginning think what may be at the end."

Although he had childhood notions of becoming an Arctic explorer, Whymper was in fact an artist before he started climbing mountains. He took his first trip to see snow-capped peaks in 1860 after receiving a commission from a British publisher to sketch scenes from the French Alps. He was so struck by the splendor of the mountains that he embarked on some serious Alpine climbing. Ultimately he scaled the Matterhorn, tackling it from the eastern face, which had been deemed an impossibility.

The disaster on the Matterhorn occurred when one of the least experienced climbers of the group slipped and cannoned into another. Both fell from the ledge, dragging two others over with them. Although Whymper and a colleague tried to secure the ropes that linked the dangling men the cables snapped, sending them to their deaths. Severely traumatized by the tragedy, Whymper nevertheless regained his nerve and succeeded in climbing the Matterhorn twice more.

From the Alps to the Andes

In 1879 he arrived in the Andes, determined to climb the Chimborazo. He soon discovered that mountain sickness—the feverishness brought about in high altitudes—was far worse in the

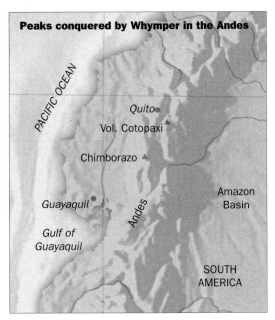

Peaks conquered by Whymper in the Andes

high Andes than on the Alpine slopes on which he had cut his teeth. Whymper and his party were confronted with two peaks on Chimborazo that from a distance both appeared similar in height. Having chosen the nearest summit, the weather suddenly changed and steep crevasses inhibited their progress. Conditions were so poor that the only way to continue was on hands and knees. "We arrived on the top of [the peak] about a quarter to four in the afternoon, and then had the mortification of finding that it was the lower of the two. There was no help for it; we had to descend to the plateau, to resume the flogging, wading, and floundering, and to make for the highest point, and there again, when we got on to the dome, the snow was reasonably firm, and we arrived upon the summit of Chimborazo standing upright like men, instead of groveling, as we had been doing for the previous five hours, like beasts of the field."

In grim weather conditions it proved almost impossible to use the geographers' instruments that they had struggled to take up the mountain. Nor could they linger long. Daylight was fading fast and they had to reach the safety of their camp before dark. According to Whymper

"we ran for our lives." It was pitch dark by the time they caught sight of the camp lights and they stumbled, relieved, toward them. It had been an arduous 16-hour marathon but it was nevertheless momentous, a day of triumph rather than tragedy.

While he had learned much about climbing in the Andes Whymper was not finished in the region yet. He chose to climb the simmering Cotopaxi, at 19,450 feet the world's highest active volcano. As he approached the top he was hampered by choking volcanic ash and sheer heat which made the ground hot enough to melt rubber. One night the intrepid Whymper crawled to the rim and peered inside.

Whymper did not restrict himself just to mountaineering. He collected plants and insects and made notes of the fauna and flora in the places he visited. But his most useful findings were in the study of mountain sickness and they helped subsequent expeditions, on mountains and in the Arctic. In 1871 his first book *Scrambles Amongst the Alps in the Years 1860–69* was published and remains in demand today. Twenty years later his *Travels Amongst the Great Andes of the Equator* appeared.

Above: *The Matterhorn would prove a useful training for Whymper's later exploits in the Andes.*

Below: *Whymper was traumatized when two fellow climbers fell to their deaths on the Matterhorn descent after ropes broke. He was ever to remain a careful and well prepared climber.*

ALFRED RUSSEL WALLACE *and* HENRY WALTER BATES

1823 to 1913

1825 to 1892

At the same time that Charles Darwin was formulating his theories of natural selection, Alfred Russel Wallace was independently coming to similar conclusions in the wilds of the Amazon. From a family of nine children, Welsh-born Wallace appeared destined for life as a surveyor or a schoolmaster until he decided to make nature study his vocation. In 1848 he contrived a trip to the Amazon, financed by the sales of collected specimens to zoos, and enticed his friend and fellow naturalist, Henry Walter Bates, to come along. The men were constantly impoverished, often sick, and continually at risk from dangerous animals and hostile Indians. Still, they relished the task in hand.

Wallace spent four years in South America collecting specimens of insects, mammals, and birds. Illness forced his return to England in 1852, but the voyage home proved a personal disaster. When the ship caught fire he watched his collections go up in smoke and then spent ten days adrift before being rescued. After recovering from the ordeal he wrote two books about his expedition when he got back to Britain.

In 1854 he set his sights in the opposite direction and remained for eight years in the Malay Archipelago. During this time he wrote

Right: Henry Walter Bates was a prolific entomologist, who discovered 8,000 insects never before recorded.

his essay *On the tendency of varieties to depart indefinitely from the original type*, which was presented to Darwin. The two scientists presented their findings to the public.

Bates's prolific work

Bates collected more than 14,000 different species of insect while he was in the Amazon, 8,000 of which had never previously been recorded. He came up with his own theories on natural selection. "Batesian mimicry," as it was known, held that harmless animals impersonated deadly creatures by adopting their bright coloration, to ward off attack. On his

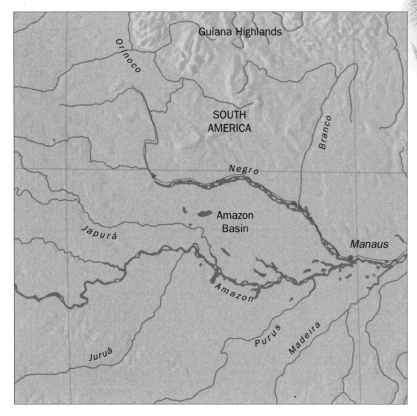

return to England he became the first paid secretary of the Royal Geographical Society and stayed in the post until his death.

Proof of Bates's literary expertise had already come in his book *The Naturalist on the River Amazons* [*sic*] which was widely acclaimed. As secretary he was responsible for editing publications at a time when exploration was going on apace across the world. Previously, Royal Geographical Society publications had been worthy but dull. With Bates at the helm their published material became lively, well illustrated, and contained accurate maps. At the RGS, for his tact and fairmindedness, he was called "dear old Bates." According to his biographer, H.P. Moon, "His great experience in travel and exploration was generously given to all who sought it, and he won the affection of everybody."

Wallace was also responsible for publishing the journals of Richard Spruce (1817–93), the botanist who collected in the Amazon and the Andes between 1849 and 1864. Spruce collected 30,000 plant specimens from South America and mapped 10,000 miles of river while traveling by canoe. He also had a keen ear for language and categorized the dialects of the Amazonian Indians. He joined Wallace and Bates on some of their excursions and also extended his travels into the Andes, where he collected seeds from the Red Bark Tree (Cinchona), which produced quinine. His seeds, dispatched to India, deprived South America of the monopoly.

Left: *It was the thinking and work of Alfred Russel Wallace that encouraged Charles Darwin to develop his theories of natural selection and the evolution of species. His editorial work with the Royal Geographical Society was an inspiration to many, as he brought to life the excitement of new scientific discoveries.*

HIRAM BINGHAM
1875 *to* 1956

By the turn of the 20th century most of the world had been explored, but there were still many archeological mysteries to be solved. Among these were the location of long abandoned Inca cities, relics of an advanced civilization destroyed by the Spanish Conquistadors. Guided by local Indians through the Peruvian jungle, Hiram Bingham found an entire Inca city never even mentioned in the chronicles of the conquistadors—Machu Picchu.

Above: *Hiram Bingham, a man who mixed with the great and good but always listed his occupation as "explorer."*

Throughout his early life Bingham was torn between an academic and religious calling. Born in 1875 in Honolulu, Hawaii, his missionary parents equipped him with some fundamental Christian beliefs and the clear expectation that once he had completed his studies at Yale University during the 1890s he would return to Hawaii as a minister to work with the sick and poor. This he did, manfully suppressing his desire for excitement and good living, but his sense of family duty was outweighed by a feeling that he was living a sham existence. When he met and fell for a society beauty, Alfreda Mitchell, he decided he must somehow earn enough money to marry her. It was a decision that set him on the road to adventure and ultimately led to one of the most important archeological discoveries in history.

Bingham returned to school, obtaining a masters degree in South American history from the University of California. He followed this with a doctorate from Harvard and, in 1905, was employed by Princeton University. He found academia dull, however, and longed to emulate the adventurous deeds of his father and grandfather, who had together sailed around the treacherous seas of Cape Horn to preach the Christian message on remote Pacific islands.

In 1906 Bingham embarked on his first expedition across Venezuela and Colombia and two years later was assigned by President Roosevelt to the U.S. delegation attending the Pan-American Scientific Congress in Santiago, Chile. This gave him the opportunity to explore Peruvian Inca territories on muleback, seeking clues to the whereabouts of the lost cities of Vilcabamba and Vitcos. Bingham and his companion found neither, but four days' ride from Cuzco they did discover some impressive Inca ruins concealed amid dense bamboo thickets. It was enough to fire the young historian's imagination.

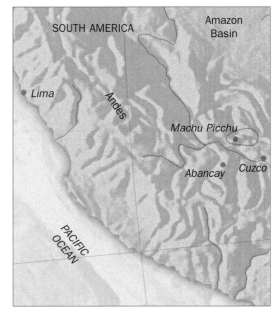

In search of Vilcabamba

In July 1911 Bingham set off determined to locate the two cities. He knew that Vilcabamba was the last refuge of the Inca as they fled the Spanish conquistadors and that it must be hidden somewhere in dense jungle northeast of Cuzco. On the morning of July 12 he was taken by a local guide called Melchor Arteaga to find some ruins said to lie beneath the peak of Machu Picchu mountain. It involved a steamy journey through thick jungle, across a rickety log bridge and up slopes so steep that for much of the time they were forced to proceed on all fours. Near the peak, an Indian family assured them that there were ruins ahead, although Bingham admits he was "not unduly excited."

His diary then records the moment he stepped into the lost city: "…suddenly we found ourselves in the midst of a jungle-covered maze of small and large walls, the ruins of buildings made of blocks of white granite, most carefully cut and beautifully fitted together without cement. Surprise followed surprise until there came the realization that we were in the midst of as wonderful ruins as any ever found in Peru. It seemed almost incredible that this city, only five days' journey from Cuzco, should have

remained so long undescribed and comparatively unknown. Yet so far as I have been able to discover, there is no reference in the Spanish chronicles to Machu Picchu. It is possible that not even the conquistadors ever saw this wonderful place."

The following year Bingham returned to the site to take photographs, and when these were published in 1913 the world hailed his achievement. The National Geographic Society called it "one of the most remarkable stories of exploration in South America in the past 50 years." Later Bingham theorized that Machu Picchu was both the site of Tampu Tocco (the mythical birthplace of Inca culture) and Vilcabamba itself. He was wrong on both counts, although this does not undermine the significance of his work. Later research suggests Machu Picchu was in fact a country retreat for Inca emperors, complete with shrines, temples, baths, and artificial watercourses.

Bingham served in World War I and led a full public life as governor of Connecticut and member of the Senate before his death in 1956. Despite mixing with the great and the good for so many years, he always listed his main occupation as "explorer."

Above: *Bingham thought he had discovered the lost city of Tampu Tocco, birthplace of Inca culture, when he came across Machu Picchu. That it later turned out to be more likely a summer residence for Inca emperors, did not lessen the magnitude of his find.*

PERCY HARRISON FAWCETT

1867 to 1925

If luck had been on his side, Percy Harrison Fawcett would have been remembered for the excellent surveying work he carried out in the heart of South America. As it happens, he led an ill-fated expedition into remote jungle and disappeared. Afterward, the name Fawcett was forever linked to ominous mystery, his previous achievements all forgotten.

By 1906 one of the last uncharted places in the world was Mato Grosso, a plateau on the Brazilian borders with Bolivia. The region was known to be rich in resources, including rubber, which was then being grown on plantations to fulfil increasing demand. Both Bolivia and Brazil were making claims on the area and tensions were rising, so London's Royal Geographical Society was asked to settle the dispute by plotting the precise position of the border. The Society's president Sir George Goldie picked Fawcett for the task.

Fawcett had been in the army since the age of 19. Already he had traveled around Sri Lanka, where he married, and in North Africa. The offer from Goldie was his notion of an ideal job. However, exciting though it may have seemed, the job was far from easy. Many of the gunslingers driven out of the "Wild West" were now living in Bolivia when Fawcett arrived to start work. Drunkenness was rife. The lawlessness of Bolivia shocked him, as did the treatment meted out to Indian slaves.

Fawcett believed a civilized approach toward Indians would elicit a civilized response. In 1910, while he was mapping the Heath river, he and his party encountered an Indian settlement on a sandbank. Fearful that whites had come to take slaves, the initial response from the Indians was hostile. However, one of Fawcett's party succeeded in bridging the hostility and language barrier by playing his accordian. The Indians put down their arrows and the belligerence was eased.

There were other hazards, including the wildlife. Back in England Fawcett regaled listeners with stories about vampire bats that would attack any flesh protruding from mosquito nets during the night. Victims awoke to find their hammocks covered in blood. Piranha lurked in rivers, ready to attack at the

Right: Faced with American gunslingers and malcontent Indians, army-trained Percy Harrison Fawcett preferred civilized discussion to guns to get his way in Bolivia.

Facing: The mystery of Fawcett's disappearance remains, whether from disease, hostile Indians, or perhaps even a fatal accident over a waterfall—he had already encountered such an incident once, and lived to tell the tale.

first scent of flesh. At one point Fawcett killed an anaconda snake which, he reported, was 62 feet in length and 12 inches in diameter.

While investigating the Madidi river Fawcett's canoe was lost over a waterfall. He survived but much of his equipment and stores was lost. "Looking back we saw what we had come through. The fall was about 20 feet high, and where the river dropped the canyon narrowed to a mere ten feet across; through this bottleneck the huge volume of water gushed with terrific force, thundering down into a welter of brown foam and black-topped rocks. It seemed incredible that we could have survived that maelstrom!"

In search of Mato Grosso

For three years Fawcett worked to establish the international boundaries. He made five further trips to South America before the doomed sixth. In 1916 Fawcett was awarded the Royal Geographical Society Gold Medal for his "contributions to the mapping of South America."

His interest in archeology grew and, after researching old documents and listening to folk tales, he became convinced the ruins of an ancient city belonging to a noble civilization lay beneath the vines of the Brazilian jungle. Preferring to travel in small groups, Fawcett recruited his son Jack and a friend, Raleigh

Rimmel, to help him find the lost city in the Mato Grosso. He left instructions that no rescue party should come after them since he considered it too dangerous. On May 29, 1925 Fawcett wrote to his wife with the encouraging message: "You need have no fear of failure." Shortly afterward the trio vanished, and their remains were never found.

By 1928 the American press reported that Fawcett and his companions had probably been killed on the banks of the Culuene river. There was no conclusive evidence, however, and many rumors circulated. According to some stories, blue-eyed Indians had been seen in the jungle suggesting that the lost men had fathered children. Other claims had Fawcett living an idyllic life in the lost city, adamantly refusing to return, or as the chief of a tribe of cannibals. The truth of Fawcett's fate has never been fully established, but it is probable that like many explorers before him he was either ambushed or died of disease and starvation in the dense jungle.

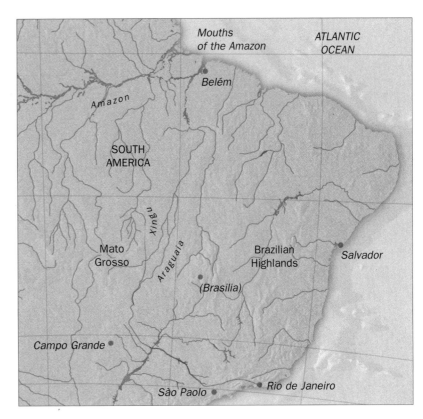

CHAPTER SIX

ARCTIC *and* ANTARCTIC

Captain James Cook made the first circumnavigation of Antarctica without ever sighting land. His closest approach was 67°15' S 39°35' E.

Atlantic Ocean

Hudson Bay

Weddell Sea

QUEEN MAUD LAND

Filchner Ice Shelf

ANTARCTICA

ELLSWORTH

Bellingshausen Sea

MARIE BYRD LAND

South Pole

South Geomagnetic Pole

WILKES LAND

Pacific Ocean

General extent of pack ice

Ross Ice Shelf

Ross Sea

Antarctic Circle

"The men whose desires lead them to the untrodden paths of the world have generally marked individuality." So wrote Ernest Shackleton, Antarctic explorer who was as much a humanist and psychologist as a strategist. The planet's poles, beset by blizzards and ice, attracted numerous pioneers. Each drove themselves to the limit of their physical endurance in pursuit of glory. In extreme places it takes an extreme kind of personality to flourish.

The polar regions are indescribably cold, with an average winter temperature in the Arctic of -91°F (-33°C) and as low as -190°F (-88°C) in Antarctica. Temperatures like these can freeze eyelashes together and perish exposed skin. Winters are shrouded in total darkness. In the opposing season the sun never sets. These are eerie places where it is difficult to tell where land gives way to sea. Thin crusts of snow and ice mask deep crevasses—posing deadly hazards for the unwary traveler. Leads, or channels, open up in the ice, suddenly leaving parties stranded. Everywhere is white, putting humans at risk of snowblindness and death through disorientation.

Many early explorers were led into danger by erroneous reports filed by misguided explorers. Often facts were thin on the ground. The perils of frostbite—painful and debilitating—loomed large. When exploration of the frozen wastes was in its infancy there were numerous dietary problems confronting the men, including scurvy and dysentery. Only bitter experience would aid subsequent generations in avoiding such

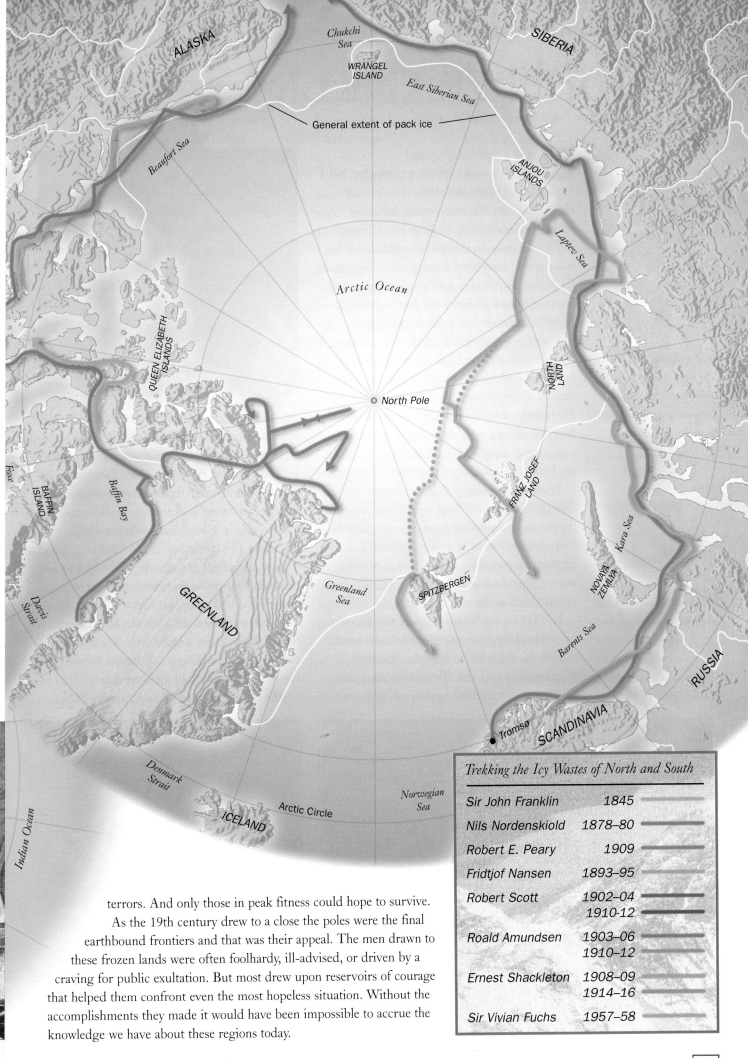

ALASKA

Chukchi
Sea

SIBERIA

WRANGEL
ISLAND

East Siberian Sea

General extent of pack ice

Beaufort Sea

ANJOU
ISLANDS

Laptev Sea

Arctic Ocean

QUEEN ELIZABETH
ISLANDS

North
Land

North Pole

FRANZ JOSEF
LAND

Foxe

BAFFIN
ISLAND

Baffin Bay

Kara Sea

NOVAYA
ZEMLYA

Davis
Strait

GREENLAND

Greenland
Sea

SPITZBERGEN

Barents Sea

RUSSIA

Denmark
Strait

Tromsø

SCANDINAVIA

Norwegian
Sea

Arctic Circle

Indian Ocean

ICELAND

terrors. And only those in peak fitness could hope to survive.
As the 19th century drew to a close the poles were the final
earthbound frontiers and that was their appeal. The men drawn to
these frozen lands were often foolhardy, ill-advised, or driven by a
craving for public exultation. But most drew upon reservoirs of courage
that helped them confront even the most hopeless situation. Without the
accomplishments they made it would have been impossible to accrue the
knowledge we have about these regions today.

Trekking the Icy Wastes of North and South		
Sir John Franklin	1845	
Nils Nordenskiold	1878–80	
Robert E. Peary	1909	
Fridtjof Nansen	1893–95	
Robert Scott	1902–04	
	1910-12	
Roald Amundsen	1903–06	
	1910–12	
Ernest Shackleton	1908–09	
	1914–16	
Sir Vivian Fuchs	1957–58	

ROBERT E. PEARY *and* FREDERICK COOK

**1856
to
1920**

**1865
to
1940**

*Below: The adventurous
Mrs. Robert Peary
accompanied her husband on
the 1891 Arctic expedition.*

onquest of the North Pole was claimed separately by two explorers who attempted the feat almost simultaneously, as often happens in exploration when frontiers are pushed back. However, the public argument that occurred between Robert E. Peary and Frederick Cook afterward did much to diminish their respective achievements. The truth was buried beneath shabby accusations of disgraceful fraud.

Indeed, latest evidence appears to prove that neither was the first to travel overland to the pole, and that the accolade should, in fact, go to a Russian and an American who made the journey some 85 years later. Both Robert E.

Peary and Frederick Cook were obsessed with the Arctic. They sought the thrill of battling the extreme elements, of going where no human had been before, and also the glittering prize of being first to the North Pole.

Robert E. Peary

By the time Peary attempted the pole he was more than 50 years old, a veteran of six previous ice-cap expeditions but far from the peak of physical fitness. Peary was born in Pennsylvania and distinguished himself as a civil engineering student, eventually joining the U.S. Navy. As a youth he was inspired by the writings of Elisha Kent Kane, the American doctor who had helped search for Sir John Franklin and aspired to conquering the pole. Peary eventually secured a six-month leave to explore Greenland. Arctic exploration proved everything he dreamed it would be and an obsession was born.

On his return from Greenland Peary visited a furrier in Washington DC, hoping to sell some hides. Here he encountered Matthew Henson (1866–1955), born in Maryland, the son of

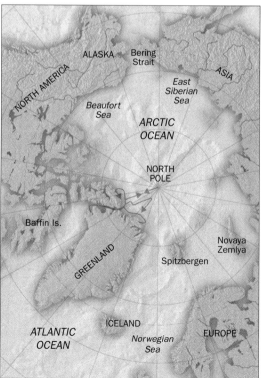

freeborn African Americans and already an experienced seafarer, and the pair found a rapport. Although Peary hired Henson to be his valet, his ultimate role was as a soul-mate.

Initially they traveled together to Nicaragua on a survey expedition.

On his return Peary married and began planning his second Arctic venture. Breaking the mold of the time, he set off for Greenland with his wife and his black partner. That their first child was born in Greenland illustrates how unconventional Peary was. On his third trip to the frozen north Peary and Henson almost starved to death. During a subsequent visit Henson pulled off his friend's boots to find a number of frost-bitten toes detached inside. Peary lost eight toes, but proudly learned to walk without a limp and was not deterred from returning to the region.

This true grit spirit went together with other altogether less noble traits. He was mightily egotistical and yearned for celebrity status. He once told his mother: "I must have fame and cannot reconcile myself to years of commonplace drudgery and a name late in life when I see an opportunity to gain it now and sip the delicious draught while yet I have youth and strength and capacity to enjoy it."

He repeatedly attempted the North Pole and time after time he was defeated by fierce weather or fickle ice. He became despondent and optimistic by turns. Peary was, according to numerous reports, a difficult man to work with. While it was Henson who troubled himself to communicate with Greenland Inuit, learning their methods of sledding with dog teams, it was Peary who declared this innovation to be "the Peary method."

Henson was undeterred by his partner's disagreeable traits, but Frederick Cook was less tolerant. Cook accompanied Peary on one expedition to Greenland—his first Arctic trip—as doctor, and found his fellow American so unpleasant that he refused to work with him again, and so became Peary's greatest rival.

Above: *Pictured in* Throne and Country *magazine in 1909, Peary was credited with being first man to the North Pole. Only later would his claims be subjected to close scrutiny.*

Frederick Cook

Cook, the son of a German doctor, grew up in the wilderness of the Catskill mountains in New York State, where he learned to respect nature at its most awesome. Proof of his immense self-will came in the hours he spent working at menial jobs to finance a spell at medical college. His first trip appears to have been triggered by the death of his wife, Libby, and baby daughter in childbirth, to escape his grief.

After first experiencing the northern ice, Cook went south with the Belgian Antarctic Expedition as surgeon and observer. When the ship was locked in frozen waters and the crew struck down with scurvy and anemia it was Cook who displayed "unfailing hope and unfaltering courage" in remedying both the diseases (he recommended a diet of raw penguin) and in forging a path to freedom. Norwegian explorer Roald Amundsen was among the explorers who thereafter championed Cook throughout a rollercoaster career.

There followed two ventures in Alaska, with Cook claiming first to have circumnavigated Alaska and then to have scaled Mount McKinley, the highest peak in North America. Later his claim was deemed bogus. The photographs presented as proof of the achievement were believed to be of a different Alaskan mountain.

Nevertheless, his reputation was sufficiently solid to attract a benefactor, John R. Bradley, whose ship took him to Greenland in 1907 to attempt the North Pole. Cook departed from the northernmost village in the company of two Inuit in February of that year and asserted that he had reached the pole on April 21, 1908, although he did not make the announcement until September 1909. "We were the only pulsating creatures in a dead world of ice," he wrote. Cook wintered in a cave before sailing to Europe to proclaim his feat.

Meanwhile, Peary in the company of Henson and four Inuit allegedly made the North Pole by April 6, 1909. In his diary Peary recorded: "The prize of three centuries, my dream and ambition for 23 years. Mine at last." Five days after Cook,

Right: An altogether more likeable man than his rival Peary, Cook's version of events in being first to reach the North Pole was nevertheless considered untrue by the public at large.

Peary announced his triumph. The ensuing controversy was as tumultuous as any Arctic storm. The prestigious National Geographic Society along with the *New York Times* backed Peary while various eminent explorers including Amundsen, Greely, Sverdrup, and Nansen vouched for Cook, as did the *New York Herald*.

Suspicions all around

There is evidence to discount both mens' claims. Peary's diary was unfeasibly clean, for example; there were only limited signs of wear and tear on a book that had, after all, traveled in the harshest conditions known to man. The writing was tidy when Peary surely must have been using a hand numbed by cold. Some key pages were blank. Questions lingered over the ability of the Peary party to take accurate readings. The speeds they would need to have reached to achieve this goal appear impossibly great. Given his advancing years, it is possible that Peary fudged his attempt to receive acclaim.

Cook's notes were also suspect. There were gaps and mathematical gaffes. Like Peary, he claimed to have traveled at great speed when the ice around the pole was drifting south and was

1554	1578	1596	1772	1790	1818	1820	1821
Hugh Willoughby freezes to death in the Arctic Circle	Francis Drake proves that South America is separated Antarctica	Willem Barents' ship becomes icebound on Novaya Zemlya	James Cook is first to cross Antarctic Circle	George Vancouver seeks northwest passage through the Canadian Arctic	Sir John Ross explores Baffin Bay	Nathaniel Brown Palmer first to see Antarctica	Bellinghausen finds Peter I and Alexander I Islands in Antarctica

fraught with ridges and fissures. In addition his sled was ludicrously pristine. One of Cook's Inuit companions later allegedly told Henson that they had traveled no further than a few miles from land. Politics played its part, too. Peary was altogether a less likeable fellow and there were many Americans who were uncomfortable with the thought that a black man had accomplished a major geographic challenge where white men had previously failed.

Both Cook and Peary had much to gain from being first to the North Pole and much to lose by coming second. A comfortable living from writing books, articles, and from lecture tours was at stake in addition to the international honor. Initial indications were that Peary was right and

Cook a liar. The American Congress was persuaded of it and Peary was awarded the rank of rear admiral before his retirement. Public opinion against Cook hardened when, in 1925, he was convicted of fraud in the oil business and jailed. He was released in 1930 and received a presidential pardon in 1940.

Much controversy exists even today over the early exploration of the North Pole. When it comes to geographic accuracies it is likely that both men were wide of the mark due to the inadequacies of contemporary technology. What is certain, however, is that Peary, Cook, and their fellow travelers were courageous pioneers who succeeded in pushing back the boundaries of knowledge in pursuit of a dream.

1823	1827	1831	1841	1845	1847	1853	1853
James Weddell discovers Weddell Sea	Sir William Parry fails an attempt on the North Pole by sled	British explorer James Ross reaches the North Magnetic Pole	James Ross discovers the Ross Sea in Antarctica	Sir John Franklin sets off to search for a northwest passage	Franklin's expedition is lost in the icy wastes of Canada	Surveyor John Rae proves King William's Land is an island	Elisha Kent Kane visits northwest shores of Greenland

FRIDTJOF NANSEN

1861
to
1930

By any standards Nansen was an extraordinary man. To ski across Greenland and then be conveyed by currents across the Arctic Sea in an ice-bound ship are astonishing exploits. Nansen did both of these and yet he is not particularly remembered for either. His name was written large in the history books years later after he won the Nobel Peace Prize for famine relief work in Europe following World War I. However, the conviction, courage and meticulous forethought which saw Nansen through the first phase of his adult life, as Arctic explorer, proved equally vital when he emerged as a statesman and humanitarian.

Nansen was born on the outskirts of Oslo in Norway. As a boy he distinguished himself as scholar and sportsman and became the national cross-country skiing champion a dozen times as well as a world-record-breaking skater. University beckoned and Nansen chose to study zoology, believing it offered better opportunities to be outdoors. The highlight of his youth proved to be a spell aboard the *Viking*, a sealing vessel patrolling the Arctic in 1882 on

Right: Fridtjof Nansen pictured returning in 1896 from his attempt on the North Pole.

Below: Nansen's Arctic expedition leaves Christiania (Oslo) in the Fram *on June 24, 1893.*

which he made scientific notes and excellent sketches that became the hallmark of his work. At the age of 20 Nansen was offered a senior museum post which, challenging though it was, kept him permanently indoors. He could not forget the thrill of seeing uncharted Greenland from the decks of the *Viking* and it was there he wanted to return. By 1887 Nansen announced that he would cross Greenland from east to west on skis,

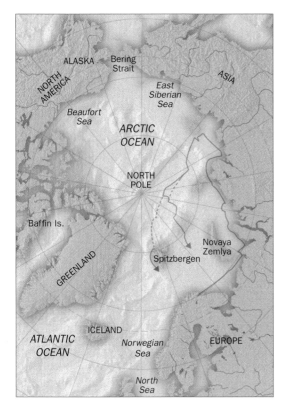

gaining the necessary sponsorship from a merchant in Copenhagen. In the ensuing months Nansen pored over plans. Attention to detail came to characterize his Arctic approach.

In the summer of 1888 a six-man team with Nansen at its head embarked on the adventure. Despite adverse weather that caused delays at the start, the men skied a distance of some 500 miles in little more than three weeks on a route from the bleak, uninhabited east coast to the settlements in the west. The direction was chosen by Nansen to ensure that there was no turning back—there was nothing to turn back to. Later he wrote: "I have always thought that the much-praised 'line of retreat' is a snare for people who wish to reach their goal... always looking back they end by getting nowhere. The traveler of the right mettle may consider well, but then he takes one road and sticks to that." The team returned from the epic journey in triumph, Nansen with sufficient material to write *Eskimo Life*, published in 1891.

Drift to the North Pole

Still, his Arctic lust remained unsatisfied. Along with many scientific minds of the era, he pondered just how wreckage from George Washington de Long's ship *Jeannette* had turned up on the coast of Greenland when it had been wrecked off Siberia, the other side of the pole. Nansen was not alone in believing that drifting ocean currents were responsible. But he stood in isolation when he proposed to leave a ship iced-up in Siberia for years to see if it followed a similar route.

When he proposed his ideas for an expedition to the North Pole that would utilize ice-pack drift to an audience comprising eminent explorers in England he was greeted with almost universal opposition. The apparent peril of the venture shocked even the most hardened explorer and their fears were echoed in America where Adolphus Greely wrote scathingly: "[Nansen's plan] seems to be based on fallacious ideas and to foreshadow barren results."

His numerous detractors counted without Nansen's painstaking planning, which took three years. Design of the ship was key. The oak and iron-clad *Fram* was squat in shape so that it would be squeezed above the ice rather than crushed by it. He allowed supplies for six years and thought out plenty of activities for the crew of 12. On June 26, 1893 the *Fram* set out from Norway and became locked in the Siberian ice shelf within three months.

The drift was excessively slow. In March 1895 Nansen decided to risk an attempt on the pole with dogs and a single companion. The pair reached a record distance north before turning back to save themselves. After wintering in a walrus hide, Nansen encountered the British explorer Frederick Jackson, who assisted their return. Nansen arrived in Norway just a few days before the *Fram*, which returned having completed its trans-Arctic journey.

Nansen worked in oceanography before becoming a diplomat and League of Nations trouble-shooter. His experiences in the Arctic equipped him well for the misery he found later in his career, as he revealed in his writings: "Deliverance will not come from the rushing, noisy centers of civilization. It will come from the lonely places."

Below: Product placement and personality endorsement is nothing new. This advertisement, which appeared in the London Illustrated News, *December 30, 1893, shows Nansen making a cup of Cadbury's Cocoa. The caption at the bottom reads: "Messrs. Cadbury have supplied about 1,500 lbs of Cocoa Essence and Chocolate in hermetically sealed tins... Dr. Nansen exercised a wise choice in selecting an absolutely pure cocoa of such typical excellence as Cadbury's."*

ROBERT FALCON SCOTT

1868 to 1912

"We shall stick it out to the end, but we are getting weaker, of course, and the end cannot be far. It seems a pity, but I do not think I can write any more."

These were the last words that Robert Falcon Scott wrote as he huddled in a tent sheltering from a blizzard in the bleak, unforgiving

Above: *Robert Falcon Scott from a 1914 calendar, showing vignettes of the ill-fated expedition. Scott's heroism spawned many commemorative items, such as the postcard on the facing page.*

landscape of Antarctica. Scott was the leader of a heroic but doomed expedition to the south pole. He was beaten in a race to be the first to the pole and lost his life while attempting to return home. Yet he remains an inspiration. While many people may struggle to recall the name of Roald Amundsen, the first man to the south pole, the exploits of Scott and his men live on because of their tragic fate.

Scott was born in Devonport, England, and went to sea at the age of 14. He became a naval officer and caught the attention of Sir Clements

Markham of the Royal Geographical Society. Markham wanted the Royal Navy to establish closer links with exploration in the Antarctic which, at the turn of the century, was still largely uncharted. In Scott he saw a man driven by honor, determination, duty, and courage. Scott had no experience of polar travel, but this fact was dismissed by Markham who saw to it that Scott headed the British National Antarctic Expedition which set out in August 1901.

Accompanied by Ernest Shackleton, Scott traveled further south across the Ross Ice Shelf toward the pole than any previous explorer. Although this was a triumphant achievement, the journey was fraught with difficulties including a debilitating outbreak of scurvy and attacks of snowblindness. Scott's inadequate handling of dog sleds also became apparent, and this was a weakness that he never overcame.

A bitter journey

On his return to England aboard the *Discovery* on November 7, 1904, Scott was promoted to captain and returned to naval duties. Four years later he married Kathleen Bruce, a sculptress. They had one son, Peter, who later would achieve fame in his own right as a naturalist. But Scott senior remained passionate about the unconquered ice cap. In 1909 he decided to

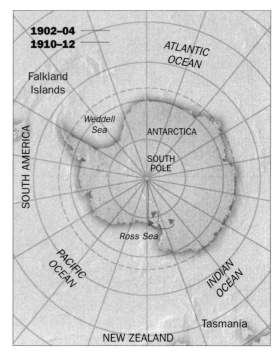

embark on a privately financed expedition to the south pole. A year later he left England for Antarctica on board the *Terra Nova*. Only when the voyage was under way did Scott learn that Amundsen was also heading for the south pole.

On November 1, 1911, Scott embarked on his expedition from McMurdo Sound; but he encountered dreadful weather that immediately hampered his efforts. Amundsen chose an unmapped route from the Bay of Whales, some 60 miles nearer to the pole, and gained a head start by setting out on October 9.

Ill-advisedly, Scott invited Lieutenant Henry R. Bowers to join the four-strong party, and this instantly placed pressure on food rations. To Scott, the glory of the endeavor was reaching the pole on foot. Scott's wish was granted when the sled-hauling Shetland ponies had to be destroyed and the motorized sleds broke down. His intrepid band made slow progress, which fatally diminished their stamina. When they finally reached the south pole on January 16, 1912 at the end of an 800-mile trek, they were confronted with a flag and a tent. Amundsen had reached the pole more than 30 days previously.

In a dejected state, the team turned back. The fate of each is well known. Petty officer Edgar Evans died first following a fall; Captain Lawrence Oates sacrificed himself after becoming disabled; and Scott, Bowers, and Edward Wilson died on or around March 29, 1912 in a flimsy tent just 11 miles from their depot. News of their disappearance did not reach Britain for months, and it was a year before the bodies were found and buried. Scott's diaries were discovered with his body. Scott's widow, Kathleen, reflected on his qualities: "There never was a man with such a sense of responsiblity and duty, and the agony of leaving his job undone, losing the other lives, and leaving me uncared for must have been unspeakable."

IN MEMORY OF THE ANTARCTIC HEROES, THE LATE CAPTAIN SCOTT AND HIS GALLANT COMRADES, WHO PERISHED MARCH, 1912, AT THE SOUTH POLE,

Beyond the track of human life,
    Away through an endless waste,
The end achieved, but lo ! sad news
    Of death most bravely faced.

Beyond the woes of earthly strife,
    Away to an endless rest—
A destiny we may not choose
    Has done it's worst, and best.

ROALD AMUNDSEN
1872 to 1928

I n the eyes of the world he was "the last Viking"—physically imposing and dauntingly single-minded. Roald Engelbrecht Gravning Amundsen appeared to have the last unexplored territories unfolding in the palms of his hands. He was not only the conqueror of the South Pole but also the first to sail through the elusive northwest passage and the equally challenging northeast passage, and he was probably the first to fly over the North Pole. Here was an explorer of pedigree.

But not everyone was impressed. Those partisan to Robert Scott believed Amundsen won the race in Antarctica through good fortune. This is no small insult to Amundsen. Sound planning and preparation were the reasons for his success. After all, he had endured similar weather to Scott *en route* to the pole. Those who accused him of unnecessary cruelty to his dogs, which were slaughtered and killed as they became exhausted, perhaps failed to observe the degree of care he took while the animals lived. They were protected from snow and frost by specially-dug shelters and were well-fed until they became expendable. Another

group disillusioned with the bold adventurer were his creditors—and there were many during his career. If he ever behaved dishonorably it was to those he owed money.

Amundsen was born in southeast Norway, and his boyhood heroes included Sir John Franklin and his ill-fated team. His well-to-do parents steered him toward a career in medicine. Amundsen did his best to oblige them while they lived, but on the death of his mother, when he was 21, he set out to pursue a life as an Arctic explorer. His first task was to equip himself with seafaring expertise and accordingly he spent three years aboard a sealing ship until he won the title of mate. With this under his belt, he joined the Belgian Antarctic expedition of 1897. It offered no tangible success but plenty of valuable experience alongside, among others, Dr. Frederick Cook. When illness beset the captain, Amundsen stepped into his role and qualified himself in that capacity for future forays.

Next he set about exploring the northwest passage. Amundsen sold his expedition as a scientific endeavor when in fact it was little more than an adventure. When worthy Norwegian institutes saw through this ruse his financial backing was compromised. Amundsen was compelled to slip out of harbor on his 70-foot sloop *Gjoa* in June 1903 to escape swooping creditors.

Beaten to the north pole

The journey through the northwest passage was hazardous. Amundsen rested at the last known camp of the valiant Franklin before facing perils of his own when harsh weather nearly wrecked his vessel. For two winters he and his six crew were ice-bound, surviving only through trade with the Inuit. Observation of this fascinating people assisted Amundsen in future ventures. The *Gjoa* finally edged through the passage and arrived to an ecstatic welcome in San Francisco in October 1906.

Amundsen had his heart set on reaching the North Pole but was thwarted by the claims of Peary and Cook that they had made it to the pole first. His thoughts turned to Antarctica but, in the knowledge that Scott was attempting

Above: Amundsen felt cheated of his real goal by the claims of Peary and Cook to be first man to reach the North Pole. Being the first to reach the South Pole did not appear to elate him as much.

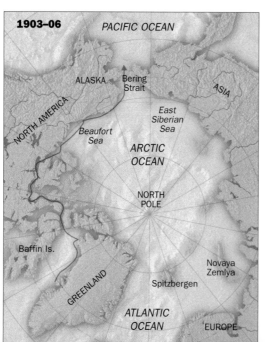

1903–06

PACIFIC OCEAN

ALASKA · Bering Strait

ASIA

East Siberian Sea

Beaufort Sea

NORTH AMERICA

ARCTIC OCEAN

NORTH POLE

Baffin Is.

GREENLAND

Spitzbergen

Novaya Zemlya

ATLANTIC OCEAN

EUROPE

the South Pole, he kept the plans to himself and only revealed them to his team as they sailed down the African coast. Triumph at the South Pole was tinged with bitterness at not having been first to the North Pole. "No man has ever stood at the spot so diametrically opposed to the object of his real desires," he wrote.

He successfully navigated the northeast passage before embarking on a drift across the polar basin on his specially-commissioned ship, the *Maud*. Although triumphant in terms of collecting scientific data, this venture was frustrated by rough weather. Amundsen himself was hurt in a fall and also had to put up a hasty

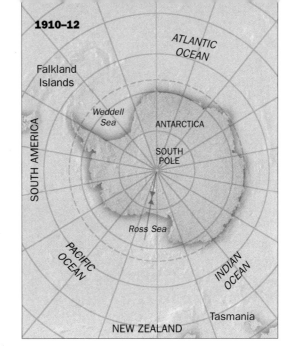

1910–12

defense against a hungry bear.

At home more financial troubles loomed. Amundsen's next diversion from his problems was the challenge of polar flight. However, it wasn't until wealthy American Lincoln Ellsworth offered him a deal that Amundsen could get off the ground. Together they flew to the Arctic Circle in 1925 and, while they did not reach the North Pole, they succeeded in capturing the imagination of the public.

The following year Amundsen was among those on the airship *Norge*, along with Ellsworth and Italian designer and pilot Umberto Nobile, that flew from Svalbard across the North Pole to Alaska. Although the mission was a stunning success, Amundsen aired a volley of complaints mainly directed against Nobile. In response Nobile flew in a balloon over the North Pole in 1928. This time the episode was marred by

tragedy. The balloon crashed onto the ice, killing six of the crew. Nobile and the remaining men awaited rescue for almost a month when their radio messages went unheard.

When he got to know about Nobile's plight Amundsen sprang into action and flew out of Tromsø by seaplane to assist. The plane was never seen again. Ironically this disaster fulfilled one of Amundsen's few remaining wishes. Just before his demise he had told a journalist: "If only you knew how splendid it is up there— that's where I want to die."

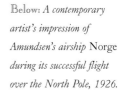

ERNEST SHACKLETON
1874 to 1922

L ike most explorers of the era, Ernest Shackleton possessed remarkable measures of fortitude, integrity, daring, and charisma. Devoted though he was to chalking up achievements in Antarctica, he refused to countenance excessive risk for himself or his men, unlike many of his contemporary explorers. Accordingly, no lives were lost in the expeditions under Shackleton's command, a significant achievement for the time.

Shackleton was born in County Kildare, Ireland. His Quaker family moved first to Dublin, where Shackleton's father trained as a doctor, and then to London where Shackleton studied at a number of establishments including Dulwich College. But any hopes that his family had of him following in his father's scholarly footsteps were soon dispelled by the 16-year-old's assertion that he wanted to go to sea. He joined the merchant marine, and by the age of 24 was qualified to command any British ship.

While the sea fulfilled his longing for adventure it failed to satisfy his urge for exploration. To this end he used his considerable powers of persuasion to convince Robert Scott and the Royal Geographical Society to secure him a place on the National Antarctic Expedition of 1901.

Shackleton and Scott enjoyed mutual respect but also exhibited a robust competitiveness. Shackleton appears to have admired Scott's tenacious spirit but disliked his adherence to separation of the ranks. Scott rated Shackleton for his impressive stamina but distrusted him, if only because he was a merchant seafarer rather than a Navy man. Their relationship was further complicated by Shackleton's illness during the 1901 expedition—he suffered scurvy due to the inadequate diet—which stopped Scott reaching the South Pole at this early date. Scott's account in his best-selling book of what he perceived as Shackleton's weaknesses was both an irritant to Shackleton and a challenge. However, both men shared the honor of having reached a more southerly point than anyone before them.

Proving his mettle

Shackleton took a leave from exploring after returning home, and became first a public speaker, then the secretary of the Royal Scottish Geographical Society and, in 1906, a candidate for the Liberal-Unionist party in the elections of that year. He failed to gain a parliamentary seat but at the same time encountered William Beardmore, who would volunteer finances for his proposed trek through Antarctica.

In 1907 the expedition aboard the sealer *Nimrod* set off with the personal blessing of the British king and queen. Shackleton took with him a prefabricated hut for living quarters, a motor vehicle (which was at this time more a novelty than a useful item), and a team of Manchurian ponies. Shackleton planned to base his headquarters at the same site used by Scott, in McMurdo Sound. In an unnecessarily proprietorial response, Scott requested that

Right: Ernest Shackleton accompanied Robert Scott on the 1901 Antarctic expedition, but Scott mistrusted him because he was a merchant navy man and not Royal Navy.

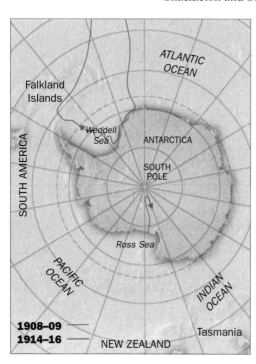

ATLANTIC OCEAN

Falkland Islands

Weddell Sea

ANTARCTICA

SOUTH POLE

SOUTH AMERICA

Ross Sea

PACIFIC OCEAN

INDIAN OCEAN

1908–09
1914–16

Tasmania

NEW ZEALAND

Shackleton went elsewhere since he himself was planning to return. The uncharitable might conclude that Scott was keen to reserve the most advantageous base for himself. Shackleton obliged, but met with severe conditions at alternative landing sites and eventually, in the name of safety, he was forced to head for McMurdo Sound.

One of the expedition's first triumphs was the ascent of Mount Erebus, never before climbed. Three men struck out to reach the magnetic pole while Shackleton was among four others who headed for the geographic pole. The trio reached their goal but there was disappointment in store for Shackleton and the others.

They lost all their ponies, the last falling to its death through a crevasse in the ice, and were forced to cut rations and make unscheduled depots with supplies that they were unable to haul. As they drew closer to the pole they were stopped in their tracks by a blizzard that confined them to their tents for two precious days. Even in their sleeping bags they suffered frostbite. Shackleton was courageous enough to realize that, even if the pole had not been reached, the limits of human endurance had, and on January 9, 1909 he turned back rather than risk a catastrophe. They were some 97 miles short of their target.

Although praise was heaped on him, Shackleton was not satisfied. He planned another Antarctic expedition to explore the Weddell Sea. However, his ship *Endurance* was crushed in the ice one thousand miles from civilization. Now Shackleton turned disaster into triumph by securing his fellow travelers in a camp on Elephant Island after five months at sea. He then set off with five others for an 800-mile journey in an open boat, the *James Caird*, to seek help. When they arrived on the coast of South Georgia they had to scale hitherto unmapped mountains to reach a whaling community. Shackleton finally made it back to rescue his comrades. His final voyage was in 1921, when he was bound once more for Antarctica, but died before he reached the continent.

Left: *Shackleton's stricken* Endurance *lies crushed by pack ice off the Caird Coast in 1915.*

KNUD RASMUSSEN

1879 to 1933

Polar exploration exposed not only vast tracts of the earth's surface for the first time but also an entire race of people with unique customs and ways. Knud Rasmussen was as much concerned with the fate of the polar Inuit as he was with finding new fjords or uncharted glaciers. His legacy was to provide information not only about the cold shores of the Arctic but also of the indigenous people, whose origin and way of life was something of a mystery until the last half of the 19th century.

Rasmussen was himself part-Inuit—his father was a Danish missionary while his mother had Inuit blood—which explains his passionate interest in them. Brought up in Greenland, Rasmussen was bilingual and a master of Inuit survival skills, including kayaking and riding a dogsled. He went to the University of Copenhagen but retained a lively interest in the Arctic folk of Disko Bay on Qeqertarsuaq Island where he was born.

At the age of 23 he joined the Danish expedition led by Mylius-Erichson, which explored the Arctic for two years. In so doing he was among some of the country's most experienced explorers, and learned much. He had already undertaken trips to Iceland and Swedish Lapland for study. Then there were a succession of visits to the polar Inuit of Cape York in Greenland, where he was ultimately adopted as a member of the tribe. His breadth of knowledge, by the age of 30, was admirable.

In 1910 Rasmussen, with fellow explorer Peter Freuchen, established the Thule station at Cape York. Thule (which means "far north" in ancient Greek) would serve as a base for seven expeditions that laid the foundations for modern understanding of Inuit culture. Rasmussen, able to talk to Inuit in their own language, had the advantage over just about every other expedition leader of the age.

The Thule expeditions

On the first Thule expedition Rasmussen crossed the Greenland ice cap from west to northeast, an arduous 500-mile trek undertaken in the company of Freuchen, two Inuit, and 54 dogs. In doing so he became the first man to cross the region by dogsled. During the epic journey Rasmussen was able—not for the last time—to correct mistakes in cartography made previously by Robert Peary.

During the second and fourth Thule expeditions, in 1917 and 1920, Rasmussen concentrated on the gathering of cultural information about the Inuit at a time when the social science of ethnology was in its infancy. He faithfully noted down songs, mythology, and rituals as told him by the Inuit. The more he learned, the more he yearned to know. Rasmussen orchestrated the fifth Thule expedition with the aim of gathering information about all Inuit settlements in the Arctic sweep before they were inundated by European influences.

On March 11, 1923 he left Danish Island to travel a distance of more than 1,800 miles in the company of two Inuit, and used the same dog team for the entire journey. By the time he reached Kotzebue in Alaska on August 21, 1924 he had studied all the Inuit settlements along the route. His conclusion was that Inuit derived from the same stock as North American Indians and had originally hailed from Asia. His detailed work earned him a Doctorate at the University of Copenhagen.

There were two other Thule Expeditions involving Rasmussen that helped to map the region, gathered cultural information and even undertook some archeology. The seventh was to be his last, however. As he traveled he suffered food poisoning and influenza, which developed into pneumonia. He died while on his way back to Denmark.

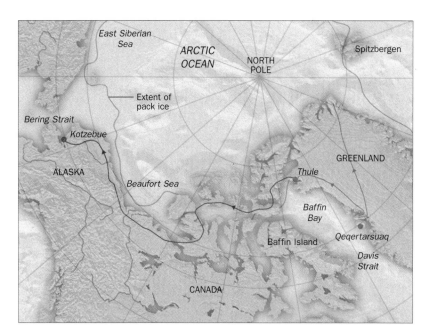

Facing: Knud Rasmussen was as much an ethnologist and archeologist as he was an explorer. His expeditions across Greenland, below, and the Arctic wastes provided a study of the Inuit who inhabited these extreme climes.

RICHARD BYRD
1888 to 1957

I n 1926 Richard Byrd was hailed a hero for flying over the North Pole in a tiny plane. Byrd was greeted with a New York ticker-tape parade after his triumph and was awarded medals by President Coolidge. The *New York Times* of May 10, 1926 broadcast that Byrd circled "the top of the world several times." However, diaries discovered in the archives of the Byrd Polar Research Center in Ohio reveal that navigator Byrd and pilot Floyd Bennett (1890–1928) in their tri-motor Fokker plane *Josephine Ford* turned back 2¼°—or about 150 miles—short of their target. And it appears that both men were aware of the fact. Students of the diaries, who discovered erased messages in the flight's official records, believe the pair probably sighted the pole but did not cross it. Byrd and Bennett turned back because of an oil leak in the engine.

Accusations that Byrd was trying to fool the public were rife from the moment the 15-and-a-half-hour flight spanning 1,360 miles returned to Svalbard. But only since the recovery of the diaries has the scandal been proven. Honors for the first man to fly over the North Pole now go to Roald Amundsen who crossed it in a dirigible just three days after Byrd's flight.

Yet although Byrd has serious critics he certainly propelled Arctic exploration into the 20th century. His efforts made aircraft a viable option to sleds and dogs. As he observed after completing the polar flight: "Men toiled for years over this ice, a few hard-won miles a day; and we travel luxuriously a hundred miles an hour. How motors have changed the burdens of man." He may have failed to conquer the North Pole outright but he distinguished himself on subsequent expeditions and thus improved his posthumous reputation.

Hoping to beat Lindbergh

The son of a lawyer, Byrd began his adventures at the precociously early age of 12 with an around-the-world jaunt financed by his parents. When he was 20 he joined the U.S. Naval Academy but was dogged by recurrent ankle injuries, which ultimately forced him to leave the service. During World War I he learned how to fly and this instilled in him a passion that lasted a lifetime. In the cockpit he pioneered methods of flying long distances, and over water instead of land, which was remarkable in that early period of aviation history.

His next project was an attempt at a transatlantic flight, which took place a few

months before Charles Lindbergh's in 1927. Byrd's plane ditched but he was deemed close enough to Paris from New York, where he began, for the 42-hour flight to be considered a success.

Afterward Byrd turned his attention to Antarctica and it was here that he achieved far greater success. He made a total of five expeditions—the first featured a flight to the South Pole in 1929. His plane was a Ford tri-motor named *Floyd Bennett* after his former colleague who had died from pneumonia.

Relying on the sun to guide him, Byrd set off with pilot Bernt Balchen, co-pilot Harold June and aerial photographer Captain Ashley McKinley. Aviation was still in its infancy and the crew had no idea whether the small aircraft could gain sufficient altitude under such difficult conditions to fly over the steeply rising polar plateau that Amundsen had reported. In the event they managed after throwing excess baggage, including valuable food and oil drums, overboard. Shortly before midnight on November 29, 1929 the *Floyd Bennett* was over the pole. This time there were no miscalculations. They flew on for a short distance, turning to account for navigational errors. Byrd dropped a small American flag onto the pole before they turned around and headed for the base.

This expedition, like others he orchestrated, was not just about being first. He carried out detailed scientific observations. His dedication was such that in 1934 he overwintered in a primitive hut in Antarctica to record weather conditions and witness the astronomical sensation of the aurora. However, radio messages alerted base camp that something was wrong. Byrd was being slowly poisoned by carbon monoxide leaking from a faulty stove and his messages were becoming garbled as the effects took hold. Despite their concerns it was months before he could be rescued. His book, *Alone*, recounting the grim experience, became a best-seller.

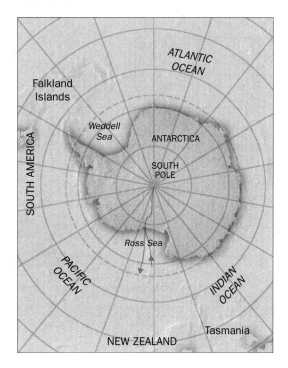

Above: *Byrd's tri-motor Fokker* Josephine Ford *being readied for take off on the 1926 North Pole flight. He claimed an overflight, but records later proved that he had turned back 150 miles short.*

Facing: *The American flyer did not make a similar mistake when it came to flying to the South Pole, and successfully proved that the future of Arctic and Antarctic expeditions would rely on aerial transport and support.*

GEORGE HUBERT WILKINS

1888 to 1958

Australian-born George Wilkins was a man who relished a challenge. His career included a spell as an engineer, a war photographer, and the exploration of the north pole on-foot and underwater in a submarine. But he is best remembered for being the first to fly from North America to Europe over the north pole, one of the highlights of the new technological age of exploration.

Born in the Australian outback, Wilkins developed a love of nature after observing the aborigines and the way they thrived in a natural environment with scant resources. He left Australia in 1908 for England and a career as a photographer. In this capacity he joined Vilhjalmur Stefansson, the unorthodox Icelandic Arctic explorer who later led the Canadian Arctic Expedition (1913–1918). For the first time Wilkins experienced the thrill of the polar regions and there he learned survival skills that he developed throughout the rest of his career. In Stefansson, Wilkins recognized some of the qualities he had found in the aborigines of his youth, for the Icelander was determined to live like the Inuit, off the land, and declared the Arctic to be a "friendly" place.

The outbreak of World War I took Wilkins back to Australia where he joined the Royal Australian Flying Corps, once again as a photographer, and rose to the rank of captain. When hostilities ceased he turned back to his polar ambitions. In 1920 he was attached to the British Imperial Antarctic Expedition and later joined Shackleton on his expedition in the same

Above: *Born on an Australian sheep ranch, George Wilkins had a keen sense of adventure, and with the gifts of a natural salesman, he found it easy to raise backing for his many expeditions around the globe.*

region. His conduct was exemplary and he was subsequently asked to head a survey of northern Australia by the British Museum.

Wilkins remained devoted to flying and could see the great advantages it brought to polar exploration. With aircraft, the most inaccessible areas were suddenly within reach. Men inside planes were sheltered not only from the cold but from the howling wind which so often defeated ground-based expeditions. Coupled with his other abiding interest, photography, Wilkins could make records of these icy wastes in a way that had never been possible before. Also, technical equipment and supplies could be dropped to assist ground-based exploration in future expeditions.

Feat of aviation

After months of preparation Wilkins and co-pilot Carl Ben Eielson embarked on their trans-pole flight, setting off in a Lockheed Vega ski-plane from Point Barrow in Alaska on April 15,

1857	1864	1871	1873	1875–6	1878–9	1895	1896
Sir Francis McClintock finds the remains of Franklin's party	Nils Nordenskiold travels further north than anyone before: 81°42'	Charles Hall discovers Hall Land and extends knowledge of Greenland	Julius von Payer discovers Franz Josef Land in the Arctic	Sir George Nares attempts to reach the North Pole	Nils Nordenskiold negotiates north-east passage on the *Vega*	Nansen attempts to reach North Pole; reaches record distance north	Fridtjof Nansen's ship *Fram* emerges from Arctic ice

1928. Ahead of them lay a 2,500-mile trip—and all the hazards the weather could bring.

Although flight was a major breakthrough for polar exploration, there were great risks, including the likelihood of fuel lines freezing, the loss of radio contact, and the engine seizing if the oil froze. Among the most treacherous conditions were white-outs, when visibility becomes so bad that distinguishing between land and sky is impossible. However, Wilkins and Eielsen were fortunate enough not to be plagued by glitches. They arrived at Spitzbergen 24 hours after take-off, having seen polar regions that had remained beyond the grasp of other expeditions.

In 1928 Wilkins was awarded the Royal Geographical Society Patron's Medal "for his many years of systematic work in polar regions culminating in

his remarkable flight from Point Barrow to Spitzbergen." It came the same year as a British knighthood. Wilkins remained tireless in pushing back the boundaries in the polar regions. Later in 1928 he made a dash across Antarctica by plane, covering 1,200 miles. Sandwiched between Antarctic trips in 1929 came an around-the-world flight on the dirigible *Graf Zeppelin*.

In 1931 he attempted to reach the North Pole by submarine. The USS *Nautilus*, a naval submarine, which he purchased for a nominal one dollar, failed to live up to expectations. After a few dives in the Arctic Sea it was beset by mechanical failure and was forced to turn back. However, his theories about the feasibility of travel under the pack ice were later proved correct, and in 1958, shortly before his death, Wilkins saw the submarine's successor, the nuclear-powered *Nautilus*, fulfill his ambition.

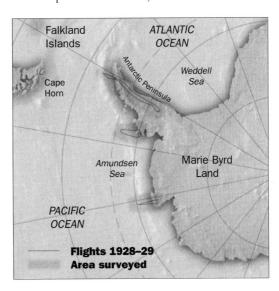

Falkland Islands

Cape Horn

ATLANTIC OCEAN

Antarctic Peninsula

Weddell Sea

Amundsen Sea

Marie Byrd Land

PACIFIC OCEAN

Flights 1928–29
Area surveyed

1897	1897	1901	1901–03	1903–06	1908–10	1909	1909
Salomon Andrée dies in attempt to fly to North Pole in a balloon	Adrien Gerlache de Gomery leads first expedition to winter in the Antarctic	Antarctic expedition led by Otto Nordenskiold, nephew of Nils Nordenskiold	Erich von Drygalski leads German Antarctic Expedition	Roald Amundsen locates North Geomagnetic Pole	Jean-Baptiste Charcot maps the Antarctic Peninsula	Robert Peary claims to reach North Pole	Sir Earnest Shackleton reaches to within 100 miles of South Pole

Sir VIVIAN FUCHS

1908 to 1999

"Nothing is ever as bad as you think it is going to be." This was the abiding philosophy of the man who achieved Shackleton's dream of crossing Antarctica. Vivian Fuchs was born on the Isle of Wight off the coast of southern England to a German-born father and an English mother. During World War I he and his family were interned on the Isle of Man because of his father's German background. Later he studied natural sciences at Cambridge University, where he was inspired by Sir James Wordie, a veteran of the Shackleton expedition. With Wordie, Fuchs visited eastern Greenland in 1929 in the capacity of geologist.

For the next decade Fuchs was in and out of Africa on numerous expeditions and in 1933 he married Joyce Connell, who shared his love of the outdoors. By then he was a strapping six-footer who looked every inch the adventurer. Bizarrely, his nickname was Bunny.

Plans for further expeditions were interrupted by World War II. Fuchs served in West Africa and northwest Europe, reaching the rank of major before he left the army in 1946. The next year he became leader of the Falkland Islands Dependencies Survey, the forerunner of the British Antarctic Survey. Now Fuchs gained his grounding in Antarctica—and he loved

every minute of it. The operation mirrored the one that Shackleton had hoped to pursue.

Sir Edmund Hillary (1919–), who would later be the first man to climb Mount Everest, led a New Zealand team that traveled from the Ross Sea to the south pole, providing supply dumps on the way for the return journey. Fuchs set out at the head of his team from the Weddell Sea. He and Hillary planned to rendezvous and then set out together for the Ross Sea. Before the joint expedition, which used mechanized transport, got under way in November 1957, there was extensive training so that all the men involved knew precisely what lay ahead. The training proved invaluable since the trip for Fuchs and his party proved to be "one of the worst journeys in the world."

Hillary beat Fuchs to the pole by 15 days. When he and his men arrived there on January 4, 1958 Fuchs was still 400 miles short of his target. Transcripts of terse radio messages indicated a row brewing between the two men. Newspapers around the world homed in on reports of a rift. Yet when they met, Hillary greeted Fuchs with the words: "Hello Bunny." The answer was: "Damn glad to see you, Ed." Later Fuchs insisted that "the great Antarctic row never existed at all."

Together they departed the South Pole on January 24, completing the journey on March 2. It had taken 99 days to cover 2,158 miles, just falling within the estimate Fuchs had made before he began. It is unlikely that being beaten fazed Fuchs. He constantly insisted that "the value of exploration lies in the gaining of knowledge, not in establishing a record."

Changing times

For a man like Fuchs, the increasing level of technology was a matter of some regret. "In the old days you had to rely on character and resources—of yourself and your companions. Now, with all the technological assistance, it is simplified." Not only was transport easier but there was also an American-run base at the South Pole by then, offering support and airborne assistance. Nevertheless the achievement was a great one in this, the world's

Facing top: British explorer Sir Vivian Fuchs stands in front of the prefabricated hut to be used on the Commonwealth Trans-Antarctic Expedition of 1955–58)

Facing bottom: Encouraging the young— Fuchs talks with Ranulf Fiennes on board the MV Benjamin Bowking at Greenwich, London before the start of the Transglobe Expedition to circumnavigate the world via both poles.

most hostile continent.

Following his award of a medal by the Royal Geographical Society in 1950 for his work in Antarctica, Fuchs was given one of the few Special Gold Medals ever struck "for his leadership of the Commonwealth Trans-Antarctic Expedition." After holding numerous prestigious posts he acted as President of the Royal Geographical Society from 1982–84. By this time he had also received a knighthood. Before his retirement Fuchs continued to work with the British Antarctic Survey.

When Fuchs died, explorer John Blashford-Snell paid this tribute: "[He] was one of the great scientific explorers, renowned for his outstanding work in the polar regions, a remarkable man in every respect."

Sir RANULPH FIENNES
*b*1944

Ranulph Twisleton-Wykeham-Fiennes has been described as "the epitome of an English gentleman—tough, incredibly determined and very funny." In 1982 Fiennes and companion Charles Burton, together comprising the British Trans-Globe Expedition, arrived at Greenwich in London after

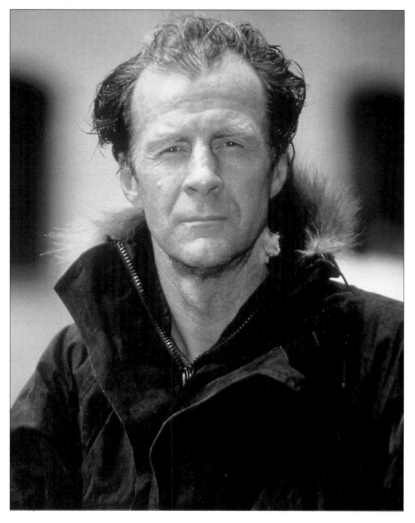

Above: *Sir Ranulph Fiennes purchased the world's most expensive cookie at an auction when he prevented a relic of Scott's from being taken away from Britain.*

circumnavigating the world via both poles. The journey was 35,000 miles long and took almost exactly three years.

A decade later Fiennes was making headlines again. He and Dr. Michael Stroud went on the longest self-supporting polar sled journey ever, in Antarctica. The distance covered this time was 1,350 miles achieved in 94 days with the

men hauling their supplies across the snow.

It hasn't been all glory, though. There were a series of failed missions, including four attempts at reaching the north pole unsupported and the expedition to walk alone and unaided across Antarctica which had to be abandoned in 1996 after Fiennes was felled by the agony of kidney stones.

In 1990 his frostbitten toes suffered gangrene, and he also nearly drowned after tumbling into a thawing ice crevasse. Despite the enormous advances in weather protection gear Fiennes is still subject to the pain of frostbite, the threat of hypothermia, bowel upsets, dehydration and other ailments. Yet still he yearns to return to the cold wastes—preferably alone—to prove his endurance skills, although he is approaching 60. "It's my job and discomfort is a part of it," explains Fiennes. Characteristic of the new breed of expedition leaders, he is motivated by raising millions of pounds for charity.

Fiennes married his childhood sweetheart Virginia Pepper in 1970 and lately the couple have been farming on a remote corner of Exmoor in England. It is there that Fiennes continues a strenuous health program focussing both on his fitness and on his diet.

Remarkably, when Fiennes and Stroud made their epic journey they ate four times more butter than health officials recommend yet their cholesterol levels stayed low and each lost about 50lbs in weight. A typical day began with porridge and butter which was followed by soup and butter for lunch, a flapjack and butter in the afternoon and a dried meal at night—with butter added. In addition they ate four small bars of chocolate a day. Although they took hot drinks like coffee, tea, and chocolate they carried no alcohol.

Fiennes has enormous respect for the pioneers who have gone before him. In 1999 he paid an astonishing £3,910 ($6,256) for a

1910	1911	1911	1911	1912	1913–18	1914	1926
Knud Rasmussen establishes Thule base in Greenland	Douglas Mawson leads three-year Australasian Antarctic Expedition	Amundsen reaches South Pole	Donald MacMillan explores north-west of Axel Heiberg Island	Robert Scott and his party die on return from South Pole	Vilhjalmur Stefansson lives above Arctic Circle, explores Canada / Alaska	Sir Ernest Shackleton is stranded when his boat is crushed by ice	Richard Byrd flies over vicinity of North Pole

Huntley and Palmer cookie found next to the body of Captain Scott. Acknowledging that it must be the most expensive cookie in the world, Fiennes said he paid up to stop the intriguing memorabilia from being taken out of the country, and he donated it to the UK Antarctic Heritage Trust. "It needs to be kept in preservative, otherwise it will crumble," he says.

For his enduring grit Fiennes credits his father, who died of wounds received in North Africa during World War II four months before he was born. "When I have a real mental battle about whether to carry on, especially when I know the next day is going to be the hundredth one of unpleasantness and gangrene has set in, I think of my father and feel it is the two of us who are trying to continue and that stopping isn't what he would do."

Pole people

The first man to visit both poles was American Dr Albert Crary who got to the North Pole on May 3, 1952 in a Dakota aircraft and the South Pole just under nine years later in a Sno Cat.

The first man to walk to both poles was Robert Swan of the U.K. who led a three-man expedition along the same path Scott had taken, in January 1986. On a subsequent expedition he went to the North Pole, and arrived there on May 14, 1989.

Englishman Robert Mear, 45, who aimed to become the first person to walk alone and unsupported across Antarctica, was forced to give up his attempt in December 1995 due to equipment failure.

Below: Ranulph Fiennes attributes his grit and determination to his father. And there are still battles ahead. Fiennes hates to give up, and recently Antartica beat his latest attempt to walk to the South Pole…

1926	1931	1935	1947	1955–58	1958	1959	1970s
Umberto Nobile, Amundsen, and others fly over North Pole in dirigible *Norge*	George Wilkins attempts to reach North Pole in the submarine *Nautilus*	Lincoln Ellsworth flies over Antarctica	US Operation Highjump extensively maps Antarctica	Sir Vivian Fuchs is co-leader of Commonwealth Trans-Antarctic Expedition	Nuclear-powered submarine USS *Nautilus* passes beneath North Pole	Antarctica is safe-guarded by international treaty	Ozone hole above Antarctica is first observed

Discovering the Great South Continent

Abel Tasman	1642–43
	1643–44
Antoine Entrecasteaux	1791–93
Captain James Cook	1768–71
	1772–75
Matthew Flinders	1801–03
Sir Charles Sturt	1828–29
	1829–30
	1844–45
Hamilton Hume	1824
Ludwig Leichhardt	1844–45
Edward Eyre	1840
	1841
Robert O'Hara Burke	1860–61

BORNEO

CELEBES

Equator

Banda Sea

BISMARCK
ARCHIPELAGO

Java Sea

Flores Sea

NEW GUINEA

JAVA

LOMBOK

BALI   SUMBAWA   FLORES

SUMBA   TIMOR

Arafura Sea

Timor Sea

(Port
Essington)

Gulf of
Carpentaria

Great
Barrier
Reef

Darwin

Indian Ocean

Coral Sea

Burketown

Cairns

Townsville

Great
Barrier
Reef

NORTHERN
TERRITORY

Flinders

AUSTRALIA

Mackay

North West
Basin

Alice Springs

Simpson
Desert

QUEENSLAND

SOUTH
AUSTRALIA

Lake
Eyre
North

Brisbane

Lake Eyre
South

Darling

Geraldton

Lake
Gairdner

Lake
Torrens

NEW SOUTH
WALES

WESTERN
AUSTRALIA

Kalgoorlie

Nullarbor Plain

Lachlan

Sydney

Perth

Great Australian Bight

Murrumbidgee

Esperance

Adelaide

VICTORIA

Murray

Albany

Melbourne

Geelong

KING
ISLAND

Bass Strait

FLINDERS
ISLAND

TASMANIA
(Van Diemen's
Land)

Hobart

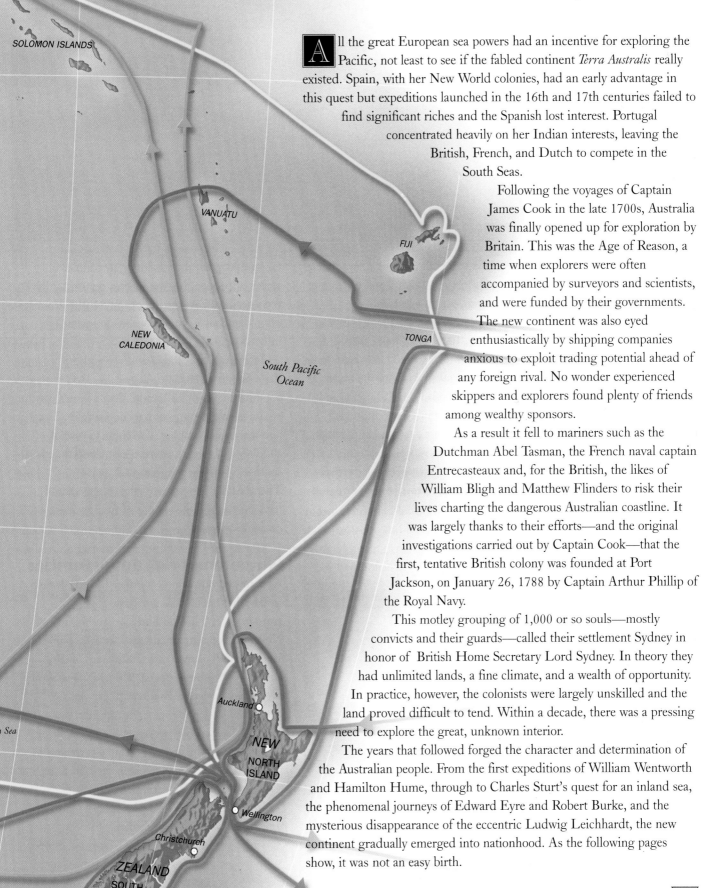

CHAPTER SEVEN

AUSTRALASIA

All the great European sea powers had an incentive for exploring the Pacific, not least to see if the fabled continent *Terra Australis* really existed. Spain, with her New World colonies, had an early advantage in this quest but expeditions launched in the 16th and 17th centuries failed to find significant riches and the Spanish lost interest. Portugal concentrated heavily on her Indian interests, leaving the British, French, and Dutch to compete in the South Seas.

Following the voyages of Captain James Cook in the late 1700s, Australia was finally opened up for exploration by Britain. This was the Age of Reason, a time when explorers were often accompanied by surveyors and scientists, and were funded by their governments. The new continent was also eyed enthusiastically by shipping companies anxious to exploit trading potential ahead of any foreign rival. No wonder experienced skippers and explorers found plenty of friends among wealthy sponsors.

As a result it fell to mariners such as the Dutchman Abel Tasman, the French naval captain Entrecasteaux and, for the British, the likes of William Bligh and Matthew Flinders to risk their lives charting the dangerous Australian coastline. It was largely thanks to their efforts—and the original investigations carried out by Captain Cook—that the first, tentative British colony was founded at Port Jackson, on January 26, 1788 by Captain Arthur Phillip of the Royal Navy.

This motley grouping of 1,000 or so souls—mostly convicts and their guards—called their settlement Sydney in honor of British Home Secretary Lord Sydney. In theory they had unlimited lands, a fine climate, and a wealth of opportunity. In practice, however, the colonists were largely unskilled and the land proved difficult to tend. Within a decade, there was a pressing need to explore the great, unknown interior.

The years that followed forged the character and determination of the Australian people. From the first expeditions of William Wentworth and Hamilton Hume, through to Charles Sturt's quest for an inland sea, the phenomenal journeys of Edward Eyre and Robert Burke, and the mysterious disappearance of the eccentric Ludwig Leichhardt, the new continent gradually emerged into nationhood. As the following pages show, it was not an easy birth.

SOLOMON ISLANDS

VANUATU

FIJI

NEW CALEDONIA

TONGA

South Pacific Ocean

Tasman Sea

Auckland

NEW NORTH ISLAND

Wellington

Christchurch

ZEALAND SOUTH ISLAND

Captain JAMES COOK

1728 to 1779

In British society's upper echelons he was respected as the man who sailed around the world. To sailors he was a savior for stamping out scurvy. To residents of Tahiti he was a revered friend. To the Hawaiians he was a god who was ultimately feared and loathed. James Cook was all of these things and more, which makes him one of the most remarkable explorers of all time.

Cook was humbly born in Marton-in-Cleveland, England, where his father worked as a farm laborer. By 13 Cook had finished full-time schooling. When he decided to go to sea as a cabin boy on the *Freelove*, a collier ship out of Whitby, he taught himself mathematics and astronomy.

In 1755 Cook switched to the Royal Navy, keen to do his duty in the Seven Years' War against France. Cook was later noticed by both the Admiralty and the Royal Society for his observations on a solar eclipse in 1766 and the way he used the phenomena to pinpoint longitude, which was still something of an enigma. Consequently, he was given a ship, *Endeavour*, and dispatched to monitor the planet Venus from the southern seas in 1768. Among the

crew was Joseph Banks (1743–1821), the botanist and future president of the Royal Society. Aboard the small ship Cook insisted on rigorous hygiene as well as abundant supplies of fruit and vegetables. In so doing he saved the men from scurvy, a merciless disease that usually claimed scores of sailors' lives during voyages. He was also disciplined without being ruthless, earning the respect and loyalty of the 94 men.

Cook's first destination was Tahiti, where a friendly welcome was assured. This became a regular port of call for Cook, who was fascinated by tribal life. Ahead of his time, he respected the traditions and religion he found there and refused to impose western ideals. Indeed, he had the foresight to realize the impact of the visitors was potentially disastrous.

From Tahiti the *Endeavour* headed southwest, discovering the Society Islands along the way. Cook then staked Britain's claim to New Zealand, having circumnavigated both North and South Islands and charted their coastlines.

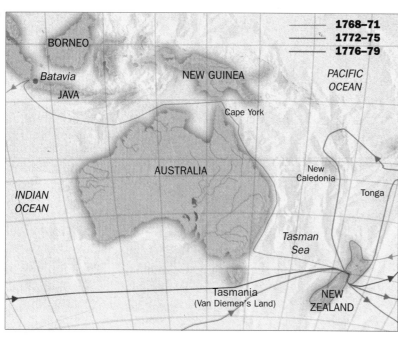

Map legend:
- 1768–71
- 1772–75
- 1776–79

BORNEO
Batavia
JAVA
NEW GUINEA
PACIFIC OCEAN
Cape York
AUSTRALIA
New Caledonia
Tonga
INDIAN OCEAN
Tasman Sea
Tasmania (Van Diemen's Land)
NEW ZEALAND

The channel between the islands is now called Cook Strait. As winter closed in Cook headed for Australia and took shelter in Botany Bay.

Holed on the Great Barrier Reef, the *Endeavour* put in at Java for repairs. Traveling home via the Cape of Good Hope, Cook's circumnavigation ended in July 1771, having taken three years and added much to the map of the world. However, it remained unclear just how far the Southern Continent—Australia—extended. Thus in 1772 Cook, now promoted to commander, set sail with two ships, *Resolution* and *Adventure*, and headed to the southern hemisphere once more.

The last continent

This time he crossed the Antarctic Circle, the first time anyone is known to have done so. Although he couldn't prove it, Cook was convinced Antarctica existed further to the south. In fact, during the four-year voyage he circumnavigated Antarctica without actually sighting the continent, Fleeing the southern winter, he visited the New Hebrides, the Cook Islands, Tonga and Easter Island, among other Pacific locations.

While Cook could have retired from the sea with honor, he chose to make a third voyage, this time to search for a northwest passage. It was to be his last. Setting off in July 1776 with two ships, *Resolution* again and *Discovery*, he went back into the Pacific after rounding the Cape of Good Hope and finally struck north, encountering Hawaii for the first time, which he named the Sandwich Islands. Once again Cook noticed an astonishing similarity in culture and language between far-flung Polynesian settlements.

In 1778 Cook and his ships sailed north up the west coast of America searching in vain for the elusive northwest passage. Before winter set in, he retreated to the Hawaiian islands for repairs and recuperation. The islanders were at first delighted to greet him. Alas, relations between them and the sailors quickly deteriorated. Cook was hacked to death in a skirmish on February 14, 1779, along with four of his men.

The voyage continued, finally returning to England in 1780. Cook was remembered for his wisdom in man-management, ethnology, navigation, map-making, botany, astronomy, and natural history.

Facing: James Cook, one of the most remarkable explorers of all time.

Below: Captain James Cook taking possession of New South Wales in the name of the British Crown, 1770.

MATTHEW FLINDERS

1774 to 1814

Above: *George Bass, whose name was given to the strait between Tasmania and mainland Australia.*

While many explorers before him had probed Australia's coastline, it fell to the outstanding British hydrographer Matthew Flinders to produce a definitive coastal map of the continent. So accurate were his charts that they remained in use for decades and his persistence in referring to the land as Australia eventually helped the name stick. Yet Flinders' all too brief life should be remembered as much for his fortitude and instinct for adventure as his abilities as a navigator. He was not the type to be easily daunted.

Flinders was born in Donnington, Lincolnshire, in 1774 and was expected to follow his father and grandfather into a medical career. Family aspirations were however demolished when the young Matthew read *Robinson Crusoe* and decided he could not resist a life at sea. By the age of 15 he had enlisted in the Royal Navy and within two years he was serving under Captain William Bligh in the West Indies and South Seas.

In 1795, as a midshipman, he was ordered to sail with the *Reliance* to New South Wales. Among those on board were the colony's governor, John Hunter, and the ship's surgeon, George Bass—two men who would play defining roles in his career. Soon after the ship's arrival in Sydney, Flinders was chosen by Hunter to help map some of the nearby bays and his aptitude for this task so impressed his superiors that he was given further commissions to survey the Furneaux Islands north of Tasmania and, later, to assist Bass in charting a channel between Tasmania and the Australian mainland. Flinders and Bass not only found and named the Bass Strait but also sailed around Tasmania, proving it was an island.

Convinced that a reliable chart was needed for mariners off the Australian coast, Flinders returned to Britain in 1800 to seek sponsorship.

His chief supporter was the naturalist Joseph Banks, a man still fascinated by the new continent 30 years after landing in Botany Bay with Captain James Cook. Banks helped Flinders secure a small sloop, the *Investigator*, and on July 18, 1801 the party left Spithead, England, on a five-month voyage to south-western Australia.

After anchoring at Cape Leeuwin, Flinders spent a month in the area, allowing his team of scientists to collect some 500 new plants and record previously unknown species of snake, lizard, emu, and kangaroo. From there he sailed east along the south coast until, on February 21, a shortage of drinking water forced him to send a landing party onto the mainland near Spencer Gulf. Neither the men nor their boat were seen again and Flinders duly named the anchorage Cape Catastrophe.

The expedition continued east along the Gulf of St. Vincent, pausing at Kangaroo Island to hunt for fresh meat, and on to Encounter Bay—

so called because it was the spot where Flinders met the French explorer Nicolas Baudin heading west. Although England and France were locked in war, the two men treated each other courteously and even ate breakfast together before heading their separate ways. Later Baudin would claim he discovered much of the coast to the west, an assertion corrected by Flinders in his later writings.

Into misfortune

The Spring of 1802 saw Flinders progress through the Bass Strait and north to Botany Bay, where many specimens were unloaded and repackaged for shipment to London. The New South Wales governor, Philip Gidley King, provided a new vessel and crew to accompany the *Investigator* on her journey north but this brig was keel-holed on the Great Barrier Reef and forced to return. Flinders meanwhile found a channel through the reef (now known as Flinders Passage) and sailed inside it for some 500 miles until making for open sea. For the next year he circumnavigated the Australian coast, surveying the northern Gulf of Carpentaria in superb detail, before returning to Port Jackson and a passage to England aboard HMS *Porpoise*.

Sadly for Flinders, the next period in his life was marked by ill fortune. First he was shipwrecked on the *Porpoise*, and had to row almost 700 miles back to Port Stanley to get

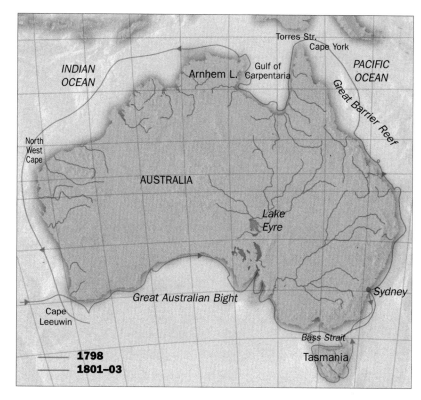

help for his comrades. He was then given a schooner by Governor King but the voyage back to England was hampered by inadequate rations and when Flinders put in at Mauritius (a French territory) he was arrested as a foreign spy and imprisoned for seven years. By the time he finally returned home he was in poor health and it took him four years to write his memoirs: *A Voyage to Terra Australis*. He died on July 19, 1814, the day his memoirs were published.

Below: The Great Barrier Reef is a major tourist attraction today. In Flinders' time it was a peril to shipping along Australia's eastern coast.

WILLIAM CHARLES WENTWORTH

1790 to 1872

Below: William Charles Wentworth pushed for self-rule for New South Wales and his campaign resulted in it becoming the first colony to achieve a measure of representative government.

Sometimes described as "The Great Native," William Charles Wentworth was a highly educated, tough and resourceful explorer. Born in 1790 on the British penal colony of Norfolk Island, he was raised by parents from opposite ends of the social spectrum. As one of the first generation of Australian-born British, he helped to lay the foundations of a distinct Australian nation.

His father, Dr D'Arcy Wentworth, was a respected Irish surgeon while his mother, Catherine Crowley, had been transported as a convict. William's well-to-do father ensured he received a good education in Greenwich, London, and Cambridge University, and by the time he returned to Australia in 1810 his success in the hierarchy was assured.

Within three years Wentworth ranked among Australia's largest landowners (his estate in New South Wales totaled more than 2,750 acres), yet he supported a political movement that sought a fairer deal for transported convicts, the "emancipists." Ex-convicts in Australia were barred from owning their own farms, and Wentworth was dismayed at the way the authorities effectively kept them in a permanent state of destitution through legal measures. As he developed a reputation as an explorer, he tried simultaneously to increase social justice in Australia.

Wentworth made his name as an explorer in the Blue Mountains, a strikingly beautiful and rugged plateau running east of the Great Dividing Range about 35 miles from Sydney. Early explorers had sought routes through the mountains to open up the lands beyond but none had succeeded. The mountains effectively hemmed in the new settlers while the land immediately accessible to them proved difficult to cultivate. The local economy was hampered by an unskilled convict workforce, while the garrison's soldiers were demoralized and ill-disciplined. During the first decade of the 19th century the entire Port Jackson colony came perilously close to starvation. Into this social minefield walked Major-General Lachlan Macquarie, one of New South Wales's truly inspirational governors.

Macquarie immediately set about raising moral standards, banning the use of rum as a currency, resisting mass acquisition of land, and showing a humanitarian attitude toward the convicts. He also encouraged exploration of the Blue Mountains in the hope of colonizing the region. Rising to the challenge, Wentworth and fellow explorers Gregory Blaxland and William Lawson launched an expedition in 1813 and

1606	1643	1721	1722	1770	1778	1788	1789
Spanish explorer Luis de Torres sights Australian coast	Dutch explorer Abel Tasman discovers New Zealand and Tasmania	Dutch explorer Jacob Roggeveen explores Pacific, first European to land on Samoa	Jacob Roggeveen discovers Easter Island	British explorer James Cook lands at Botany Bay	James Cook explores Pacific Ocean and discovers Hawaii	Britain transports the first ship of convicts to Australia	The crew of the British ship *Bounty* mutiny

discovered it was possible to reach the far side of the mountains by following ridges rather than valleys. Wentworth found virgin grazing lands that stretched out to the west as far as the eye could see.

Fast-moving times

His discovery created a huge shake-up in the Port Jackson community. A squatter breakout resulted when farmers scrambled to claim their patch of land and, in the years that followed, political power moved increasingly toward the "squattocracy." This eventually led to the establishment of the state of Victoria and a series of measures inspired by free settlers designed to curb the squatters' activities, most notably the introduction of land title legislation. Wentworth found himself in the thick of the political debate and he recognized more than ever the need for Australia to develop an effective constitution.

In 1816 he traveled to England to study law and the British constitution, hoping to draft a similar framework for Australia. Wentworth described this project as "a new Britannia in another world," and by the time he returned to Australia he had developed ideas for the devolution of government. In 1824 he helped found one of the world's most distinguished newspapers, *The Australian*, and used it as a powerful mouthpiece to campaign on behalf of emancipists against self-interested government officials and free settlers. He also pushed harder for self-rule and, in 1842, was largely responsible for New South Wales becoming the first Australian colony to obtain representative government.

The irony for Wentworth was that he became suspicious of the very democracy he had helped to create. Though a champion of self-rule, he had an inherently conservative streak and was more comfortable with a benevolent, patrician government rather than the advanced political system he had seen take root. In 1862 he retired to England, although when he died, ten years later, his body was returned to Sydney for burial.

Above: The Three Sisters in the Blue Mountains of New South Wales. By sticking to the ridges rather than the valleys, early explorers broke across this natural barrier to the interior of Australia.

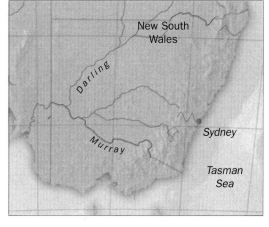

1793	1801	1804	1808	1813	1814	1816–30	1819
First free British colonists arrive in Australia	Flinders circumnavigates Australia	Colonization of Tasmania begins	The Rum Rebellion is staged against Governor Bligh	Gregory Blaxland crosses Blue Mountains	Samuel Marsden establishes first European settlement in New Zealand	Botanist Allan Cunningham explores New South Wales	John Oxley surveys coast of Australia

Sir CHARLES STURT

1795 to 1869

In the early 19th century the first serious attempts were made by Europeans to penetrate deep into Australia's interior. Colonists had noted the distribution of the continent's southeasterly rivers and there was general speculation that because they flowed away from the coast a vast inland sea awaited discovery. The man charged with testing this hypothesis was Charles Sturt, often known as the father of Australian exploration.

Sturt was born in Bengal, India, in 1795 but was educated at Harrow school, England. He made captain in the army and served in Spain and Canada prior to a garrison posting to Ireland. In 1826 his 39th Regiment was assigned to guard convicts in New South Wales, where Sturt quickly fell in love with the wild, open country. He was appointed military secretary by Governor Sir Ralph Darling, whereupon his interest in geography, and fascination with the activities of local explorers, inspired him to make several forays inland. On November 10, 1828 he launched his first major expedition accompanied by the 31-year-old (though already vastly experienced) bushman Hamilton Hume.

Sturt and Hume headed across the Blue Mountains to the Macquarie Marshes and pressed on to find a vast river, which Sturt

named the Darling. Its directional flow and saltiness left him still more convinced of the existence of an inland sea and he returned to Sydney in April 1829 keen to prepare for another trip, this time further south along the Murrumbidgee river.

This second expedition in November 1829 started inauspiciously with a trek across uninspiring country. Sturt later noted how "neither bird nor beast inhabited these lonely

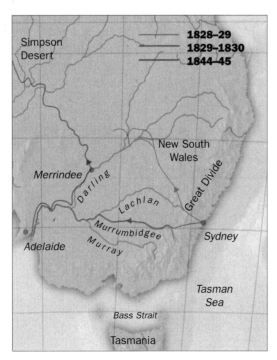

and inhospitable regions, over which the silence of the grave seemed to reign." Nonetheless, he pressed on to the Murrumbidgee, constructed a 27-foot whaleboat and, on January 7, 1830, began a breathtaking, whitewater ride downriver during which many provisions carried in a small supply boat were lost in rapids. It was more than a week before Sturt came to a junction with a "broad and noble" river that he named the Murray (after Secretary of State for the Colonies, Sir George Murray). The flow was northwesterly and the party assumed it would lead them to the inland sea.

First encounters

In fact the Murray took them to the Darling river before veering sharply south to the huge Southern Ocean estuary, which Sturt called Lake Alexandrina. This section of the journey was enlivened with plenty of high drama; not least when a 600-strong aborigine war party lined the banks of the river chanting battle anthems. Fortunately for Sturt the current carried his boats clear of attack, after which a second group of aborigines arrived to chase off the aggressors. This puzzling episode was partly unraveled by anthropological experts who later found that Sturt was regarded by the second tribe as a living incarnation of the god who had led them to the river's mouth.

Sturt had hoped to find a passage through Lake Alexandrina and out into the open sea for a coast-hugging voyage back to Sydney.

However, no obvious route appeared and instead the party had to sail and row 900 miles back upstream, arriving home as heroes in May 1830. By discovering a navigable waterway across southeastern Australia, Sturt speeded up settlement of the Gulf of St. Vincent and the founding of Adelaide.

He married back in England, retired from the military, and then returned to Australia with the aim of running a 5,000-acre farm. This backfired, however, and in 1839 Sturt was hired by the South Australia Survey Department to carry out detailed mapping work.

His last major expedition—an attempt to reach the center of the continent—was launched in 1844 and followed the Murray and Darling rivers as far as Menindee. From here Sturt and his 15 fellow explorers struck northwest only to find themselves in the middle of a severe drought. Water holes disappeared as temperatures topped 130°F. They were forced to dig an underground shelter to escape the sun and waited for six months until rain finally arrived. Sturt and four colleagues then pushed on a further 450 miles to become the first white men to see the Simpson desert, but exhaustion and scurvy at last forced them to abandon their mission. On January 19, 1846 Sturt arrived in Adelaide on a stretcher, badly sunburned and almost blind. He never fully regained his health and died in Cheltenham, England, in 1869— just before being awarded a knighthood.

Below: A paddle steamer on the Murray. Sturt described the river as "broad and noble," and named it after the British Secretary of State for the Colonies.

HAMILTON HUME
1797 to 1873

Hamilton Hume exemplified the spirit of the early Australian explorers. Born in 1797 at Parramatta, New South Wales, his family had left their roots in the Welsh valleys at a time when his father Andrew was appointed a convict superintendent. With no privileged background, and a limited education, the young Hamilton must have seemed an unlikely young man to lead dangerous expeditions into the outback. In fact he proved a naturally-gifted bushman with an insatiable appetite for probing the unknown.

Right: *In opening up the Southern Tablelands to ranchers, Hamilton Hume proved that an ordinary bushwacker could rise to mix with the new elite of Australia.*

Hume got his first taste of exploration at the age of 17, when he roamed the country south and west of Sydney, and soon graduated to become an official government guide. In the ten years to 1824 he plotted extensive routes through the Bong Bong and Berrima districts, the Sutton Forest, and rivers such as the Clyde and the Goulburn. In 1819 he joined John Oxley and James Meehan on a journey to Port Jervis and three years later was one of the first Europeans to set eyes on the Yass Plains. His first major solo expedition—for which he was declined government support—began in 1824 when he teamed up with a sailor, William Hovell, and six convicts transported from Britain to travel across the mountains between Sydney and Port Phillip Bay.

After leaving Lake George the party crossed the Murrumbidgee on October 22, using their wagon and a tarpaulin to make a crude raft. From there they pressed on to discover a river they named the Hume—the same river that in 1830 would be renamed the Murray by Sir Charles Sturt (in fairness, Sturt didn't recognize the waterway as that found by Hume and, unfortunately for the latter, it was the name "Murray" that caught on). The two explorers were, as it happened, acquainted and in 1828 had partnered an expedition across the Blue Mountains and Macquarie Marshes to find the salt waters of the Darling river.

Hovell and Hume declined to follow the Murray's southwest course and instead took a bearing due south to cross the Ovens and Goulburn rivers. Around the Goulburn they found valuable grazing land and, after narrowly escaping death in the midst of a bush fire, successfully negotiated a pass through the Great Dividing Range and a route to Geelong in Port Phillip Bay.

An unending feud

The entire two-month trip was soured by Hovell and Hume's constant squabbling; the former (wrongly) believing that his own bush skills were superior to those of his comrade. The feud simmered on for decades until in 1855, after retiring to a farm granted by a grateful Governor Darling, Hume published his definitive account of the trip with the neatly understated title *A Brief Statement of Facts in Connection with an Overland Journey from Lake George to Port Philip*. Even this was not the final word since Hovell soon responded with his own tome, punchily titled *A Reply*.

Hume's main achievement was to open up the Southern Tablelands for cattle rearing and, when cattle were established, to make vast tracts of Australia's interior accessible. Along with John Kennedy, Charles Throsby, and others, Hume created the means by which the colony would one day assert its independence—indeed

so successful were the explorers' efforts that the authorities tried to impose a moratorium on new settlement. By 1826 the government had imposed a boundary extending along the Manning river in the north, through the Mount Royal and Liverpool ranges to Wellington and

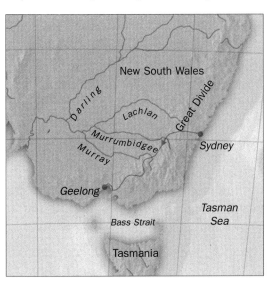

finally turning eastward to shadow the Murrumbidgee and Moruya rivers. In theory, settlement was permitted only on the 90,000 square acres within this area; in practice it was a strategy doomed to failure. For one thing, a population explosion of cattle and sheep forced farmers to move further out onto new grazing land. In addition a vast improvement in the comfort and safety of passenger ships, together with the falling price of fares, had opened up the colony to a new generation of free Britons. In their thousands, these colonists ignored the settlement boundaries and built new homes and farms ever further inland.

Though his last years were marred by poor health, Hamilton Hume had the satisfaction of knowing that in the new Australia an ordinary bushman could rise to mix with the great and the good. He served as a magistrate and, before his death in 1873, was elected a Fellow of the Royal Geographical Society.

Above: *Mustering cattle in Australia, 1871. Within years of Hume's overland trek that mapped out the extensive grazing lands beyond the coastal mountain barrier, cattle ranchers began to settle and create an economy that would help the colony grow through new immigration from Britain.*

LUDWIG LEICHHARDT

1813 to 1848

Below: A deserter from the Prussian army, Ludwig Leichhardt led several overland expeditions, but his poor leadership qualities and navigational skills eventually led to disaster in the Simpson Desert, right.

One of the more eccentric and, it must be said, inept explorers to set foot in the Australian outback, Ludwig Leichhardt arrived in Sydney in 1842 with a colorful early life behind him.

Born in Trebastsch, Prussia, in 1813, Leichhardt was a talented scholar who switched effortlessly from studying philosophy to natural sciences during his time at the universities of Berlin and Göttingen. He subsequently deserted the Prussian army and emigrated to the newly-colonized continent, scratching a living from lecturing while indulging his passion for collecting plants. He was instantly recognizable to fellow colonists by virtue of his distinctive Malay coolie hat and the sword carried at his side (he was scared of guns). The mystery of his eventual disappearance in the bush, along with six other explorers, has never been solved.

Leichhardt's arrival in Australia coincided with efforts to discover an inland route between the southeast and Port Essington (near modern-day Darwin). It was felt that this would open up valuable new trading links with the Spice Islands and help establish new and bigger settlements in Queensland and the Northern Territory. Leichhardt was originally due to join an expedition planned by the surveyor general of New South Wales, Sir Thomas Mitchell, but frustrated by delays—and to Mitchell's great anger—he announced plans to lead a party himself. In October 1844 his entourage of of ten men, 17 horses, 16 bullocks, and some dogs assembled at Jimbour Station on the Darling Downs for the long trek northeast.

Leichhardt later wrote of how they were "launched buoyant with hope into the wilderness of Australia." It soon became clear that they would need all the optimism they could muster.

From the start Leichhardt's survival techniques were atrocious—just like his sense of direction. His incompetence allowed the bullocks to escape, poorly-secured loads to spill, and members of his party to get lost. There was daily squabbling and it transpired that most of the provisions had been eaten well before the half-way stage. Unsurprisingly, Leichhardt's character inspired no confidence. Soon he was both distrusted and despised by many of his colleagues.

On June 25 this sorry state of affairs took a turn for the worse. Having crossed the Great Dividing Range, and reached the Mitchell river east of the Gulf of Carpentaria, the group was attacked by aborigines who speared to death the ornithologist John Gilbert and wounded and clubbed two others. For the survivors the remainder of the journey must have been an unimaginable form of torture, yet they managed to reach Port Essington alive on December 17, 1845. The journey had taken 14 months and 17 days—twice as long as Leichhardt had planned and one of the longest overland treks in Australian history. Despite his many failings it seems the German's knowledge of natural science had mustered some imaginative food sources, although most of his men showed symptoms of scurvy.

Hero's welcome

Leichhardt was feted on his return to Sydney and presented with a handsome financial reward. Typically, the expedition sponsors cared little about his hopeless leadership and poor bush skills and instead dwelled on his report of "an excellent country, available, almost in its whole extent, for pastoral purposes." This was what they wanted to hear. Indeed, such was the heroic status bestowed on Leichhardt that even the Prussian king pardoned his desertion from the army.

In 1846 Leichhardt concocted a plan to

1826–9	1829	1837–9	1850	1851	1854–62	1859	1861–2
Jules Dumont d'Urville surveys coast of Australia and New Zealand	British claim the whole of Australia	Sir George Grey explores northwest coast of Australia	Britain's Australian colonies are granted self-government	Colonists discover gold in Victoria state	Alfred Russel Wallace collects specimens in Malay Archipelago	Dispute over land sparks second Maori war in New Zealand	John McDouall Stuart crosses Australia south to north

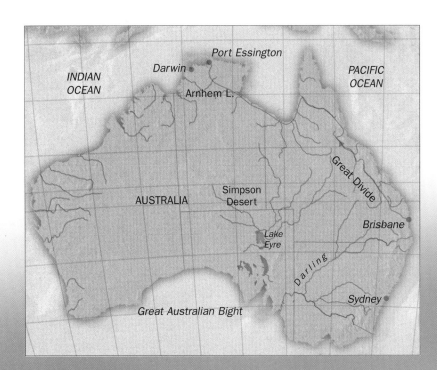

travel east-to-west across Australia using a tortuous route that would take him along the Barcoo river, north to the Gulf of Carpentaria, west to the coast and then south to the Swan river. His first attempt was a spectacular failure in which he covered barely 500 miles in six months. Undeterred he tried again in March 1848, leaving McPherson Station on Darling Downs with six other explorers and almost eighty pack animals.

The last sighting of the party was on April 3 as they headed west along the Condamine river. Search parties later found the remains of two camps on the Barcoo, although there was no conclusive proof of a link to Leichhardt. Rumors abounded; some believed the party had mutinied, killing the German, and then dying themselves at the hands of aborigines. There was talk of one lone survivor, Adolf Classen, living in the bush. Other theories had it that the group died in flash floods or bush fires. Perhaps most likely, considering Leichhardt's navigational qualities, is that they got hopelessly lost in the Simpson Desert and died of thirst.

1865	1867	1873	1876	1901	1905	1907	1914
Wellington is established as the capital of New Zealand	Last shipment of British convicts is sent to Australia	British annex Fiji in South Pacific	Outlaw Ned Kelly is executed	Australia gains Dominion status in the British Empire	Papua New Guinea is annexed to Australia	New Zealand becomes a Dominion	Australian troops occupy German New Guinea

EDWARD EYRE
1815 *to* 1901

Right: Explorers of Australia's interior were beginning to understand its vast scale and the dangers of its outback. Edward John Eyre left his name behind on several geographical features after one of the most grueling treks anyone had undertaken.

As Australia's sheep and cattle stations expanded in the mid-19th century so farmers recognized the need to tap new markets, utilizing minimal transport costs. The solution was the time-honored technique of droving—moving stock overland along routes that offered sufficient grazing and watering holes. Within southeast Australia this was reasonably straightforward; the problem lay in herding cattle across more than 1,000 miles of western Australian desert to the settlements around Albany. The man who volunteered to pioneer such a route was Edward John Eyre.

Eyre was a priest's son who emigrated to Australia in 1833 at the age of 18. He ran a sheep station in the Hunter Valley, near Canberra, and in 1838 he became the first farmer to move stock overland from Sydney to Adelaide. He settled in Adelaide the same year and quickly set about investigating new grazing lands to the north, together with a possible droving route to the west.

Eyre's first two expeditions were of only limited success. In May 1839 he led a party along the Flinders Range to Mount Arden, later crossing the mountains and the Eyre peninsula to Streaky Bay on the eastern edge of the Great Australian Bight. The following year he set out to explore the center of the continent, hoping to eventually reach Port Essington on the north coast. Unfortunately the party became bogged down, quite literally, in the salt marshes

and mud flats of Lake Eyre and were forced to turn back. Eyre's despondency is reflected in the names he gave to two mountain peaks—Mount Desolation and Mount Hopeless.

On February 25, 1841 Eyre began the trek that would make his name. He set off from Adelaide with his sheep station manager John Baxter, four other white men and three aborigines, one of them only a boy. As

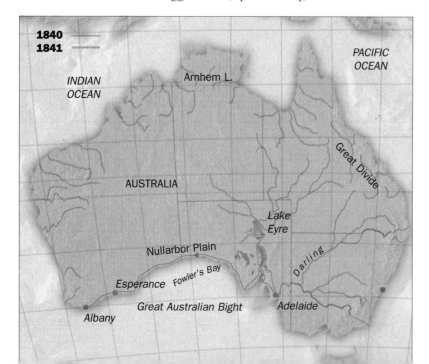

1840
1841

PACIFIC OCEAN

INDIAN OCEAN

Arnhem L.

Great Divide

AUSTRALIA

Lake Eyre

Nullarbor Plain

Darling

Esperance Fowler's Bay

Great Australian Bight Adelaide

Albany

expedition leader, Eyre had agreed to pay half the costs of the expedition himself; the rest came from private sponsors with some government support. The party headed west across the dry, mostly treeless Nullarbor Plain on a route just north of the Great Australian Bight coast. They took along 13 horses, 40 sheep, food for three months and some 70 gallons of water pulled on a dray. These supplies were to be bolstered by a government ship, which they planned to rendezvous with in Spencer Gulf. From there they would set out on the long road to Albany.

The first stages of this journey went well, but by the time they reached Fowler's Bay Eyre felt a smaller group would cope better with the hostile conditions. He sent most of the white men back to Adelaide and pressed ahead with just Baxter and the three aborigines, searching constantly for water on the way. It was a journey of appalling hardship and, as the pack horses tired in the endless sands, they were forced to leave some of these pitiable animals behind,

Starvation and mutiny

Even worse was to follow. On April 28 the two adult aborigines, who had appeared sullen and mutinous for some time, murdered Baxter and vanished with most of the supplies and remaining firearms. Only the aborigine boy, Wylie, remained loyal and over the next seven days both he and Eyre must at times have wished they too were dead. There was still no water and they survived by hunting kangaroos, even eating a dead penguin found on the shore.

After a further three weeks, and with the winter rains at last commencing, Eyre and Wylie found the going easier. The end of the long Bight cliffline meant they had access to the sea, and the chance to catch fish and crabs. On June 2 they spotted a French whaler anchored near Esperance and were permitted a two-week rest on board with plenty of food and wine. Though the final 300 miles to Albany remained a challenging goal—this time, ironically, because of the cold and wet—they now had enough strength to complete their task.

Below: A desolate view across the great salt flats of Lake Eyre.

along with firearms, spare water bags, horseshoes, and clothing. Attempts to conserve water by sucking gumtree roots and collecting dew in sponges only prolonged the inevitable and with the trek barely half-complete their water supplies finally ran out. Their crisis was worsened when they slaughtered and ate a sick horse, which made both Eyre and Baxter seriously ill.

Though he failed in his attempt to open a droving route Eyre's incredible journey was acknowledged by the Royal Geographical Society, which awarded him its gold medal. He later became lieutenant-governor of South Island, New Zealand, and governor of Jamaica where his actions in executing 400 rebels in 1865 provoked outrage in England. He retired to England in 1874 and died in 1901.

ROBERT O'HARA BURKE

1820 to 1861

The story of Robert O'Hara Burke is one of the greatest tragedies—and most avoidable—in the annals of global exploration. Bad leadership and bad management combined to claim the lives of three brave men and reminded Australians of the outback's cruel and unforgiving nature. Burke and his party won their place in history as the first to cross the continent from south to north, but they paid a terrible price.

Born in St. Cleram, Galway, Ireland, in 1820, Burke was educated at London's Woolwich Academy and later served with the Austrian Army and the Irish Constabulary. In 1853 he emigrated; first to Tasmania but later settled in Melbourne, Australia. There his career experience ensured rapid promotion within the Victoria police force and he became an inspector responsible for supervizing the Orens and Beechworth gold prospectors. Later he was made superintendent and became an influential public figure.

In 1860 the Victoria state government appointed Burke leader of an expedition to find an overland telegraph route to the north coast.

He was under pressure to succeed, and to do so quickly. Two years previously John McDouall Stuart had reached the center of the continent on behalf of the South Australia government and on March 2, 1860 Stuart left on a new expedition, also intending to establish a north-south telegraph road.

Burke's expedition was billed as the best-equipped and most expensive in Australian history. He set out in high spirits from Melbourne on August 21, 1860 with 18 men, 24 camels, and 21 tons of supplies. However, by the time he reached the Darling river settlement of Menindee, 400 miles north, his party was riven by squabbling and discontent. Much of this could be attributed to Burke's feisty personality and it did not bode well for the task ahead.

Burke's deputy, George Landells, quit along with the expedition's camel master and doctor. The Irishman responded by splitting his party into two. He would lead five men on to establish a halfway depot at Coopers Creek while the rest of the party, under the leadership of William Wright, would follow a few days later with more supplies. This arrangement quickly fell apart

and, with Stuart's progress at the back of his mind, Burke decided he could not wait at Coopers Creek. He again divided the group, leaving William Brahe in charge of the depot with instructions to wait as long as possible for his return. Wright, meanwhile, was still biding his time in Menindee.

Death by misadventure

Burke's journey north was a hellish experience, undertaken in 140°F of dry heat. Nonetheless he and his comrades William Wills (his new deputy), John King, and Charles Gray made it to the mouth of the Flinders river in February 1861, so completing their goal. They now had to return south in weather that had shifted dramatically to heavy rain and electrical storms and, with rations desperately low, they were soon reduced to eating their camels and Burke's horse. They could not have known it, but when Gray died from dysentery it effectively sealed the fate of all of them. They spent a day burying his body and when they arrived back at Coopers Creek on April 21 they found a message cut into a tree which read: "DIG—3 FEET N.W." Burke's team dug up some supplies and a letter revealing that Brahe had left just eight hours earlier. It was a devastating psychological blow.

Burke knew they were too exhausted to catch up. He decided to rest, regain strength, and make for a remote cattle station 150 miles away. It was soon obvious that even this would be impossible and the party began wandering in circles, surviving on a diet of nardoo seed and fish caught with the help of some friendly aborigines. This meant that they missed the return of Brahe and the unreliable Wright to Coopers Creek on May 8. Incredibly, Brahe did not even check to see whether the supplies he'd left had been dug up. He simply assumed his fellow explorers were dead.

Burke, Wills, and King returned to Coopers Creek 20 days later in the hope that help would arrive. It did…but far too late. Burke and Wills died of starvation within days of each other at the end of June 1861. King survived under the care of aborigines and was found alive by Alfred Howitt's search party on September 18.

Despite his failings of leadership, Burke is today regarded as one of the great Australian explorers. His bravery is recorded on a memorial standing near Melbourne's Parliament House.

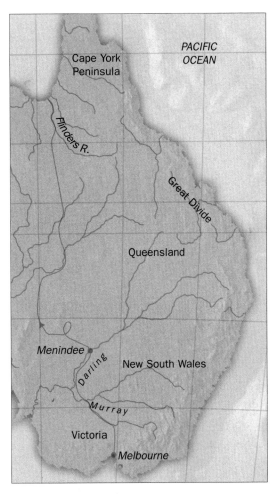

Facing above: *Burke set out with one of the best equipped expeditions ever and with the highest hopes of success, but through poor decisions and human frailty, it became a mortal disaster of epic proportions.*

Facing below: *The Burke and Wills team sets out from Royal Park, Melbourne on August 20, 1860.*

Below: *Carving on a tree at Coopers Creek in memory of Robert O'Hara Burke.*

CONCLUSION

Today the world seems much smaller than it did to our forefathers. When we travel we know precisely where we are going and we have the means to get there, fast. The heroes of history's greatest expeditions would view us with envy. Yet the ease with which we traverse the globe now merely serves to heighten the immense achievements and strength of character of those who explored remote places. The expedition leaders who made this all possible were as diverse and individual as any group of human beings. There was little similarity, for instance, in the personality of Mary Kingsley, who memorably maintained her Victorian dress code in the jungles of Africa, and the rough-and-ready mountainmen of North America. Mystic Alexandra David-Néel would have struggled to empathize with the morally crusading David Livingstone. But there must have been a kernel of their characters that linked them, for all faced adversity and hardship—indeed they chose to—in order to expand mankind's knowledge of the world. There was disease—the scourge of every expedition to far-flung places—hostile natives, wild animals, even wilder elements, shortages of food and water. The detrimental effect on their bodies and minds was huge, and their tremendous tenacity deserves immense credit.

For most explorers, the carefully drawn maps and published journals that resulted from their expeditions was reward enough. As we have seen, numerous men and women lost their lives in pursuit of making them. Only the lucky few received medals from geographical societies and international fame as tribute. Their ultimate aim has, however, been achieved—Earth is an open book, and every page of the atlas is complete.

Now we look to the future. The two views from space of Lake Chad and Nepal that appear on these pages, and two regions much explored by people discussed in this book, are made possible by space-age technology. (How Hugh Clapperton and Francis Younghusband would have loved to have been in possession of such accurate maps.) Soon, mankind will leave the Earth's atmosphere in search of new destinations, and a new era of discovery will commence. The men and women who will take part in these future expeditions to far-flung planets will differ from their forebears immeasurably. Their planning, preparation, and training will be intensive, the craft at their disposal will be sophisticated beyond imagining. And yet there will be similarities: the frailty of humans

Below: This color composite photograph taken from the Landsat-1 satellite on December 14, 1972 shows the eastern third of Nepal, a mountainous country between India and Tibet. The red arrow indicates North.

that leads to poor judgment and decision-taking will still be present; no matter how careful the preparation, laws of happenstance will still dictate success or failure. They will still be heading into the unknown with no certainty of the outcome.

In the past, as explorers set off toward the infinite horizon, they expected to meet other peoples, and when they did they found their languages and customs strange. Future explorers of space are unlikely to meet any other race—no signs of alien cultures inhabiting our galaxy have been seen. But if these future expeditions do indeed discover new races, we may be certain that the inhabitants will be much stranger than the Indians Columbus met in the Americas. Hopefully, *vive la difference*.

Above: A vertical view of Lake Chad photographed by Frank Borman from Gemini VII. It demonstrates the reduction in size of the once giant body of water in Chad and Nigeria. The red arrow indicates North.

Index

INDEX